Look at God!
My Hollywood Walk of Faith

ROZ STEVENSON

To Gayle —
Who I wake to
every morning.
Enjoy,
Roz Stevenson 5/25/2021

RSPublishing

Los Angeles

This book is dedicated to my parents, Roscoe and Clara Steverson.

Thank you for teaching me to:

*Trust in the Lord with all your heart,
and do not lean on your own understanding.
In all your ways acknowledge him,
and he will make straight your paths.*

Proverbs 3:5-6 (ESV)

CONTENTS

FOREWORD

Rosalind Stevenson is truly something special. I first met her in the mid-nineties, when, as a young man, I was in the early stages of a fledgling career as an A&E journalist. I sought out Roz to help me navigate that path, believing that she could help make a difference with a few principal goals that I had for my life. At the time, she was already a legend. She was a PR giant, who served as the Senior Broadcast Publicist in the Motion Picture Marketing Department at Universal Pictures, which was an enormously rare find in Hollywood then and now.

During our meeting, I shared my growing portfolio and my ambition to be included on the highly coveted list of journalists invited to cover junkets for her studio's new releases. Let me explain: For an entertainment journalist getting on such lists represents an essential rite of passage that can open up doors to the type of access and opportunity to grow a full-fledged career. Roz opened that door for me and then provided me with counsel on how to get added to similar lists at all the major studios, networks and distributors. Her belief and support were indeed game changers that launched my career into overdrive. I amassed over fifty national magazine covers and had my byline appear in even more A-lists national newspapers and magazines. In other words, her actions seeded my career with the resources to create a life for myself.

Over the years I have been a witness to her doing the same for countless others. This has included people from all origins who now occupy prominent positions in some of the most important areas of entertainment. And I only hope that the work we do with the African American Film Critics Association (AAFCA) mirrors that. Reflecting on the value she has brought to so many lives, without ever asking for anything in return, I know that Rosalind Stevenson is more than just something special. She is actually an angel right here on earth.

Gil Robertson IV
Founder & President
African American Film Critics Association (AAFCA)

PREFACE

In my pursuit of my Hollywood dream, I never included the biblical principles taught to me as a child. I went about living life according to the whims of the flesh. At age twenty, I was married and excited to get out on my own and make my own choices. One of the first things I did was put Christianity in a box and pushed the word of God out of my mind into a dark corner. That was no longer part of my life plan; I was living the Hollywood dream. I tried everything to win, except *seeking* God.

Fast-forward two decades later, one Sunday morning I found myself feeling emotionally defeated, sitting in the back row of a neighborhood church; at the closing altar call, I walked up to the front of the sanctuary, stood at the altar and re-dedicated my life to Christ.

This book is a testament to the instantaneous change — from inside out — and the many miracles that began. My life was redefined according to scripture, "exceedingly and abundantly above all that I had imagined."

And thus, this story begins to tell of God's glory.

Initially, it was no easy task as I struggled to follow the voice of the Holy Spirit, compelling me to write *my story*. Honestly, I felt inadequate to bring forth the biblical truth that He wanted me to share. However, deep in my heart, I knew that is what I had to do. I turned to my daily devotional for the word of the day, and, lo and behold, I received the confirmation I needed. God spoke directly to my insecurities. That day's message was entitled, "Please Send Someone Else," which is what Moses prayed in Exodus 4:13, when he was reluctant to go where God told him. I was blown away. The writer took the words right out of my mouth. The prayer for that day read the following:

> Our Creator and Sustainer, the very idea that you would call us into service is often overwhelming. It is such a privilege, and yet the responsibility is awesome. Help us not to fear those things that you would lead us to do if we keep our eyes on your divine purpose instead of our human frailties. Lord, work through our fears and insecurities so that we may faithfully serve you and be a blessing to others. Amen

That prayer gave me the confidence to move forward with the work. I now realize that when I feel inadequate, He will equip me. I know that it was not what I can do, but rather what God can do through me. I moved forward thanks to the Holy Spirit that lives inside of me. I have committed myself to doing God's will.

Even in Hollywood, God will make the crooked places straight. He made a way for me and He will do it for you. My praise song every day is, "To God be the glory for the things he has done." One of my favorite gospel hymns is the song "I Love the Lord," which the late, great Whitney Houston sang so beautifully in the movie, *The Preacher's Wife*. Every time I hear her sing this song, tears begin to flow, because it speaks so deeply to my situation.

> *I Love the Lord, He heard my cry*
> *And pitied every groan, long as I live*
> *And troubles rise, I will hasten to his throne.*

From an early age, I was taught that prayer was my most powerful weapon. In Chronicles 7:14 the Jesus encourages us: "If my people, who are called by my name, will humble themselves and pray and seek my face and turn from their wicked ways, then I will hear from heaven, and I will forgive their sin and will heal their land." The biblical principle of the importance of prayer is quite clear. Application is another thing. For me, it went in one ear and out the other and there was no daily application.

This is the story of the pitfalls I encountered as I tried to push my way into the film industry, never considering seeking God's help to direct and guide me into His purpose for my life amid the world of glitz and glamour. This is a story of dreams coming true after I surrendered all and began to walk in faith. I watched God's hand work in my life as I stepped into His purpose.

I hope by reading my story you will be inspired to not only trust God with your goals in life but to watch with anticipation as God makes your dreams come true, too. They may not happen as you planned, but when you surrender to God, I'm a living witness that God can surpass your wildest dreams and goals. I have enjoyed working with "stars," but most importantly, I've enjoyed watching my director, God, produce a story I couldn't make up or even dream up. With God, it is all possible. And I'm so happy I've been able to live this life—and live to write about it.

Blessings to you,
Roz Stevenson

PROLOGUE

What do Denzel Washington's *American Gangster* and *Inside Man*, Eddie Murphy's *The Nutty Professor* films, Will Smith's *The Pursuit of Happyness*, Vin Diesel's *The Fast & Furious I, II & III*, Queen Latifah's *The Last Holiday*, Eminem's *8 Miles*, Gabrielle Union's *Bring It On*, Samuel L. Jackson's *Coach Carter* and *XXX* films, Dwayne "The Rock" Johnson's *Gridiron Gang, The Scorpion King* & *The Mummy*, Regina King, Kerry Washington and Jamie Foxx's *Ray* and many, many others have in common? They all have had the distinction of being blockbuster films successfully marketed by Roz, a warm, loving Godmother to black stars and the black entertainment press in Hollywood. She was President/CEO of Roz Stevenson Public Relations (RSPR), a highly respected PR firm, which served every major studio. RSPR specialized in creating and implementing film strategies, which propelled African Americans nationwide to support films, resulting in box-office gold.

She is a black woman, who started in a community acting workshop, which gave her an opportunity to work in the industry as an extra. She started at the bottom in search of a credible career in the film industry. After a ten-year struggle (seven years in TV production), she finally discovered her gift of marketing films. Roz's journey took her on various career paths for which she had limited success and, ultimately, unsatisfactory outcomes. How did she finally discover her God-given purpose and begin to win? Only when life brought her to her knees, and she was forced to seriously soul search. Her life had been going in a downward spiral after she was shattered by divorce, left with bad credit and had two boys to raise. However, she found a glimmer of hope, as she entered into a second marriage. This caused Roz to yearn even more to get every aspect of her life right. It was when she returned to God that the miracles began to happen. Her career moved forward, and she achieved more success than she ever imagined.

This book is written to encourage anyone who has ever felt that it is too late. If you have ever wanted to give up, professionally and personally, because you have experienced too many rejections, too much heartache, too much stress and too much drama, she wants to assure you that you can still win. Roz was a late bloomer who refused to wilt and die. Even while carrying baggage of previous failures, with God on her side, all of her dreams have come true.

Once she said "yes" to God, everything changed. She realized she had been trying in her own power. She had not sought the God she grew up knowing. She had backslid. She realized she had to "let go and let God," then His true purpose for her life began to manifest.

In this memoir, she will share what her life was like growing up in Compton, California, in a Christian home from childhood to age nineteen. Then she focuses on the hills and valleys she experienced in Hollywood, when she did it her way. Lastly, she shares the victories she experienced after she re-dedicated her life to Christ at age forty. Today, when she glances in the rearview mirror, all she can say is, "Look at God!" He showed up and showed out! He made the crooked ways straight in every aspect of her life!

ACT I:

GROWING UP IN COMPTON

CHAPTER 1:
Daddy and His Girls Attend 1964 Oscars

Whenever God sets the stage,
you can be sure it is going to be miraculous.

I was a young black woman barely out of my teens in my sophomore year at Cal State Los Angeles, living in Compton, California, in our family's modest tract home complete with three small bedrooms and one bathroom. My life had been going along routinely, but all that changed in 1964 when, out of the blue, my daddy was given five tickets to attend the 37th Annual Academy Awards. He received them from his client, Sam Brown, who was the Executive Director for the Academy of Motion Picture Arts and Sciences, at that time.

My father, Roscoe Steverson, worked as a postal worker by day; however, he also had a lucrative janitorial business in the evenings and on weekends that specialized in window cleaning and waxing floors. Mr. Brown admired my daddy's work ethic and devotion to family. My father was a gentle giant, six foot, seven inches tall, whose whole life centered around being with his wife, kids, friends, church and serving as a Boy Scout leader. It was an exceptionally kind gesture to bless my father with the tickets.

Daddy decided he would take "his girls," which included my mother Clara, my sister Carol better known as "Cookie," their goddaughter Connie Van Brunt and me. I have one brother, Richard, who was away at Central State College in Ohio at the time. Cathy, my younger sister, who was only six years old, was too young to go.

To say it was a big deal is an understatement. As we sat down for dinner, daddy was grinning from ear to ear. He said, "Mom, girls, you're not going to believe what happened today... I don't know if you realize it, but Mr. Brown is a big man in Hollywood. As a matter of fact, he is about as big as they get. He is in charge of the Academy Awards. I am always telling him how much you love movies and if you could go to something like that, it would be beyond your wildest dreams. Well, he was kind enough to give me tickets for our family to attend the Oscars!"

We were screaming and hollering when daddy shared the news. From that moment on, all we could talk about was what were we going to wear. We wanted to look glamourous and sophisticated, and we wondered how we could acquire a glitzy outfit.

I was a sophomore in college and made a little money working part-time. For the occasion, I felt I was forced to use my newly acquired charge card for May Company. I trotted over to the department store where I hunted and hunted for something impressive that I could afford. Finally, on the sale rack I found a sparkling pink jeweled top, but that was all. I charged it, then I went to the yardage store and got pink crepe fabric and lining to make a formal length skirt on my trusty Singer sewing machine.

I still needed a proper cover-up. I convinced myself I had to go back to May Company where I charged a silver fox fur stole. It was expensive, but I had to have it to top off my outfit, I reasoned. I had no idea how I was going to pay for it with my meager income. And I didn't stop there. As I was leaving the store, I also spotted a pair of tortoise shell opera glasses. Since we had balcony seats, I decided I had to have them, too. Once, again, I whipped out my charge card before heading for home. I was now ready to look fabulous for my special night with Oscar.

On the day of the Academy Awards, I went to my hairdresser, Marguerite Rand, to get my hair done up in a heavily teased bouffant hairdo, which was all the rage at that time. Everyone in the shop was buzzing with excitement about my extraordinary opportunity. Marguerite, who was a fashionable woman about town, bought jewelry she thought I might want to borrow. I selected a pair of fabulous rhinestone earrings with a matching bracelet. I was set! Later I put on my makeup with expert precision. Once I finished, I looked in the mirror and I was proud at how amazing I looked.

Daddy squeezed us into his big Lincoln Continental, and we headed north on the Harbor Freeway, then west on the Santa Monica Freeway to a far-away land we had never seen before. We had the official pass prominently placed on top left windshield, which allowed us to enter the restricted area. As we approached the Santa Monica Civic Auditorium, we were blinded by the swirling searchlights that danced across the evening sky. We tried to be cool as we strolled down the red carpet with all the other beautiful people. We were in awe, as we took in the sights and sounds of Hollywood's biggest night. It was beyond exciting.

The most historic moment of the evening was when my heartthrob, Sidney Poitier, become the first African American to win Best Actor for his performance in *Lilies of the Field*. I must have stood longer and clapped louder than anyone else in the auditorium. I could not have been prouder to be there at this moment in time. He won despite having steep competition from iconic movies with four of the finest actors on the big screen that included Albert Finney for *Tom Jones*, Richard Harris for *This Sporting Life*, Rex Harrison for *Cleopatra*, and Paul Newman for *Hud*.

Anne Bancroft, who had won Best Actress for *The Miracle Worker* the year before, presented Sidney with his Oscar statuette. Years later I learned that when she congratulated him with a kiss on the cheek, it was a gesture that apparently caused a mild scandal among the show's most conservative audiences. That detail was lost on me. Nothing could have bought me down.

After the show ended, we headed down to the lobby and I saw my namesake, veteran actress Rosalind Russell. I rushed right up to her and said, "Hello, Miss Russell. My name is Rosalind, too. I spell my name just like yours." She looked at me like I was crazy. She merely nodded her head, then quickly turned away and disappeared into the crowd. I should have felt embarrassed, but not even she could dampen my spirits during my extraordinary evening with the stars.

Daddy splurged and took us to dinner at a beautiful Santa Monica restaurant called The Gates of Spain, which was on the rooftop of the Huntley Hotel, eighteen stories high. We were about as close to heaven as we could get. As we ate, we had a spectacular view of the moonlit

Pacific Ocean glistening before us. It was the perfect end to a dream evening.

When I got back to my tiny bedroom, I couldn't go to sleep. I kept re-living the entire evening in my head over and over again. They say it takes just one small spark to set a fire. That night a fire storm was set ablaze in my soul that could not be extinguished. I was determined to somehow find my place in the glamorous world of Hollywood.

CHAPTER 2:
Long Walk from Compton to Hollywood

*I knew my purpose could be found in Hollywood,
but I was just looking in the wrong direction.*

My fascination with Sidney Poitier started long before the Academy Awards. I was just twelve years old in 1955 when I sat in the movie theater mesmerized by Sidney, who was the star of the hottest new film, *Blackboard Jungle.* I fell madly in love with his smooth chocolate skin, which was a rare sight on screen. He was the only "negro" — as we called ourselves in those days — in a classroom full of unruly teenagers.

Sidney played Gregory Miller, a tough guy with a cool swagger and piercing eyes. Chill bumps popped up on my preteen arms as I watched him defend himself against his teacher's false accusations. I was bursting with pride when he stood firm under her attack. Most of all, my young heart was racing with my first crush. At that moment, though I didn't realize it, the greatest love formed that day was not just for the man, but also for a life in the motion picture industry. Yes, my first bite of the Hollywood bug came by way of Sidney Poitier.

My obsession began that day. I was Hollywood bound with illusions of being on the big screen opposite my heartthrob. I didn't realize the youthful black face I was swooning over was actually a thirty-year-old man. The fact that Sidney had been a struggling actor for more than ten years eluded me.

The bright lights of Hollywood were just twenty miles away from Compton, a short thirty-minute drive, from my parents' tract home.

For a young black girl like me, it might as well have been on the other side of the world. Well-meaning adults advised me to pursue teaching, social work or something else sensible rather than an acting career in Hollywood. Their advice meant nothing. I did what many who have been "bitten" do. From that day forward, I started taking baby steps toward Hollywood, first in my mind, then in earnest.

In the fifties, when I was a child, all roads led to Bel-Vue Presbyterian Church on 118th Street and Stanford. It was a wonderful church located near our home, deep in the heart of South Central, Los Angeles. Every week we went to Sunday School, followed by the regular church service, then later that day, we would return for Youth Fellowship. We were also a part of the church's scout troops, the junior usher board and the young people's choir. You name it; Cookie, Richard and I were there.

When my father acquired the church as one of his janitorial accounts, his reluctant cleaning staff consisted of my sister, brother and me. My father taught us how to vacuum correctly and, most difficult, how to wax floors to a bright shine by maneuvering this huge, cumbersome buffer in the church's social hall. We had to strategically move the buffer's handle up to go one direction, then slowly move it down to go the other direction. The goal was to make a straight, shiny line, then move up to the next line. Each of us lost control of that big, roaring monstrosity more than once. We hated it! My favorite responsibility (if there was such a thing) was dusting the pews. I'd dust the pews by placing the dust rag on the bench, then I would sit on it and wiggle and slide from one end to the other.

When we became adults, we realized what a blessing those experiences were. They taught us valuable lessons about a sense of accomplishment, teamwork, hard work, pride and tenacity.

On occasions, when I was around twelve years old, I joined the band of rowdy teenagers from the neighborhood for wild movie-going adventures. Unsupervised, we rode the red bus from Compton to the end of the line in South Central Los Angeles at Manchester and Broadway Boulevards. There were two magnificent movie houses in the area, The AAA and the Manchester. We always went to the Manchester. It was big fun to go and see the latest movie and act a fool. Once inside, the first thing on my agenda was to go into the ladies' bathroom to transform myself from an innocent schoolgirl to a "fast heifer." First, I would pull out white tubes of my mama's Avon lipstick samples, pick a color and smear it across my lips. Then I would use a Maybelline pencil to draw in my eyebrows and eyeliner. Once I thought I looked grown, I would strut into the darkened theater to join the group. In between watching the movie, we would dance in the aisles, kiss boys, use bad language and puff on cigarettes.

While all the extracurricular activities were fun, most of all, the movie and the stars on the screen had me hypnotized. That is when my wheels first began turning about one day being a part of the Hollywood scene. Some of my Saturday afternoon favorite movies included *Carmen Jones*, starring the drop-dead gorgeous, sepia actress Dorothy Dandridge; *Island in the Sun*, starring tan and sexy Harry Belafonte; *The Girl Can't Help It*, starring blonde bombshell Jayne Mansfield; *Rock Around the Clock*, featuring the rock 'n roll music star Bill Haley & the Comets; *Rebel Without A Cause*, starring blue-eyed bad boy James Dean and sweet-as-pie Natalie Wood; and, of course, every Elvis movie from *Jailhouse Rock* to *King Creole*.

Most of the boys loved the scary, sci-fi fare. That's where we parted ways. I absolutely had no interest in movies like *King Kong*, *The Blob*, *Creature from the Black Lagoon* and *The Thing*. My movie tastes were very distinct. They had to be satisfied with comedy, drama, music and/or romance.

It was years before I made it to Hollywood. I never became a successful actress, nor did I ever share the screen with Sidney. After a ten-year struggle in Hollywood, I eventually discovered my true show business, God-given purpose. I became a publicist and had a very fulfilling career. Most people don't know what a publicist does; however, it is a part of the marketing campaign, the final part of the filmmaking process. So, yes, I did eventually work for Sidney as a publicist on the last film he directed, but more about that, later.

For every actor on a movie set there are several hundred people behind the scenes. I, as others do, started out wanting stardom. Though acting looks simple, it's not. Not everyone has the gift to perform. Studies have found that public speaking and performing are among the greatest fears people have, even greater than a fear of snakes. The idea of making a presentation in public is the number one fear reported by people in the United States.

I was quite talkative and fearless when I was with my friends. However, when I crossed that line to performer or public speaker, I panicked, every time. There are many successful actors who say they have jitters, but they quickly go away once they begin to perform. They learn to use the nervousness to propel their performance. But for those of us without the gift, the fear never subsides. I tried to succeed on screen, but when the nervousness never left and the rejects began to pile up, that dream began to fade away. I was finally forced to let go of the acting dream and find my true calling and place within the world of entertainment.

CHAPTER 3:
Too Cute for My Britches

With time, I went from being an awkward child with
huge feet into a stunning and tall woman.

When I was a kid, my head and feet were always disproportionately bigger than the rest of my body. The first time I realized my head was larger than my peers was when I needed an extra piece of felt to make my Brownie beanie fit. The feet situation was even worse. After extensive searching, I rarely found cute, stylish, shoes in my size. This was long before the internet when a myriad of choices opened up online.

All those embarrassing days ended in high school, as I began to stretch out taller by leaps and bounds. When my growth spurt finally ended, I was sixteen years old, five-foot-eleven and, I was told, absolutely stunning. Finally, everything came together.

The gorgeous beauty I had become was a life-changing experience. Family, friends, and often strangers, would say I should be a model. I forged ahead. Several well-known black photographers took my photographs. I began to participate in fashion shows and enter local beauty contests, most of which weren't particularly well organized. More than anything, they were moneymakers for the organizers, because contestants were required to sell a large number of tickets and ads. Two of the pageants I entered were Miss Bronze Beauty and Miss Photogenic.

Of the two, Miss Bronze was more legitimate. It was run by a well-known photographer named Howard Morehead, who was popular because he was connected to Jet magazine and got girls in the centerfold as the Beauty of the Week. That was a big deal in the black community. I don't remember the winners getting prizes of any real consequence.

I didn't place, however the winner of Miss Bronze was Pearl Robinson, who was a popular, statuesque beauty from our Compton neighborhood. She went on to become an Ebony Fashion Fair model and to have a lucrative modeling career under the professional name of Elizabeth Robinson.

When we were growing up, her father, Jesse Robinson, was the most highly respected Compton resident. He had the distinction of being the first African American postmaster for the City of Los Angeles. Her mother, Myrtle, was a prominent elementary school principal.

Pearl was an only child, who had a warm and friendly personality. The family lived in a large, two-story Spanish Craftsman house with a swimming pool, sprawling grounds filled with colorful flowers and lots of tall trees. We were proud to point their home out, because it was a rarity in Compton, which was best known for miles and miles of cookie-cutter tract homes.

Top social events were often held at the Robinson home. When I was a teenager, I remember attending an extravagant Hawaiian Luau around the pool in their beautifully manicured yard. My sister, brother and I were invited as members of the South Central Chapter of Jack and Jill, as was Pearl. Jack and Jill is a national organization of African American mothers whose goal is to nurture their children to become future leaders. Many consider it to be a "bourgeoisie" organization for the sons and daughters of black doctors, lawyers and judges. But in South Central, our parents were primarily hard working, community active teachers, social workers or, like my mom and dad, civil servants. In Jack and Jill, we participated in many cultural programs and performed useful community services. More than anything, we made lifetime friends with young people who went on to make great contributions to society. Pearl was one of them.

I don't recall who organized the Miss Photogenic pageant, but I do remember the year I entered, I won first place. I was ecstatic when I was presented with a gigantic trophy, which stood almost three feet tall. However, when I got back to the dressing room and took a closer look at it, my delight quickly turned to dismay and anger. There was a golden statuette of a woman leaning over with a bowling ball on top.

Then I noticed the writing on the trophy, and I realized I had been given the organizer's old bowling trophy! I was livid as I stormed out of the dressing room with the bogus trophy in tow. I searched in vain for the organizer, who was nowhere to be found. I threw the trophy in a trashcan as I left in tears and total humiliation. I was never given a replacement trophy, but I did learn a hard lesson about exploitation. From then on, I became more discerning.

My junior and senior years of high school, I became a member of both the Speech, Debate Squad and Drama Club. I was I secretly preparing for my future life in Hollywood. In my senior year, I began doing humorous readings, which I did successfully in competitions throughout the school district.

After I graduated from high school, I entered Cal State University in Los Angeles. I majored in Sociology, however in the back of my mind, I still had Hollywood dreams. Along with my required courses, I managed to squeeze Acting 101 into my schedule.

I was very naive about guys at that time. Because of my height, I was often hit on by men, who were much older than me. Foolishly, I thought I was mature enough to handle them. I had one older boyfriend who I thought was really hip. I met him at a party at a classmate's house. He was her older cousin, who had dropped out of high school years before I attended. He dressed nicely, bought me nice gifts and, most of all, he had a cool MG sport's car. Since he didn't look his age, my parents didn't realize he was too old to be dating me. One day I confided in his cousin that he was nice most of the time, but sometimes he was really moody. She said, matter-of-factly, "That's what happens when that heroin kicks in." "Heroin!" I exclaimed. My eyes almost popped out of my head! I couldn't believe how naive I was. I had never been around a drug addict, so I didn't have a clue what was going on with him. However, I had sense enough to drop that guy like a hot potato.

It wasn't long though before I had another boyfriend, who had just come out of the Navy. I was seventeen years old and he must have been twenty-four or twenty-five years old. He laid his hair down in a smooth, wavy style called a "process" that I thought was fabulous. But when he came to my house in his convertible car, my father flipped his lid. He demanded to know, "How old is that man?" I couldn't lie, so

I mumbled his age under my breath and my father snapped. "What in the hell would a grown man want with you?" My father put his foot down. "You are not going anywhere with that man!"

I cracked open the door and gave the guy a lame excuse about not being able to go out. I closed the door with tears streaming down my face and I screamed at my daddy, "You don't even know him and you're making judgments about him!" My tears didn't impress my father. He said, "I don't need to know a damn thing about that old fart, and he better not come back here again." I sobbed hysterically. Yes, I was a real drama queen.

Thinking about it today, I was really gullible. Thank goodness my daddy saved me from myself that night. Years later, when I became a parent, I was thankful that I only had boys, no girls! From all my "soap opera" experiences, I knew first-hand how young girls could get themselves into some dangerous situations, especially when we think we are attractive to men. Foolishly, I thought I knew-it-all when it came to matters of the heart. While daddy was adamant about me not dating that one guy, over the years there would be a lot more of those incidents. Daddy wasn't always around, so I had to learn the hard way. Even though I was an excellent student and considered one of the smart kids at school, in the School of Life, I had a lot to learn. It took me years before I snapped out of it and sought guidance from God the Father.

ACT II:

I DID IT MY WAY

CHAPTER 4:
Life with Pretty Mel

Young lovers are not always wise.

A funny thing happened on my way to Hollywood: Marriage. When I first flirted with a good-looking college basketball player named Melvin Woodruff, I was still in high school. He had come to my house with a buddy to visit my older sister, Cookie. They all attended Los Angeles City College. When I peeped in the front room and saw the two fine, male specimens, I strutted through wearing my sexy drill team outfit. The guys did a doubletake as I sat down on the couch and forced my way into their conversation. Annoyed, my sister rolled her eyes, however the guys didn't seem the least bit impressed with my conversation. I was still a young girl.

Nevertheless, I still learned that Melvin went by the nickname of "Pretty Mel." He was truly a cutie-pie, but even more importantly, he was tall, six-feet, six-inches. Rarely did I meet guys that much taller than me. Based solely on his height and good looks, I decided, then and there, that I was going after that tall, dark and handsome man. Godly counsel? No way, I just forged straight ahead.

A few months later, my best girlfriend, Saundra Lang, and I attended a college Kappa fraternity party. The party always followed the popular Frat Basketball Games, where the black fraternities — Kappa Alpha Psi, Alpha Phi Alpha, Omega Psi Phi and Phi Beta Sigma — competed. Lo and behold, there was Melvin standing on the wall in the Kappa House. I was wearing a sophisticated St. John knit dress with a leopard skin belt, which I had received as payment for a modeling gig. I thought I looked sharp, so I had no trouble sashaying up to him.

"Aren't you 'Pretty Mel'?" He looked me up and down and said, "Hey, I know you. Aren't you Cookie's little sister?" Since I was considerably taller than her, I said with my best Mae West impression, "No, sugar, I'm Cookie's big sister."

I was happy to find a tall guy to dance with me. I had no idea Melvin couldn't dance. He refused to dance with me, and I later learned he had two left feet and not an ounce of rhythm. He never budged off that wall. He proceeded to ask me stupid, insulting questions like, "Do your parents know where you are?"

Although he didn't dance with me, I felt redeemed when he asked me for my phone number at the end of the evening. However, I never heard from him and I wondered why. Later I found out his grandmother had suddenly passed away, and he had moved back home to Memphis, Tennessee. When he returned to school a year later, I was happy when he called me. Melvin's timing was perfect. By this time, I had gone through more drama with guys than I cared to remember. We started to date.

Although I was barely out of my teens, finding a husband had become an obsession with me. After a very brief courtship and against the wishes of my parents, Melvin, at twenty-two years old, and I, at twenty years old, got married in 1964. I don't know why. I guess I wanted someone to call my own.

God gave me all kinds of signs that getting married to Melvin wasn't a good idea. The first biggest problem was (duh!) neither of us had real jobs. I was in college and working part-time as a Student Worker for the County of Los Angeles Road Department. During that time, I made a $1.66 per hour and I only worked four hours a day. Melvin worked sporadically for his stepfather, who was a remodeling contractor. I foolishly figured we could straighten out those minor problems once we got married.

When we first started dating, he lied and told me he was a building contractor, but he actually worked as a painter and sand blaster. Melvin was good at that job, but all he really wanted to do was to be the remodeling salesman. He joked, "Manual Labor? Who is that? A Mexican?" He loved dressing up in business suits and ties to go out on the job leads. He did earn great commissions on the contracts he wrote but those were inconsistent.

Melvin was a real charmer with a winning smile, who "could sell a refrigerator to an Eskimo." So, as he signed more and more jobs, he did less and less of the painting and sandblasting. However, there were serious problems with the contracts Melvin wrote. He would consistently underbid the jobs in order to get the homeowner's name on the dotted line. It annoyed the hell out of his stepfather. After Melvin got the jobs, he had to constantly go back to the homeowners with various excuses to get more money to complete the job.

Even more foolish, Melvin and I got department store credit cards and charged up whatever we desired. I am embarrassed to say that we never paid for the items we charged.

On one occasion Melvin charged a brocaded satin smoking jacket with an ascot so he could look suave at a holiday party we hosted in our tiny apartment. He looked ridiculous, but he was convinced he looked debonair. To top off "the look," he sat around puffing on a cigar with thick circles of smoke swirling around the heads of our annoyed guests. He got a kick out of being a pain-in-the-butt. Yes, Melvin was a character — the life of the party — but, nonetheless, a real character. He and I were kids pretending to be grown-ups.

Since Melvin worked on commission, I kept trying to convince myself that he would sign a big job and all our financial worries would be over. But it never happened. I cared about paying debts, and I would be terrified when the relentless bill collectors would call and badger us about paying our delinquent bills. I would say, "We have to pay or gas and electric bill or they are going to cut them off." His solution would be, "Put the check for the gas bill in the electric bill, and the electric bill in the gas bill. By the time they figure it out, we will probably have the money!" What?

When I would try to talk to Melvin about their threatening calls, he would simply laugh and say, "May Company has more money than me. They can try and catch me if they can." And, one day they did. I will never forget the two of us going to the department store to charge up some items and they confiscated our credit cards. Honestly, I was relieved. God knew he had to save us from ourselves.

The straw that broke the camel's back was when my car payment was behind. Melvin had promised to get the money, but he didn't come through. I don't remember what the excuse was on this occasion, but it wasn't uncommon for him to gamble away his entire weekly paycheck, trying to double his money and come home empty handed.

With the threat of repossession looming, I had to scramble to pull together the money due to my credit union. I was relieved when I was able to use my paycheck from my part-time job and borrow the rest from a co-worker. I got to the credit union at five p.m., just as they were closing and paid the back due amount.

At that time, we lived in a ten-unit building and we stayed upstairs in the last apartment. My sister Cookie and her husband, Willkie Tucker, lived downstairs in the first unit. That night, we heard noise coming from the parking lot. Melvin looked out and saw two guys hot-wiring my car.

As Melvin ran out bare foot after the guys, who were at that point pushing the car into the street, I called Willkie to help. He ran and jumped in his car. By now the guys got it started as Melvin ran down the middle of the street on foot.

The driver gunned the car and it let out a loud popping noise, causing Melvin to think he had been shot by the thieves. He fell back on the ground as Willkie swooped up.

He screamed, "They shot me, Tuck!" as he held his throbbing leg and eased into the car. Later he realized he wasn't shot; he had merely pulled a muscle, and he presumed the sound of the car backfiring was a gun shot. Anyway, they were in hot pursuit of the car thieves, who sped over to the nearby police station, jumped out my car and ran inside.

The thieves presented paperwork, showing the car was being repossessed for non-payment. Willkie was mortified, because guess what? Willkie was a police officer and they had driven to the 77th Precinct where he worked. Sorry, brother-in-law. Apparently, I had paid so late, the order to repossess hadn't been rescinded. Even though I had proof I paid, the car was still impounded until the credit union opened on Monday and my payment could be verified.

After that, Willkie and Cookie were done with us and our habitual drama. Because our financial situation was so shaky, I decided to quit school and turn my part-time job into a full-time secretarial position at the Los Angeles County Road Department, much to my family's dismay. I figured I had to take action to make ends meet.

After Melvin and I divorced, it took me years to untangle the credit problems we immaturely created, primarily, for only a few thousand dollars of unnecessary purchases.

While we were married, the Watts Riots erupted. It was 1966 and Melvin and I had moved to a large duplex on the Westside, nowhere near the riot zone. However, as things heated up, I got a frantic call from Fannie, my mother-in-law, who lived on the east side. She was scared to death because all the businesses around her were on fire and looting was rampant. She begged me to come and get her. Melvin wasn't around, so I jumped in the car with his pregnant cousin, Vernita, to pick up Fannie. I witnessed the riot firsthand.

We couldn't believe what we saw. People were looting and casually strolling down the street with anything they could get their hands on from the stores in the area. It didn't take much to convince us we needed a few items, too. After all, we reasoned, we had to sustain ourselves until the crisis passed.

Fannie wanted beer, so Nita and I walked into the liquor store and got Fannie a few cases of her favorite Budweiser. Once we had her beer, she was ready to go, but we wanted to get items for us, as well, non-sense like sodas, chips, candy and Old Taylor bourbon for Melvin. Nita's baby was due soon, so we also decided to go into the Thrifty Drugstore and get everything we thought her baby would need – diapers, bottles, powders, oils and outfits. We were walking gingerly on piles of rubble and soot among the mob of shoppers. Armed National Guardsmen were walking up and down the sidewalk, looking right at us, but they made no attempt to stop us from looting. At that point, I decided I also needed makeup, soap, toothpaste, aspirin and anything else I could fit into my hand cart. For years after the riot, I wore makeup from containers that were grey from soot and contained the lingering smell of smoke. As time went on, I asked God to forgive me for my transgressions.

When we returned to the car, Fannie was freaking out, so we reluctantly left. Finally, we got back home where Melvin was waiting and curious about all the items we had. We made up some lame story about looters leaving them on the front lawn of one of Fannie's neighbors.

"The lady asked us to please take the stuff, so she wouldn't get arrested," we lied. He believed our story and was so excited that Old Taylor was among the items we found. "Imagine that. Just what I drink," he said. We looked at each other and smiled knowingly. Melvin prided himself on being a conman, yet he failed to realize when someone was conning him.

Years later, I foolishly told my sons about me being a looter in the Watts Riots. Much to my dismay, that admission came back to haunt me when they did the same thing in 1992 during the Rodney King uprising.

CHAPTER 5:
Saga Continues with Pretty Mel

Young lovers may not make the best decisions
but some good can still come from them.

One of the most enjoyable and memorable moments I had while married to Melvin had to do with the popular game show on TV "Let's Make A Deal." I wrote in for tickets to the show, because at that point, it was about as close as I could get to Hollywood. I asked my sister-in-law, Pat Steverson to join me, and she happily agreed. The first order of business was to have a great costume. Hundreds of contestants would be there, but only a select few would be chosen as participants on the trading floor, and I was determined to get on the trading floor.

I dressed as Raggedy Ann, the rag doll from the popular children's books. I matched her look perfectly. I wore a sailor hat, a red checkered blouse and blue shorts. She had red yarn hair, so I simply wore my own hair, which was dyed "sparkling sherry" red at the time. I used bright red lipstick to paint on her red triangular nose. Melvin was a great sign painter, so he made me a red, white and blue sign that read, "Rags to Riches or Bust – Let's Make a Deal." I was ready! My sister-in-law was cute, too. She dressed as "The Queen of Hearts." She wore two poster boards, one across her chest and the other on her back, a replica of the queen from a deck of cards.

When Pat and I got to the NBC studio in Burbank, there was a mob scene. We were instructed to line up behind a wide yellow line so the show's organizers could get a look at us and decide who would be selected to go on the trading floor. When one of the organizers approached our section, I went berserk. I started hitting him over the head with my poster, screaming, "I wanna make a deal! I wanna make a deal!" Pat was horrified by my outlandish behavior, but there was no shame in my game. As she stepped back, giggling in utter embarrassment, I was given a card to go to the trading floor. At that point, I thought, "Yes sir, the squeaky wheel gets the grease, baby!" I jumped up and down and acted an absolute fool.

Amazingly, by the end of the show, Monty Hall, the show's host, had awarded me the "Big Deal of the Day," which was a roundtrip for two to London and Paris. I also won six-pieces of hot pink Ventura luggage (it was definitely easy to find in baggage claim!). To top it off, I got spending cash, a thousand dollars. The co-host, Jay Stewart, peeled off ten crisp, new one hundred-dollar bills and put them into my wet, shaking hand.

As the show came to a close, I got paranoid that someone would be waiting to hit me over the head and take my cash money. So, I tore open the lining at the bottom of my purse and hid the money under it. However, when I was instructed to come backstage to fill out some paperwork, I was surprised when they asked for the cash money back. Apparently, the cash was only "for show" during the taping and they said they would send me a check. That's when I turned beet red. I had to empty out my purse, pull up the lining and dig out the money. A few months later, Melvin and I flew out on PSA Airlines to London and Paris, where we had a grand time. The trip was a magnificent gift from God, and I failed to thank Him at that time.

Hollywood Comes to My Hood

In my life there have been countless opportunities that have literally fallen into my lap. That was certainly the case in Fall 1968. While still on maternity leave from my job, one day I was walking to the neighborhood market, when I saw the newly opened Performing Arts Society of Los Angeles (PASLA). I curiously walked inside where I was greeted by the workshop's director, Vantile Whitfield. He invited me to observe as he went over a scene with a group of aspiring actors.

I learned that the acting workshop was funded by the Anti-Poverty Program, which was established by the federal government after the Watts Riots. As a matter of fact, there were many new opportunities

24

afforded the black community at that time. I soon discovered more important and critical information about PASLA. I didn't have to pay anything to enroll in the classes. They had babysitting service while classes were going on and the movie studios came to them when they needed black actors to work in TV and films. I signed up that day, and that was the beginning of a new life for me. Surprisingly, Melvin said he didn't care about me going to the acting school. His only stipulation, "Don't expect me to babysit." I assured him that was not a problem.

The classes were wonderful. We did readings from popular black plays of the day, which spoke to the unrest our community was experiencing at that time. Our live productions usually consisted of an evening of one-act plays or spirited monologues. In class we constantly worked on scenes from plays like *Ceremonies in Dark Old Men, Amen Corner, A Raisin in the Sun, The Dutchman, The Blacks, The River Niger, Big Time Buck White, Norman Is That You?* and other works from black playwrights.

It was a time of Black Power and everyone was "Black and Proud." Almost everyone in the workshop adopted African names. Vantile's African name was Motojicho. However, I decided to keep the name my mama gave me. I had black pride, too, however I didn't feel the urge to change my name.

A few years after I joined, we were disappointed when Van closed the workshop and left Los Angeles. Apparently, the grants for Los Angeles were no longer offered. However, he gave us no explanation; he simply returned to his hometown of Washington, D.C., where he started the Black Repertory Company with actor Robert Hooks. While there, he married an aspiring actress from Howard University, Lynn Smith, who hailed from Baton Rouge, Louisiana. She later became the successful actress we know as Lynn Whitfield, best known for her Emmy-nominated portrayal of Josephine Baker and as Samuel L. Jackson's wife Roz Batiste in the critically acclaimed film *Eve's Bayou*. Most recently, she starred on OWN's series, *Greenleaf*, as the first lady of the church.

A few of the actors who trained at PASLA went on to have decent careers in film and television. Most notably, there was Marla Gibbs, who played the hilarious maid, Florence, on the popular TV series

"The Jeffersons" and as Mary Jenkins on "227"; actor/director Eric Laneuville, who starred on the series "St. Elsewhere" and still directs episodic TV to this day; Ta-Tanisha played Pam, a student on the series "Room 222"; Nathaniel "Jitihari" Taylor played Rollo on "Sanford and Son"; Ji-tu Cumbuka landed his first top role in the movie *Uptight* directed by the late director Jules Dassin. Ji-tu is famed for roles in movies such as the films *Harlem Nights, Brewster's Millions, Mandingo* and *Bound for Glory*. In television, Ji-tu is acclaimed for roles in major shows as "Roots," "Knots Landing," "The A-Team," "The Dukes of Hazzard," "Walker Texas Ranger" and "CSI: Crime Scene Investigation." In total, he appeared in more than a hundred films and television series.

Lady Sings the Blues

Incredibly, I got my first chance to work in Hollywood as a policewoman in the film *Lady Sings the Blues* and my idol, Diana Ross, was starring as troubled singing great Billie Holiday. The day started rather strangely at the crack of dawn. In those days, most black extras were cast by a little wheeler-dealer named Eddie Smith. He had given me the assignment the night before with very specific directions. First of all, he said it was imperative to bring my own black lace-up shoes. Not a problem, I lied. I didn't own any black lace-up shoes. My mother-in-law agreed to let me have an old pair of her white nursing shoes. I bought black shoe polish and spent the entire night turning her shoes into black police oxfords.

Also, Eddie said I would be working at Paramount Studios; however, he needed all of his people to meet him at 4:30 a.m. at his house near the studio. I was skeptical. I had Melvin, who was six-foot-six and two hundred fifty pounds, take me to his house. As I suspected, Eddie came to the door with his potbelly spilling over his droopy boxer shorts. Once he got a look at Big Mel, he made a U-turn and jumped into his pants. He moved swiftly to his car and never made eye contact with us, gesturing for us to follow him. In a matter of minutes, we were at the Wardrobe Department at Paramount where I was the first to arrive. Eddie whizzed away and Melvin waited with me in the cold morning air until someone else arrived. What would have happened if he hadn't come with me? I guess Eddie wanted a little casting couch action to thank him for a little extra gig. I'm glad I didn't have to find out. Yuck!

The first thing I noticed, despite what Eddie had said about the shoes, there were hundreds of pairs available. I quickly realized that he was stacking up to be a big-time hustler of black extras. I decided then and there I didn't want to be under his control ever again.

In the makeup and hair department, the hairdresser used a ton of bobby pins and hairpins to create 1930's finger waves. While there I became acquainted with several friendly white women who were playing police officers, too. They freely shared with me how I could become a member of the Screen Extras Guild by signing up with Central Casting in Hollywood. They said after I worked a certain number of hours, I would be eligible to join the union. That was good news to me. Eddie had led me to believe it would take an act of Congress to get into the extras' union.

All of us who were playing policewomen were summoned to the set. They gave each of us something to do. My new best white friend was told to hold Billie Holiday up as she came wobbling through the jailhouse door. I was playing the booking officer. Since I was the only black policewoman, the assistant director had instructed me to recognize Billie as she was being booked in jail. After the director, Sidney Lumet, said, "Action!" I stared and blurted out, "Oh, no, is that Billie Holiday?"

"Cut!" he screamed, and suddenly I was surrounded by an angry mob of crew members.

"You spoke! Extras don't speak!" the assistant director yelled.

"Just nod. React!" another yelled.

It was my first extra assignment in Hollywood, and I committed the cardinal extra sin. I spoke. I thought I was following instructions. I naively thought I was lucky to get a speaking part on my very first casting assignment. Their vicious verbal attack caused me to hyperventilate. The assistant barked at me to do it right the next time.

I had barely regained my composure when the director screamed, "Action!" again. Shaking in my police oxfords, I leaned back on the wall, then as Diana re-entered, I stood up straight, squinted my eyes and gave a puzzled look to indicate I recognized her. This time the director said, "Cut. That's a take."

Whew! They were pleased with my silent bit.

The next day they were going to do another jail scene of Billie flipping out as she came off drugs cold turkey. The assistant director said he wanted me to put her into a straight-jacket and get her in a padded cell.

I thought it was incredible that he was giving me another chance. However, a big discussion ensued between Motown founder Berry Gordy and the director Sidney. Berry insisted a black woman would not have been a policewoman in New York in 1934. In the end, Berry won out and my gig was snatched away, just like that. It was a wrap for me. When the film came out, a year later, there was no sign of me anywhere. Working in Hollywood that day had been the fulfillment of a dream, but, when it was all said and done, I ended up on the cutting room floor.

After that fateful day in 1971, I became a zip-lipped extra for three long years. I never uttered a word. Now I can reveal what it ultimately took for me to discover God's purpose for my life and become successful in Hollywood.

Following the advice of the ladies I had met on the set, the next day I sent my picture and a cover letter to Central Casting. Within a few days, I was registered to work on television and movie sets. In my mind this was a start. My next goal was to get into the Screen Actors Guild and become a full-fledge actress. However, things didn't pan out that way. Much later, I learned that being an extra in Hollywood often had a stigma attached to it and extras very rarely moved on to speaking parts and to become serious actors.

Lessons that I learned from my first day in Hollywood sustained me throughout my Hollywood journey. I learned to be prepared for whatever came my way and to remain positive even when things go wrong. I learned to develop relationships with a network of people. I learned to be pro-active and seek information that could help me get to the next level. Most importantly, I learned to be patient. I realized that, more than likely, I would not reach my goal as fast as I had hoped. Finally, I learned that Hollywood definitely wasn't for the faint of heart. Nevertheless, I felt I was up for the task. It never occurred to seek the direction of the Holy Spirit living inside of me. I was in for a bumpy ride.

Jason Meets Linc

By 1972 I had two sons, a bubbly toddler, Damon Woodruff, was almost two years old, and Jason Woodruff, who was turning five years old. One of the most memorable moments in my marriage to Melvin happened on February 5, 1972, when our oldest son, Jason, was celebrating his fifth birthday at the Beverly Amusement Park in Los Angeles. That park no longer exists. The popular Beverly Center shopping mall sits on the spot where it used to be. In its day, the Beverly Amusement Park was the trendiest place in town to take your kids. Many celebrities frequented the park, so it was a great place to star watch, too.

In preparation for Jason's birthday, I secretly wrote a letter to Clarence Williams III, the black actor who played Linc on the popular TV series "Mod Squad." I told Clarence that he was my son's favorite person on TV, and I would love for him to surprise him and come to his party. I was too embarrassed to tell anyone that I had written a fan letter. I was disappointed, but not surprised when I never heard a word from Clarence Williams III.

However, on the day of the party, Clarence strolled into the park accompanied by his wife, actress Gloria Foster, and a park official. One of the parents spotted him first, "Look, it's Linc from 'Mod Squad'!" I was shocked. When they reached our party, Clarence introduced himself and told me how touched he was by my letter. He explained that for security reasons he didn't respond and added that he never would have come had it been in a private home.

I quickly beckoned Jason so he could meet his hero, but he shyly pulled away and hid behind me. I smiled and gently tugged at him to come around and shake Linc's hand. Finally, when he adamantly refused, I bent down and said, "Honey, Linc came here specially to wish you a happy birthday." Jason quietly whispered to me, "Mommy, if Linc is here, there must be crooks in the park." Everyone laughed, but Jason was dead serious. I tried to explain to him, but at five years old, Jason couldn't understand how Linc got out of our television. He innocently asked me, "Did he come down the cord?"

I learned that day how shy some people get when they meet celebrities, while others act a darn fool. In particular, the parents were embarrassing because they were more excited than the kids. After that party, my friends began to look forward to events that I hosted, because they never knew who they might meet. Years later I was working on a film set with Clarence and I reminded him about coming to Jason's party, which he vividly remembered. We had a good laughed about my son's innocent reaction to him.

As a matter of fact, the same thing happened for Damon, my younger son's seventh birthday, when I had actor Ralph Carter, who played Michael on "Good Times," come to his party. Though Damon knew him well, his friends were afraid of someone they had only seen on TV.

Things Got Ugly with Pretty Mel

Not even memorable times for our children, or an opportunity to work on a Hollywood movie, courtesy of a free performing arts school right in my neighborhood, or an amazing international trip with all expenses paid couldn't salvage my deteriorating marriage. Throughout our eight-year union, Melvin and I had more drama than the then popular soap opera "As the World Turns," or as my mother called it, "As the Stomach Churns." We would break up and get back together, time and time again. We were knee deep in financial trouble, and there were never ending arguments and tension in our home. To top that off, things got real stupid when I found out Mel had two girlfriends on the side. He wasn't good at hiding his infidelity. In order to get back at him, I immaturely decided to sneak around, too. My attitude was, "What's good for the goose, is good for the gander!" I hadn't yet learned that when you do harm to others, you do harm to yourself, as well. I was stressed out to the max.

Finally, by 1972 I knew I needed to get a divorce. By this time, we had two darling sons. I didn't know how my boys and I were going to make it, but I knew I had to end the marriage. Since we owned no property, it was simple. Unbeknownst to Melvin, I went to the local bookstore and bought a *Do-Your-Own-Divorce* book. I typed up the forms on my manual Royal typewriter. I put together the money needed to file and had the papers served on Melvin while we were still living together.

Early one morning the doorbell rang, and I knew it was the process server. I said, "Melvin, that is probably one of your painters. Get the door." He stumbled out of bed and made his way to the door. When they served him, he was stunned because he never thought I would do it. That was the beginning of the end of our marriage, and, praise God, the beginning of the rest of my life. It was sad, because he truly was a fun guy; however, he spent the bulk of his time flaunting, gloating and trying to impress people who didn't really matter.

Over the years, I learned that I liked Melvin like a brother, but not as my husband and provider. I simply couldn't depend on him. Although he loved our boys, and they loved him, after our divorce, he rarely provided for them. With him, you couldn't expect the traditional methods of payment, like mailing a check or money order. I had to badger him and make him feel guilty. On rare occasions he would tell me he would give me, say four hundred dollars. He would suggest we meet at some place near, usually a bar. I had to get there quickly because every few minutes, the amount he was giving went down. I was lucky to get two hundred dollars by the time I arrived. It really wasn't worth the effort. As in our marriage, we were always at odds with one another over money.

At one point, Melvin leased a big house in Baldwin Hills, and he said instead of paying me — which he didn't — he wanted to take care of the boys. He hired a lady named Hattie to take care of them. One day when I went to pick them up, she was looking unhappy. I asked what the problem was, and she said Melvin had not paid her for weeks. I apologized and told her I would be speaking to him about it. I called him and this is how the conversation went:

"Melvin, why aren't you paying Hattie for taking care of the boys?"

"I've paid her! I let her select whatever she wanted from the expensive women's clothes I had. So, she was paid more than enough."

"Melvin, was it clear to her that the clothes were in lieu of being paid, because she's sitting there looking very sad."

"Roz, she looks sad because she is an ugly lady. That's how she looks."

"What?"

I realized he had ridiculous answers for everything, so I just brought my boys back home. I left him to figure out how he was going to deal with Hattie's pay.

After we divorced, Mel continued to conduct his business unethically. He managed to get a license and become a remodeling contractor. Yes, he was a contractor with an emphasis on "con." His company eventually failed because of his unsavory business practices. Legal action was taken against him for embezzling large numbers of homeowners, and he went to jail. After he served his time, he lost his contracting license and the opportunity to work in the State of California.

Eventually, Mel moved to Dallas where he heard there were opportunities for minority contractors. I don't know how it happened, but somehow, he ended up northeast of Dallas in Palestine, Texas. Instead of work, he found the love of his life, Lenice Mims, a hair salon owner. He never really worked while he was there. However, he was a great help to Lenice with her children, all of whom were extraordinarily smart and athletic. Since she worked long hours in her beauty salon, he supervised her household. He also became active in local politics, sports programs and community affairs. He even ran for public office, but he didn't win.

According to Mel, he ran an extraordinary campaign and even arranged to give voters rides to the polls. He said he and his campaign team took over one hundred people. However, when he only received eighty-five votes, he fumed and he wanted to know "which dirty 'MFs' took his ride, then didn't vote for him." He never lost his sense of humor.

In 1997 Melvin was still living in Texas when we learned he was having serious health problems. He was never one to go to the doctor. Pressured by his girlfriend, he finally went and discovered he had stage four prostate cancer. During the next few years, he continued to joke around and pretended he was fine. When the boys would talk to him by telephone, he was always upbeat. However, Lenice kept telling them that he was gravely ill and rarely got out of the bed.

As God would have it, on September 26, 1999, our oldest son, Jason, was getting married to his long-time girlfriend, Nikki. Jason said he wasn't getting married without his daddy in attendance. So, Melvin made a fateful trip to California for the wedding. The airplane trip took a tremendous toll on his failing health. He attended the wedding, but he was in such bad shape that he was unable to attend the reception. Prior to coming, he had had a biopsy that seemed to have sapped the life out of him. When Jason saw him, he cried, "What did they do, give my daddy a lobotomy?" After the wedding, Melvin went to stay at his mother's house. He got in the bed and never left, except to be taken via ambulance to the hospital in the end. Melvin was taking strong doses of painkillers, which made him delusional, and he was constantly talking out of his head.

During that time, he became sentimental and thanked me for being a wonderful mother to Jason and Damon. He also kept telling me as soon as he got out of that bed and made some money, I was the first person he was going to pay. He meant well, but it was too late. Most importantly, during that time his mother's pastor came by to serve him Holy Communion, and that day he accepted Christ and asked for forgiveness for his sins. From that day forward, his favorite pastime was listening to various pastors' sermons and gospel music on cassette tapes. That was a blessing.

It was a very sad but special time for my boys to spend time with their daddy, who had been gone for years. His girlfriend, who had come with him for the wedding, had gone back home. He constantly asked for her. She arranged to return in November for Thanksgiving. At that point he was getting weaker and the hospice nurse had said he only had a few weeks left to live. Lenice arrived on the Monday before the holiday, and he was beyond happy to see her.

His mom had been serving his meals on a small plate and he would eat bite size pieces with his fingers. When Lenice saw this, she was horrified. She said, "Oh, no. I always feed him." She got down on her knees on the side of the bed and spoon fed him. The look of love in each of their eyes was a revelation to me. It was evident that he truly loved and respected her, and she loved him even more.

After that night, he never spoke another word and he slowly faded away. Melvin died early on Thanksgiving morning, November 26, 1999. I was grateful to God that he got a chance to spend his final days with our sons and Lenice, the love of his life. I was deeply moved by their devotion to one another. Before that time, I was convinced that Melvin was incapable of loving anyone, but I had to admit I was wrong. It was eye opening and I learned a great lesson; there is a perfect love for everybody. I am thankful that they found one another.

CHAPTER 6:
Extra! Extra! Read All About It!

Quick, fast and in a hurry—love can be found.

After my initial extra assignment on *Lady Sings the Blues*, my first job call from Central Casting was to be a nurse on the popular TV show "Marcus Welby". When I finally landed the job, I was thrilled, because it was a grueling process to get booked. We were required to call the job lines between 2:00 p.m. and 6:00 p.m. You simply said your name and hoped they would say, *"Hold on,"* which meant they had a job assignment for you. However, ninety-nine times out of a hundred, they said the dreaded words, *"Try later."* Then you would call back again and again to see if they had something for you. In those days we didn't have touch-tone phones or redial capabilities. We had rotary phones, so we had to put our finger in the hole and dial each number one at a time over and over again. It was nerve-racking. Soon I learned that there were three additional extra casting offices, which I joined once I was in the union. Now I had four numbers to call for work assignments. Yikes!

When you were working on a show and needed an assignment for the next day, you had to sneak away and find a pay phone to call in. There would be a long line for the phone, so you would have to wait your turn.

Most extras were jokesters with wicked senses of humor. It wasn't unusual for someone who was told to "try later" to keep talking, pretending he or she got a big job assignment. No matter how many times they pulled that trick, we would fall for it and we would go crazy to see what he or she got. We would just shake our head when we realized we had been had, again.

The job of an extra was a true hustle. When you did get a call, the goal was to make as much money as possible on that particular job assignment. You got base pay for "making crosses." That meant you were a faceless person in the crowd walking up and down the street over and over again. Nobody wanted to merely do that. In order to make more money, extras had various perks like "a car call" where your car was used in the scenes. Also, if you got a "dress call" you would be required to wear formal clothes and were paid extra. Best of all, if you were asked to participate in the scene with the actors in a way that was crucial to the storyline, you got a "silent bit," which is still the ultimate goal of an extra when he or she sets foot on a movie set.

Further, to avoid having to call in every day and have a more stable job situation, the best thing was to be a "stand-in" for an actor or actress. It required that you be his or her skin tone, size and height. You would stand-in for the actor while the lighting director and cameraman set-up their shots, leaving the actual actor to study his or her lines. Right away, I began to look for an opportunity to be a stand-in.

The first time I became a stand-in was for a six-foot tall actress named Tamara Dobson, who starred in blaxploitation film called *Cleopatra Jones*. I was especially happy to get that gig because it was Christmas time and I really needed the cash to buy my kids Christmas gifts.

However, three weeks into the production, I made a big mistake. I left the set at lunch time with my friend, Ann, who was the hairdresser. We got lunch, and then she told me she had to make a "quick stop" at someone's house. I waited and waited in the car. When she finally came out, I could tell she was under the influence of drugs. I was livid and wanted to kick myself for getting involved with someone who had a drug habit. I knew I was in trouble because the stand-in was the first person needed on the set when the lunch period was over. When we reached the set, one of my friends was serving as the stand-in and I was fired, just like that! I learned a hard lesson that day. That was the first and last time I was ever fired from a job. I needed to learn discernment.

Getting Back Out There

While I was in the process of getting a divorce, I realized that the movie sets were great places to meet guys. There were more men than women on the sets, so it was simple to strike up interesting conversations. The key thing was finding out if a guy was actually single, and most weren't.

One guy I met was a handsome hair stylist name Robert Louis Stevenson. He was working on the TV show "Emergency" where I was playing a nurse. It started simple enough. He complimented the natural wig I was wearing. "It looks so real," he said, as he patted my afro.

When he told me his name, it stopped me in my tracks for several reasons; obviously, it was the name of the famous author of *Treasure Island* and his last name, Stevenson, and my maiden name, Steverson, were almost identical. I learned that he lived near me in Inglewood. He was honest about the fact that he was married, and he had a young daughter named Kendra Stevenson. I told him I was in the process of getting a divorce and I had two sons. Over the course of the day, we continued to talk, and our friendship began. Every time I worked at Universal, I "accidently, on purpose" sought him out. He was handsome with a large afro, thick eyebrows and a sexy mustache, and he dressed really cool. I liked that fine man.

Later I was working on "Ironside," starring Raymond Burr with black actor Don Mitchell, playing his office assistant. Lo and behold, Robert was now permanently working on the show primarily as Don's hair stylist. Robert and Don's huge afros looked identical. As a matter of fact, the two looked like twins.

Robert and I resumed talking and he had lots of questions about how my divorce was coming along. He said he had broken up with his spouse, too, and he was very interested in how things were working out for me. It didn't seem like a come-on. He was serious. At the end of the day, he asked for my phone number. That night, as I was unlocking the door, the phone was ringing. It was Robert. Wow! That was the beginning of the rest of my life.

I was surprised to learn Robert's back story. He was the oldest of twelve brothers and sisters. He was born in Louisville, Kentucky, however his parents followed his grandmother's lead and moved to Los Angeles when he was a toddler. Robert grew up in the housing projects in Watts. He was well known as a track star at David Starr Jordan High School. He was the boyfriend of the student body president, Gwendolyn Lett. So, life was good. However, when his mother suffered and died of cancer at age thirty-four, his life was up ended. Their father pretty much abandoned the family, and his grandmother raised his brothers and sisters, moving them to East Los Angeles. But Robert bounced around, living with friends and in time got his own apartment. When he was drafted into the Vietnam War in 1965, the popular couple married. He was lucky to spend his military deployment in Korea, where he served as a gunner and a cook.

Upon return, he took advantage of several G.I. courses, computer programming was one. However, when his good friend's dad, who was a successful barber, suggested they study cosmetology because it was more lucrative, he thought he would give it a try. Surprisingly, he was good at it, and he thought it was cool, fun and creative. After graduating, he worked in a shop on Crenshaw Boulevard. On one fateful day, he heard an announcement over the radio for blacks interested in careers at the movie studio to come and sign up. Always pro-active, he went immediately to the location, signed up for hair and several other careers. As luck would have it, a friend who had also signed up learned someone they knew, lawyer Charles Hack, was in charge of hiring at Universal. Robert called him, Charles pulled his application, and the rest is history.

After initially working only on the Universal Studios lot, Robert's talent, pleasantness and work ethic soon had him traveling to various film locations. How much he would travel was yet to be seen, but as time went on, I came to realize our future life together would be dictated by his numerous travels near and far. For me, it started off simply. In the winter of 1974, he was the hair stylist on a western being filmed in Sonora, California. It was a TV pilot called "Bridger," starring Ben Murphy, James Wainwright and Sally Field. It was the true story of Jim Bridger, the legendary pioneer mountain man who opened the west for settlement in the 1830s by blazing a trail from Wyoming to the California coast.

As would often be the case during the early years of his career, Robert was the only African American on the crew. He would be gone from home from several weeks to three months. While it would always be an exciting adventure, he often found himself lonesome. I promised to visit. The best way to get to Sonora was by Greyhound bus. It was a five-hour ride that took me from Los Angeles to stops in Bakersfield, Visalia, Fresno and, finally, Sonora in Central California. He laughed when I told him I must really like him because I travelled through "Hee-Haw" country to be with him. Sonora was a quaint little town, and Robert was staying at a historic inn called the Gunn Hotel. It felt like we had been taken back in time and landed in the 1800s. Our rooms had ornate, dark antique furnishings with tasteful décor from way back when.

It was a great escape, and I enjoyed my time on the location. Robert was only responsible for styling Sally Field, since the actors were playing mountain men, there was nothing he had to do with their hair. I went on the set with him where I met Sally, who was very friendly and talkative. We bonded over the fact that we both had two sons and had recently gone through agonizing divorces. Once her scenes were completed, she and Robert were free to go back to the hotel. One day, it started to snow, so she offered for us to ride back with her driver, instead of waiting for the crew van. As we got almost back to the hotel, the snow fell to a point that the traffic was moving along at a snail's pace. With the hotel in view, she decided she wanted to walk. Robert didn't think it was safe, so he decided to walk with her. After all, she was well known as the star of "Gidget" and "The Flying Nun." As they moved out, I didn't budge. I informed Robert I didn't have the proper shoes or winter wear to walk in the snow. I didn't care how long it took; I was riding in the car. He was okay with that.

Over the next several days, Robert and I had romantic dinners, loving nights and plenty of uninterrupted time to get to know one another better and share our hopes and dreams for the future. The trauma we were going through with the break-up of our marriages was taking a toll. The undoing of a marriage was the most stressful experience either of us had ever experienced, especially since it involved upsetting the lives of our children. We yearned for peace in our lives and that's what our relationship offered us. As my visit was coming to an end, I didn't want to leave. When I did go, I left Robert feeling it was possible to find love, again. My future looked bright. But now it was time to get back to my boys.

Robert's divorce was a much longer process, which was emotionally taxing for him. Every day we talked through our challenges and helped each other get through our situations. Our relationship came together in record time and as I write this, it has been forty-five years since we first met. We got married in 1977 and Robert has been my very best friend and the most wonderful husband I could ever ask for. Together we have built a wonderful life. I thank God every day for sending him to me — quick, fast and in a hurry!

We have one son together, Teron André Stevenson, who was born on September 15, 1979. We blended our families, my boys Jason and Damon, and his daughter, Kendra, who continued to live with her mother. We have lived in our home in Ladera Heights, California, for over forty years. Both of our careers blossomed to greater heights after we got together. Robert has always been my biggest cheerleader and I have been his. Most importantly, our Christian walk began during our marriage and continues to be the backbone of our relationship today.

While we were dating, Robert started to work on feature films and began taking projects at other studios. It began at Universal when he was a hair stylist on Richard Pryor's film *Car Wash*. After that, Richard asked for him to serve as the supervising hair stylist on some of his greatest films: *Greased Lightnin'* (Warner Bros.), *Which Way Is Up* (Universal), *Blue Collar* (Universal), *Some Kind of Hero* (Paramount), *The Toy* (Columbia), *Superman III* (Warner Bros.) and *Harlem Nights* (Paramount).

As Robert's reputation grew, he also began having memorable experiences as the hair stylist on movies for Eddie Murphy *(Coming to America, Another 48 Hours, Harlem Nights)*, Angela Bassett *(What's Love Got to Do with It, Strange Days, Waiting to Exhale)* and his longest, fourteen years with actor Samuel L. Jackson. With more than one hundred fifteen film credits, other stand-out movies include *The Color Purple, Sister Act I & II, Amistad, Flashdance, A Time to Kill, Jackie Brown, Eve's Bayou, Jarhead, Three Kings, Coach Carter* and *The Butler*. Robert worked non-stop in the business for four decades from 1969 until he retired in 2009.

Robert also supervised several television movies for which he was recognized for Emmy Awards. In 1985 he won a Primetime Emmy for "The Jesse Owens Story," starring Dorian Harewood and Debbie Morgan. Additionally, he was nominated for two more Primetime Emmys for "The Atlanta Child Murders" and "The Jacksons: An American Dream." In 1998 Robert applied and was accepted as a voting member of the Academy of Motion Picture Arts and Sciences. Highly respected, he also served on the Executive Board for the Makeup Artist Branch of the Academy.

Lastly, in February 2019, he was honored as the first African American to ever be selected for the Lifetime Achievement Award by his union. That evening during the Make-Up Artists and Hair Stylists Guild Awards (MUAHS, IATSE Local 706), he spoke about the circumstance surrounding his opportunity to become a film hair stylist and the challenges he had faced. The following is some of what he shared with the audience:

> In 1969 the federal government conducted hearings with the Hollywood studios about their minority hiring practices. The EEOC's research found 19,000 people working at the studios, of those only 400 minorities, mostly in maintenance and entry level jobs. To right that wrong, the studios agreed to a federal mandate, which required the studios to offer job opportunities by advertising in minority newspapers and on minority radio stations. I knew none of this; however, when I heard the announcement on the radio, 'If you are interested in working in Hollywood, come and sign up at Contract Services,' I went and filled out an application and eventually was given a three-year apprenticeship. I was met with resistance. The situation at that time was all makeup artists were white men, who wore white shirts and ties. The hair stylists were all white women, who wore dresses and their hair pinned up. Imagine the sight of me, a black, male hair stylist with my big afro, bell bottoms and platform shoes! However, as time went on, I was helped by some of the best makeup artists and hair stylists in the business. While I shared with them how to style black hair, they guided me and helped me so that I developed into a successful film hair stylist.

All our family and many friends attended, among them his two sisters who followed in his footsteps, makeup artist Joanetta Stowers and hair stylist Linda Khan. He also has a niece, Jataunia Schweitzer, who gave up a career in public health to become a makeup artist. Also, in attendance were his brothers Jackie Stevenson, Bernard Stevenson, his uncle Harold Joyner, sister Connie White and niece Shonita Stevenson. In particular, he recognized a few of his friends who also came into the industry under the federal mandate and have had successful careers. His friends include the following: Norm Langley, a cameraman and lifetime achievement recipient; Stephanie Colin, who was a young teenage mother when she started working in wardrobe and now her son has a successful career in wardrobe; Cheryal Kearney, who was the first African American Set decorator and an Emmy winner, and his golf buddy, Alan Oliney, who was a champion gymnast at their high school in Watts and started his career as a stuntman when Clarence Williams III on "Mod Squad" insisted they find him a black stunt double. Alan went on to be an outstanding stunt coordinator and has doubled some of the biggest stars in the business. Robert's insightful speech and award were both a beautiful end to a career that took him from the projects in Watts to all around the globe working with Hollywood's best.

Back to Me

In the Screen Extras Guild, I had an edge over many of the women because I had a professional appearance. Most of the black female extras were former showgirls, dancers and singers and they tended to dress flashy, wear a lot of makeup and huge, showy hairdos. I was always selected when they were looking for a black business professional. I found my niche.

My longest running job was playing a teacher on a popular TV show called "Room 222." I loved that show, starring Lloyd Haynes, Michael Constantine, Karen Valentine and Denise Nicholas. We had lots of fun on the show, which was filmed at 20th Century Fox Studios.

"Room 222" was produced by Gene Reynolds, who was a University of Southern California (USC) alumnus. He made it a point to hire the Trojan football stars to work as extras during the summer months. It was a good deal for both. The ball players could earn some easy Hollywood money and Gene gained clout with his alma mater. When I was on the show, both wide receiver Lynn Swann and quarterback Pat Haden worked during the summer. Lynn was about nineteen years old and he was intrigued by me, although I was nine years older than he was. I had a "big sister" relationship with him and we remained good friends for many years.

While Lynn was working on "Room 222," he lived at the home of former USC football great O.J. Simpson and his first wife, Marguerite, with their two young children, Arnelle and Jason. O.J. was playing professionally for the San Francisco 49ers at that time. I remember Lynn wondering if he would ever be as famous as O.J. He talked about what it was like to go into restaurants with O.J. If the restaurant staff didn't treat him like royalty, he'd really get pissed off. Of course, today Lynn would not want to be as notorious as O.J. has become since being found not guilty in the highly publicized criminal trial for the murders of Nicole Simpson and Ron Goldman. Back then, no one would have ever dreamed O.J.'s life would turn upside down the way that it has.

Another regular classroom extra was a young kid named Brian Grazer, who ultimately became an Academy Award-winning filmmaker as the head of Ron Howard's Imagine Films. Years later, when I became a publicist at Universal Studios, I would run into him because we released most of Imagine's movies. However, he didn't seem to remember me from our days on "Room 222." One day I casually said to him, "Brian, I just spoke with Lynn Swann from the Pittsburgh Steelers. He used to work with us on 'Room 222.' He told me to tell you hello." He was stunned and stammered. "Oh, my goodness, that was a long time ago. I didn't realize you worked on the show. Tell Lynn I said hello." With that, he scurried away quickly, as I secretly chuckled.

In 1978 when Robert worked on a film called *The Fish Who Saved Pittsburgh*, and Lynn came on the set to visit one of the stars of the film, basketball great Dr. J. Lynn was pleasantly surprised to see me. He was kind enough to give my family tickets to see him and the Pittsburgh Steelers play at Three River Stadium that coming Sunday. When I told my two sons where we were going, they were not the least bit impressed. "Oh, okay," they said casually. However, once we arrived at the stadium, they realized the magnitude of football and the Steelers in that city. Even more surprising, they were stunned when they realized what a big star Lynn was. It was an unforgettable experience. From that day forward, they talked about "their good friend, Lynn

Swann."

The last time Lynn and I were in touch was during the filming of *The Color Purple* in 1984. He was a huge fan of the book and he wanted to visit the set. My husband was the supervising hair stylist on the movie, so he arranged for Lynn to visit. Lynn went to the location in Madison, North Carolina, and hung out for a week. Most of all, he enjoyed talking with director Steven Spielberg and all the cast members, and he especially loved horseback riding around the set with Danny Glover.

I recently spoke with Lynn when he visited my church after he returned to Los Angeles as the athletic director of USC. He resigned that position in 2019. At sixty-eight years old, I am assuming he is now happily retired.

Extra Odd Jobs

As an extra, I had the most fun playing extreme out-of-character roles. For instance, black females were most often cast as hookers. One day I got a call to play a prostitute for the "Kojak" TV show on the Universal Studios' back lot. I put on my boots, mini dress, huge afro wig and headed to work.

There was a dozen or so pimp and hooker-types on the call. One of the hookers was played by a transgender actor, Eva, who used to work in the business as Eddie before her sex change. None of the "pimps" wanted Eva to be their girl. The assistant director had no idea about the situation. He told a stuntman named Alex to team up with Eva. Alex screamed, "Oh, hell no! I have swung through the tree on 'Daktari' with that negro. I'll be damn if he's going to be my girl." The assistant was puzzled as we all fell out laughing. Eva took out a can of mace and exclaimed, "I'll spray your ass, Alex, if you don't shut your mouth." It was crazy. In the end, Alex reluctantly walked with her at arms-length. In those days, people weren't as thoughtful and politically correct as they are today about those types of issues. The assistant director was totally perplexed until someone pulled him aside and whispered in his ear.

On one memorable occasion, I had played "a neighbor" in a 1930s period landmark film called, *The Sting*, starring Robert Redford and Paul Newman. The wardrobe department issued me an old robe, flannel gown and house shoes to wear. We were taken to the studio back lot where we were instructed to wait for the film company to arrive from another location. It was freezing cold, so to keep ourselves warm, we started to sip on some peach cognac. By the time the film company arrived, we were all "drunk as skunks."

For the scene we were filming, Johnny Hooker (Redford) comes into the black neighborhood to meet up with his con partner, an old black man named Luther, played by Robert Earl Jones, who was actually the father of famed actor, James Earl Jones. In the film, Luther had taught Johnny everything he knew about running con games, but now the old man yearned to get out of the business. However, before he could escape and before Johnny arrived, he was killed by some people he had conned, and they threw him out of the window of his second story apartment.

When Luther's wife arrives home, she sees her husband's bloody, lifeless body lying on the ground and she begins to scream hysterically. I played one of the neighbors, who was snooping around to see what was going on. Well, given that I was highly intoxicated, I truly over acted. I am prominently seen in the movie tiptoeing behind his wife with my eyes bugging out and my finger stuck in my mouth. I looked ridiculous.

Every time that movie comes on television, my husband falls out laughing at my moment in the "dim" light. I worked on hundreds of shows, but that one will live on as the most hilarious moment I am seen on film.

Extras are a tight knit group, no matter your age or race. Some of my best girlfriends were white. On one occasion we were all cast as townspeople in "Hec Ramsey," a Richard Boone TV western. However, once we got to wardrobe department, my white girlfriends were issued beautiful satin and lace dresses with full petticoats carrying matching parasols and donning fabulous hats. I was looking forward to getting a gorgeous dress, too, but it was not to be. Instead, I was issued a slave outfit. I got a long, drab gray, cotton dress with an apron, a head rag and a broom.

All day, as my white girlfriends pranced up and down the street, twirling their parasols, I walked with my head down sweeping the dirt street. My girlfriends laughed at me until they were in tears that day.

However, I couldn't stop thinking about how terrible my ancestors must have felt to really be relegated to that station in life. I was humiliated "playing" the part for just one day.

One of the more peculiar and lucrative ways I found to make money was as a hand model. I had always been complimented on my beautiful hands. When I found out it could be a moneymaker for me, I jumped at the chance. On the television series "Get Christie Love," starring Teresa Graves as a black female detective, I got my first opportunity to be her hand model. Apparently, Graves was a nail biter, so I was asked to double for her hands. They filmed my hands shooting guns, opening safes, searching through drawers, thumbing through magazines and whatever hand shots were needed. After successfully working on "Get Christie Love," I decided to advertise my hands.

I even went to the expense of creating a composite sheet featuring my hands, with photos of me handling a mirror, putting on face powder, putting on sunglasses and handling a camera and spraying hairspray. Those jobs paid four-times what you would receive for regular assignments, so it was quite lucrative. Eventually I had the odd, distinct honor of becoming "the black hand" in commercials. Most often, I worked alongside a veteran hand model named Michelle, who was "the white hand."

Michelle clued me in on the important tricks of the hand-modeling trade. For instance, in order for your hands to look as smooth, soft and pretty as possible, we used rich moisturizing lotion while on the set. After generously lathering it on and rubbing it in, we would lock-in the moisture by sitting on our hands until we were needed. Once we received direction, we would hold our hands high up in the air to flatten any protruding veins. Then when the director shouted, "Action," we would quickly bring down our hands and do the necessary action. Among the other commercials with products that featured my hands were: Kodak, Wrigley's Gum, Tropicana Orange Juice, Bic Lighters, Sara Lee, Sprite, Coke Cola, Salem Cigarettes and many more.

After a time, I became over-confident about landing the hand modeling jobs. On one audition for Frigidaire, I was thrown a curve ball. I didn't realize my hands were going to be used to double a petite black actress named Vernee Watson. I am very tall with long fingers. When the director asked to see my hands, I boldly set them out flatly on the table, spread wide. He shook his head and said, "Oh, no. Your hands are way too big for our actress." Then he laughed and said, "If we need someone to palm a basketball, we'll call you," as he quickly ushered me out of the door. I was stunned. After that experience, I learned to hold my hands up delicately, like I was holding an object, rather than laying them out flat.

Sometimes we were asked to do things that required a steady hand, and mine, unfortunately, sometimes shook when I got nervous. I remember doing a commercial for a vegetable stew product. I was instructed to put the spoon in the bowl and specifically pick up a piece of beef, two green peas, a pearl onion and a piece of carrot, then raise the spoon and move it out of camera without spilling anything. Invariably, the gravy or one of the veggies would drop off the spoon onto the tablecloth, and we would have to do it over. Re-starting required another bowl of stew where the food stylist would painstakingly add brightly colored vegetables with tweezers on top of the stew to make it look colorful and appetizing. When we finally got some good takes, I couldn't get out of there fast enough.

On another occasion, I had to fill a glass with orange juice starting with the pitcher at the top of the glass, then lifting it up about a foot for a steady stream of orange juice without it splattering everywhere. So, you see, though hand modeling paid well, I earned my money.

Since I never knew when a hand-modeling job might come along, I went to great lengths to keep my nails in good shape. For most jobs they wanted short, nicely trimmed housewife hands with clear polish. However, I kept them somewhat long, just in case. Then I would cut them, as needed, for the job. I did my housework wearing rubber gloves to keep my hands lovely, moist and fresh. If I broke a nail, it was a major catastrophe.

I was proud of my work, but my family found it laughable. While I was at a family dinner, one of my hand commercials came on the television. I screamed, "That's my hands! That's my hands!" My family was absolutely embarrassed for me and they teased me to high heaven. I was working in Hollywood, and all I had to show for it was my hands in a commercial. They shook their heads. "That is sad," my mother said. "Very, very sad," the others laughed.

When you get an extra assignment, your hope is to be converted to a speaking part, "going SAG," they called it. I "almost" got my chance when I was working on the 1973 blaxploitation film, *Scream, Blacula, Scream*, starring William Marshall. Rubin Watt, the black assistant director, was always looking for an opportunity to get one of us converted. He told my girlfriends and me he needed one of us to scream when we saw Blacula's latest victim falling down the staircase. My friends Annette, Doll and I were asked to "audition" for the role. Doll went first and she gave a weak scream. Annette was so excited that her throat closed up and she barely got out a whimper. He then asked me to scream. I opened up my mouth wide, let out a blood curdling scream. When I finally stopped, he said I had the role. I was beaming about getting my first "speaking (screaming) role." However, when the time came, the director pointed to one of the actresses, who was already being paid to act, and told her to scream. That quick, my opportunity to "go SAG" was snatched way.

Some movies used the same extras from the beginning until the end of filming. To get on such an assignment meant a guaranteed two to three months of continuous work and pay. The very last jobs I auditioned for was to be a village peasant in a pirate film called *Swashbuckler*. Fifty or so black extras were being selected. The casting office didn't send me on the audition, and none of my black friends told me about it. Nevertheless, I heard about it from one of the white extras. I realized I didn't have the dark skin tone to be considered a Caribbean peasant. So, I wore darker makeup and I dressed the part. I wrapped my head in a raggedy old diaper I normally used for dusting. I wore a lifeless potato sack blouse and a wrap-around gauze skirt. At the audition, I stood bare foot with no makeup, looking downtrodden. I was picked. Yes! It felt good to use my ingenuity to get selected.

What was even better, a few days later, I went to the wardrobe fitting. I was fully made up and I wore a beautiful outfit with a stunning head-wrap. The costume designer said, "You're too pretty to play a peasant. Why don't we make you the pirate's wench. The pirate turned out to be James Earl Jones! I wore a beautiful pink satin corset and a long flowing lace skirt. It was a fitting end to my career as a movie extra. It was time to move on.

CHAPTER 7:
Then There Were Good Times

*I went from in front of the camera to behind the desk
and learned even more about the entertainment business.*

After three years of struggling as an extra, I finally got it through my head that acting was not my gift and I had little or no chance of becoming a full-fledged actress. I thought God must have a greater purpose for my life. While it had been fun, I knew I had to get a real J-O-B. More than anything, I was struggling as a single parent and the pressure was ever-present. I began putting feelers out among all my friends. Finally, I got help from Pat Edwards, who was my friend from the world of black theater and worked on the popular television show "Good Times." She was moving up to the position of stage manager, so she informed me about her old spot as assistant to the producers. I interviewed for the position and (Praise God!) I got it. It was hard to go back to a nine-to-five after freelancing on movie sets. As a matter of fact, I felt sick and perspired profusely my very first day on the job.

My fear subsided once I met the welcoming, warm and friendly staff. Central to my immediate comfort were the two veteran producers I was hired to work for, Jack Elinson and Norman Paul. They were an odd but darling team. Norman was a seasoned comedy writer, who was also a stumbling, bumbling alcoholic. He spurted out hilarious punch lines like a machine gun. Jack was the organizer. He structured the storylines and typed the comedic dialogue provided by, more often than not, Norman. Jack typed with unbelievable speed using only two fingers on a manual typewriter.

Then There Were Good Times

Jack's history as a comedy writer went back to the earliest days of television, beginning with "The Colgate Comedy Hour" in 1953. Among other landmark shows he wrote for were "The Andy Griffith Show," "The Real McCoys," "Hogan's Heroes," "Make Room for Daddy" and "That Girl." Norman had a long list of classic shows he had worked on, too, including "Topper," "George Burns and Gracie Allen Show," "The Doris Day Show," "Get Smart," "Gomer Pyle," and "Francis the Talking Mule."

Learning to work with the two veteran writers required figuring out their unique style. Norman never sat at a desk, nor did he use typewriter, paper or a pen; he just talked. He would lie on the couch discussing the story lines while Jack sat at the desk typing. I sat outside of the office they shared eager to do whatever they needed me to do. Without warning, Norman would swing open the door and charge out with a red, flushed face and eyes glazed over. I would ask, "Can I help you?" but he wouldn't utter a word as he looked right passed me. I soon realized that he was allowing Jack to catch up with him on the typewriter. He would silently pace in front of my desk, then he would spin around and head back in the office and shout, "Then J.J. would say," as he slammed the door behind him. Some of the funniest lines ever delivered on "Good Times" came from the mind of Norman, including J.J.'s signature phrase, "Dy-no-mite!"

Norman was old and wrinkled with a potbelly and a flat butt. Many times, when he jumped up, his pants would slide down, exposing half of his behind. So, when he ran out of his office, sometimes I had the odd duty of urging him to pull up his pants and tighten his belt. Every day with those two was wild!

Often, I would get calls from bars or restaurants where Norman had been the night before, because he would drop his wallet containing his credit cards and money. He was well known and respected wherever he went, so they would call me, and I would send a messenger to pick up his belongings.

Norman had an elderly wife who was bed-ridden, whom I never met. He was committed to taking care of her; however, he had a beautiful, young, red-head girlfriend on the side. In the office, we referred to her as the "gold-digger." Her biggest claim to fame was having worked in every Elvis movie. We all surmised that she had possibly been the girlfriend of someone in Elvis' camp. She was the only woman we ever saw Norman with. When he suddenly died in 1979, we all attended his funeral. For the first time we saw his wife sitting on the front row. Where was the girlfriend? She was sitting on the very back row of the chapel wearing large, dark glasses.

Norman was Jewish. At his funeral, I experienced a cultural ritual they did during the burial ceremony. After they lowered the casket, it is considered an honor for each guest to shovel up some dirt and toss on top of the deceased person's casket. It was a touching gesture, which, I thought, would never, ever work with black folks. I imagined one of us crying uncontrollably as we tried to toss the dirt, and someone would end up falling in the hole on top of our dearly departed love one. It would be utter chaos.

There was another young, fun-loving team on the writing staff, Kim Weiskop and Michael Baser. Kim was the son of Robert Weiskop, one of the famous writers from the classic "I Love Lucy" series. Michael was a hippie type with a huge, floppy head of curly hair. Every day, while writing their teleplays, they sat in their office tossing a sponge basketball through a plastic hoop held on the wall with suction cups.

When I first joined the staff, the show's executive producer was Allan Manings, who had a sharp, sarcastic tongue. He was a very opinionated Jewish man, who continually caused dissention among the African American cast and staff. He particularly had a bug up his butt about Esther Rolle, who he thought spoke too proper to be Florida Evans, playing the mother of kids in Chicago's Cabrini Green Housing Projects.

Additionally, Esther constantly challenged him on the direction of the show. "Good Times" was Esther's spin-off from the "Maude" show, where she had played her maid. She, rightfully, felt "Good Times" was her show. However, when the public was drawn to J.J.'s character, which was played by comedian Jimmie Walker, the writers started making the show more about him. Esther was angry and challenged every new script that put the spotlight on J.J. Allan arrogantly made it clear that he had the final say on the direction of the show, and that didn't sit well with the Esther or John Amos, who played her husband, James. There were rarely complaints from Ber'Nadette Stanis, who played

J.J.'s sister, Thelma, and young Ralph Carter, who played J.J.'s brother, Michael, on the show. However, Esther and John routinely, vehemently, questioned the scripts, storylines and dialogue.

There were other times when their complaints didn't have anything to do with the storylines. Sometimes the black cast and staff just got pissed-off at the gall and insensitivity of the producers. For instance, on tape night we recorded two shows before a live audience; one taped at 5:00 p.m. and another taped at 8:00 p.m. In between the shows we went into the rehearsal hall for a catered dinner. Esther questioned why we always had a caterer with tasteless, bland food, which the majority black cast and staff didn't care for. She felt, we could change up sometimes and use a caterer who served tasty, healthy soul food, which we would enjoy much more. However, the producers ignored her and continued to have caterers of their choosing. Esther then went to the associate producer, George Sunga, to request a caterer she wanted. Finally, he gave in.

The first night the black caterer came, there were huge smiles on all our faces. The Jewish producers, on the other hand, were a different story. They abruptly walked out rather than eat her food. After years of eating their food preferences, we were stunned by their rudeness. However, the bottom line was we really didn't care. Let them go somewhere and get some kosher food, if that is what they wanted. Our yummy soul food spread was prepared by a North Carolina native named Loni Kay Harkless. The cast and crew dived into her food like there was no tomorrow. She had prepared all our favorites that included the following: fried and baked chicken, greens, candied yams, macaroni and cheese, topped with peach cobbler for dessert. When word got out about our delicious spread, the next thing we knew, in walked Rob Reiner and Sally Struthers from "All in the Family." Others joined, too. When our producers returned, they were shocked to see the invasion of other white folks, who wanted to partake of the delicious soul food meal. We won that battle and Loni Kay continued to cater.

Tape day was always an exciting, but tedious time, because we taped before a live audience twice a day within a three-hour span. After the end of the final taping, we would go over any mistakes and determine which scenes had to be re-done. It could be a long night.

This was a dilemma for me as a working mother. On normal workdays, I had Jason and Damon in sports activities, and I would pick them up after I got off. However, if Robert was working out-of-town, my boys would be left unsupervised later in the evening. To solve the problem, I hired a driver to bring them to the television station. Their driver was a guy named Mel, whose mother owned the answering service I used, and she also owned the Yellow Cab company in Culver City. Mel and the boys got to be buddies as he brought them to KTTV for me every Thursday evening. Other staff would have their children there, too. The kids would have fun hanging out in the dressing rooms with the cast. There was also a room where they could eat snacks and watch the taping on a monitor. Things ran smoothly.

During the week there could be problems between the cast and producers leading up to tape night, but they would be resolved by Thursday. In particular, John was always angry with the producers and there was one occasion when he took it out on the show's director, Herb Kenwith. Herb was a tiny, soft spoken guy, who tried his best to keep peace on the set. On this particular occasion, John came back from lunch with an attitude. Herb was starting to block a new scene. He saw through his peripheral vision that John was in a funky mood, so he worked with the rest of the cast and said sweetly without looking at him, "John, I'm going to need you in a minute." John sat there with an angry scowl on his face, not uttering a word. Herb kept blocking the scene until he had to have John. He went over and touched John. "I need you now." John grabbed Herb by both arms and lifted him off the floor. Herb whimpered, "Please put me down" and John abruptly put him down. Everyone's mouth fell open. Herb was more shaken than anything, as was everybody else. John was a pistol. He did things just to annoy the producers. The producers annoyed him and he, in turn, did things just to let them know he wasn't taken their mess lying down.

On another occasion we were doing a two-part show. We did the first part, then the show went on a one-week hiatus. When John came back, he had grown a mustache. Herb casually said to John as rehearsals went on, "We'll need to match the first look, John. You'll have to lose the mustache." John ignored him. Finally, tape day came and Norman Lear, the top man at Tandem Productions, came down on the set. He said, "John, will you please shave your mustache?" John said, without hesitation, "Sure," and went to the makeup artist and had her shave it off. This time the mission was accomplished without an explosion.

However, we weren't as fortunate the next time. We did an episode called "The Family Tree," which was about John's character, James Evans' biological father finding him and seeking his forgiveness after abandoning the family when he was child. Unbeknownst to any of us, this was John's true-life experience and he exploded when he read it. He felt the writers had purposely written about his personal life. The truth was our black staff writer, my good friend Bob Peete, wrote that teleplay, and he had no idea John had been raised in a single-parent household and his father had abandoned the family. The bottom line, fathers not taking responsibility for their children is a common scenario. Nevertheless, John made a huge scene. He overturned the table at the reading and scared the hell out of everybody. The yelling, cursing and screaming between John and the producers began and ultimately everyone went huffing, puffing and moving into separate corners.

Always the peacemaker, Ja'Net DuBois, who played the popular, spunky neighbor Willona Woods, would plead with everyone to get along and act civil towards one another. It was very unsettling for all of us to work in a virtual war zone. Everyone wanted a peaceful set, however the arguments continued. The producers didn't try to neutralize the situations, they kept stirring things up and the cast bucked at their gall. The bottom line, the producers really did not feel that the black actors had any say-so, and the cast felt disrespected.

Sadly, after things got so bad, the producers — in a blatant show of authority — killed off John's character and, in my opinion, essentially killed the show. As tough as John was to work with, the James Evans character was dearly beloved by the TV audiences. The show continued for a couple of more seasons, but it was never the same without John. We missed him and the show started on a downward spiral.

I remember my own personal run-in with Allan Manings, which got me kicked off the staff for a minute. On New Year's Day, Esther Rolle had co-hosted the Tournament of Roses Parade on KTLA, Channel 5. She wore a beautiful white diamond mink coat with a matching mink hat. She looked great and did an excellent job. However, the next day Allan walked into the other producers' office and started loudly ripping her apart. In addition to making fun of her coat and hat, he negatively bashed her for the way she spoke with a "fake English accent." I was boiling. I had taken about as much of him as I could take. When he turned to go back to his office, he could see the scowl on my face.

"What's wrong with you?" he asked.

I blurted out, "How do you think it makes us feel to hear you tearing Esther down like that?"

He blew his top, "This is my show and if you don't like what I say, you can get the hell out!" Then he stormed into his office and slammed the door. I got my belongings and headed out the door. Once I got to my car, his secretary ran after me. She said he thought about his rude comments; he was sorry and wanted me to stay. Whew! I was glad because I really needed my job. I humbly returned to my desk. He didn't say anything further to me that day, and I didn't say anything, either.

Despite all the drama, I looked for ways to advance my career. I volunteered to assist with Norman Lear's Minority Writers Program, a national search for black writers. Bob Peete, the only black writer on staff at that time, administrated the program. My main responsibility was sending out an encouraging rejection letter to those whose stories were not being considered. I also would help read scripts and make a recommendation, if a submission had some merit. Those were few and far between.

More importantly, I wanted to be a writer, so my husband Robert became my writing partner, and we were granted an opportunity to pitch five story ideas. The producers liked one and gave us the green light to write a teleplay we entitled, "Penny's Christmas" for the fifth season of the show. It was the story of Willona's soon-to-be adopted daughter, Penny, played by Janet Jackson, who was pick pocketed when she went to buy her mom a Christmas gift. Without the money she had saved, Penny took a necklace and slipped it into her pocket, which was seen on the security camera. Subsequently, the theft jeopardized the adoption plans. However, the social worker attended the Evans family's loving Christmas party, and in the end, she concluded that Penny lived in a positive and a healthy environment.

Janet was nine or ten years old when she was selected to play Penny. She was shy and very sweet, much like her mother Katherine, who accompanied her to the set, along with their friend and driver named Mickey. The Jacksons were devoted Jehovah's Witnesses.

When we did the first table read of the script, Janet came to me and said she wasn't sure her mother would let her do an episode about Christmas. She said, "We don't celebrate Christmas." I said, "Well, Penny does." She realized that she was an actress playing a part and it had nothing to do with her being a Jehovah's Witness. I was so glad, because it was my first teleplay, and I didn't want any confusion that could mess up my opportunity to be a writer. I had hoped to become a staff writer, but I was never given another opportunity.

We were not deterred. Soon after that, Robert and I were motivated to join the Writers Guild of America's Open-Door program for aspiring minority writers. When the year-long program ended, Robert won first place for his western *Half Moon* about a runaway slave living with an Indian tribe. I won third prize for a script called *Lady T*, which was the true story of my friend's mother, Mrs. Torrance, who ran a deluxe boarding house in Los Angeles for black entertainers and railroad men in the forties. After the winners were announced in the trades, we got requests from producers to read our winning scripts, but no deals were made.

We were most proud of the children's stories we wrote for Ebony Jr., the newest magazine from Johnson Publishing Company that targeted school- age children. We had seven stories published before the publication ended in 1985, including the following: "I'm Mean Willa Jean," "Fast Hand Kendra" "Kung Fu Willie," "The Fox That Came Out of the Hole," "Me and Jerry T." "Edwin Sure Can Lie" and "Getting Even with Jimmie Ray."

Write on! Write on!

Some People

Flavia Weedn's poem, Some People, aptly describes my friendship with playwright Judi Ann Mason. We met when she was just a twenty -year-old writer and had won the Norman Lear Writing Competition for Comedy, which was an additional effort initiated at colleges nationwide to find black writers. As the grand prizewinner, she came to work with our staff of writers to develop her winning teleplay, which would air on "Good Times." It worked out extremely well, and she joined the staff as a full-time writer. Judi Ann became the youngest person ever to join the Writers Guild of America. She was a bubbly, old soul who was perceptive beyond her years. She was the only woman and one of two black writers on our staff at that time. The other black writer was Bob Peete, a Chicago native.

Judi Ann and I who had a beautiful friendship that lasted over thirty years. When she first bounced into our offices, she had so much enthusiasm that she blew us away. She was a graduate of Grambling University, who hailed from Bossier City, Louisiana, and had a warm, down-home, southern manner. She introduced herself to each of us and inquired about our jobs, our families, our boyfriends, husbands, etc. After that, she was led to her office where an IBM Selective typewriter awaited her. Immediately she started typing fast as can be. Soon she emerged from her office with poems about each person. She totally captured each person's personality and remembered every detail about his or her life. We were amazed and totally impressed.

We worked with comedy writers who were veterans. To have someone on staff who was poetic and thoughtful was unusual. The poem she wrote about me was spot on, about my "caregiver" personality, my young sons Jason and Damon and my soon-to-be husband, Robert.

Judi had so much hope in the beginning. She remained on the staff of "Good Times" until the show ended. Later she worked as a producer/writer for "Generations," the first black soap opera. She was on the staff of "A Different World," while still writing and producing plays. She started moving away from comedy and started writing teleplays, such as "I'll Fly Away," "American Gothic," "Clover and Sophie and the Moonflyer." However, her biggest credit was for the film *Sister Act 2*, starring Whoopi Goldberg. Her original script was actually based on a true story she had written about the Los Angeles music teacher, Iris Stevenson, at Crenshaw High School. Disney had been negotiating with her agent to do it as a film but quickly realized the heart of the story could be fashioned into the sequel for the hit Whoopi Goldberg film *Sister Act*. Though Judi really wanted her own film project to be made, it was an opportunity she couldn't pass up. After that, she had many projects in the works, but, for various reasons, nothing ever materialized.

She had married an aspiring actor from Las Vegas, Lanyard

Williams, and they had two children, Mason Synclaire Williams and Austin Barrett Williams. I was delighted when she asked me to be the godmother for her daughter, Mason. In an attempt to make her marriage work, she moved back to Louisiana and taught at the university level. She was convinced she could get projects off the ground there easier. However, eventually the marriage ended, and her career path got rocky as well.

I believed in her and I continued to be a "Judi Ann" cheerleader for many years, because I truly felt she was an extraordinarily talented person. I felt it was just a matter of time before she would shine brightly in the national spotlight. But on July 10, 2009, my young friend died suddenly of a ruptured aorta at the age of 54. Only after her death did I learn the extent on the personal problems she had endured. Even though she had been under enormous personal and professional pressure, she still wrote and dreamed. She continued to put together complete budgets, shooting schedules and even created soundtracks for film after film.

Prior to her death, she called me on June 25, 2009, because she was distraught over the untimely death of Michael Jackson. It was the first time we had spoken in more than two years. She talked to me about the status of her latest project, *The Motherland*, one of the many films she had written. She said, "I shouldn't say anything until the money is in the bank in the next few weeks." After a week, the money was indeed in the bank. At last, a long-awaited project was totally ready to go. The next day she died. I couldn't get over it. In death she was written about in the *Los Angeles Times* and *Written By*, the Writers Guild's magazine, as a "trailblazer for black writers in Hollywood." She was highly respected; she had a recognizable name but very little tangible success in the last ten years of her life. The memorials for her were huge – both in Los Angeles and in her hometown in Louisiana.

Before I move from this chapter, I want to also acknowledge Michael Moye from New Haven Connecticut. He was another black college student who won the Norman Lear contest for writing a "Good Times" script. He went on to have an extremely lucrative career on our show, then worked as a writer/producer on "The Jefferson." Michael was also the co-creator, producer and writer for "Silver Spoons," "Married with Children" and other shows. I am so grateful that he bought a script from me in 1984 called 'Getting Back to Basiks' for "The Jeffersons." It was about George Jefferson learning that one of his employees was a functional illiterate. The script ended up being nominated for a Humanist Award for tacking the subject of adult illiteracy.

CHAPTER 8:
My Life with My Hero, Roberto

Now, I was a wife on the set, traveling whenever and wherever I could.

By the end of 1976 my personal life was looking promising. Robert and I, along with my two sons, moved into a large townhome in Culver City. We leased it with an option to buy. After a year we purchased the property in Robert's name only. I still working to resolve the credit problems I had stemming from my first marriage. I didn't want to jeopardize our chances, so I decided not to be on the deed. I later had second thoughts about it. I felt Robert loved me and I trusted him to do the right thing. However, I had two sons to consider and I didn't feel I had made a wise decision to buy property that I didn't have a legal stake in. It was something we resolved the later.

More importantly, in my heart, I wasn't comfortable living together, not being married. I shared my feelings with Robert, who had barely gotten his divorce. I said I would like to be married by June of the next year (six months), or I would have to move on. Robert was stunned, but after thinking about it for a few days, he agreed that we should get married.

We tied the knot on a Friday, April 29, 1977, at the home of Judge Xenophon Lang, Sr., who was my best friend Saundra's dad. On that Sunday, May 1, 1977, we had a huge reception at the Pacifica Hotel in Culver City. It was a fun and joyful occasion. We had an awesome live band and singer who kept the ballroom rocking. Robert said it was one of the happiest days of his life, and I felt the same way.

After Robert and I married, I left "Good Times." I teamed up with

Bob Peete, my writer friend from the show, to produce his original play, *It's Called Survival* at the Ebony Showcase in Los Angeles. Bob had several comedian friends he cast in the production, among them a funny guy with a dry sense of humor named Grant Wilson, Esther Carroll, and Bob's cousin Margaret Hudley, whom I knew from college by her nickname, "Buttons." We held open auditions for the rest of the cast. We got several unknown actors who went on to work in TV and film such as Taurean Blaque, who later had a long-running role as Dr. Neal Washington on the popular police series "Hill Street Blues," Justin Lord, who continued to work as a character actor in television for years, and Dianne Dixon, who had starred in Sidney Poitier's *A Piece of the Action.*

I found out I was pregnant during the production, however that didn't stop me. I stayed with the play, wobbling up and down the stairs until the end of the successful run. My sons, Jason and Damon, had a fun time working in the box office and running errands for the actors, who often wanted snacks from the nearby convenience store.

Though Bob had lots of interest from potential filmmakers, somehow it never panned out. So, we both moved on. After all, "it's called survival." Not long after the play closed, I gave birth to my eight-pound, thirteen-ounce baby boy, Teron. We became one big happy family. I still wanted to make my mark in entertainment, but now motherhood took priority.

When we had a luncheon after our baby was christened, Nellie Hannible, the mother of our friend Connie, pulled me aside and wisely suggested I needed to find a church home for our family. She recognized that so many wonderful things were happening for Robert and me, but we were not acknowledging that it was because of God's grace and mercy. She said, "He is pouring blessing after blessing over your lives. You should open your heart and let Him in." I said I would, but it would take a little longer for me to take action.

Richard Pryor

During this time Robert worked on films starring actor and comedian Richard Pryor. Robert and I, along with actors in his films and other crew members, were invited to spend Saturday afternoons at Richard's mansion.

He owned a sprawling 9,000-square foot property known as the Wrigley Estate on Parthenia Street in Encino, California. What we didn't realize was it was one of many homes owned by the Wrigley family throughout the United States. The family's wealth came from Wrigley chewing gum and having been the owners of the Chicago Cubs.

Richard's amazing property sat on 2.2 acres of land. The compound had six buildings that included a main house, a guest house, a pool house, a gym/dance studio, an office and a children's playhouse. The property also had a three-car garage and kennel. Outside, there was a pool with a spa, a waterfall and a slide, a BBQ pavilion, tennis, tetherball and basketball courts, and a putting green. The gated property was surrounded by lush gardens.

Richard purchased the property in 1974 and lived there for ten years. The most infamous incident occurred at the estate in 1980. After days of freebasing cocaine, Richard poured one hundred fifty-one-proof rum all over his body and lit himself on fire. While ablaze, he ran down Parthenia Street until the police got to him. Two years later, Richard would joke about the horrific incident in his comedy concert, *Richard Pryor: Live on the Sunset Strip,* and used it as source material in *Jo Jo Dancer, Your Life is Calling*, a fictional account of his life.

Our Saturday visits included playing tennis, swimming, outdoor barbequing, eating, hanging out and playing cards. Robert, who was an excellent tennis player, had been the hair stylist on Richard's films, including the latest *Greased Lightnin'* with Pam Grier as his co-star. She was also his girlfriend at the time.

Richard would host tennis tournaments with trophies and all. We were excited to be among the group. Most of the women were terrible tennis players, including me. The female players included many of Richard's leading ladies from his films such as Pam, Margaret Avery *(Which Way Is Up?)*, Beverly Todd *(Moving)*, Lonette McKee *(Which Way Is Up?)* and her sister Cathy, who was a popular newscaster. Richard's friend and attorney David Franklin from Atlanta was always there. Paul Mooney, a popular comedian and his dear friend; David Banks, his humorous close friend and Richard's assistant, Tony Berkeley — who made sure all went well — were also always there. Sometimes Richard's relatives from Peoria, Illinois, were visiting, too. His Aunt

Maxine was his favorite. She was a large, tall, fair-skinned woman, who never failed to speak her mind. I was glad when I finally met her because every time I came around, Richard would say I looked just like her. Amazingly, it was true.

Richard never attempted to play tennis. He would sit quietly and watch us play, while directing his staff in the grilling of steaks and preparing for the yummy lunch that always followed the tournaments. He didn't talk much, and when he did, he wasn't particularly funny. He was a people-watcher, so he quietly and pleasantly checked everybody out as they were having fun.

Often his young daughters would be there along with their mothers. One thing I learned about famous celebrities was that their significant others continued to be a part of their lives. Being with and sharing a child with someone as legendary as Richard was exciting and the children's mothers enjoyed still being in his world. His daughter Elizabeth Pryor, who became a college history professor, was always there with her mom, Maxine, who was the daughter of his one-time Jewish manager. There was also his daughter Rain with her mother Shelley Bonus, a photographer/hippie. Rain was a dead ringer for her dad. Later we would meet Jennifer Lee, the interior decorator for his home, who became his most enduring wife. Then there was Deborah McGuire, who Richard allegedly met after he first saw her provocative photos in Larry Flynt's *Hustler* magazine. It was said that he had someone call Flynt to ask who she was and how he could get in touch with her. Later there was also a sepia tone beauty from Washington, D.C., named Flynn Blaine, who he married briefly and with whom he had several children.

Through Pam we also got to know her best friend and one of our favorite singers, the late Minnie Riperton, who came with her music producer husband, Dick Rudolph, would hang out with us, too. At that time Minnie was undergoing treatment for cancer; however, we were confident she would beat it because she was so young and vibrant. To soothe her condition, she always smoked marijuana. Occasionally, we would join in, too, puffing on the joints with no medical excuse, except we wanted to do what Minnie was doing. She was lots of fun to be around.

It was a very sad day in 1979 when we learned of her passing at the young age of thirty-one years old. Although she had become a spokesperson for the American Cancer Society, no one thought her condition was terminal and her life would end so soon. She was so talented with a wonderful husband and two young children, Maya and Marc. For many years I had a small standee in my family room of Minnie from her final album, simply entitled "Minnie." My favorite selection was "Memory Lane," in which she effortlessly demonstrated her four-octave vocal range. Her voice was incredible. She could hit a note so high it could break a glass. Today artists, like Mariah Carey, never fail to pay homage to Minnie as an inspiration. Minnie's daughter Maya went on to have a successful career in TV and film as an actress/comedienne on "Saturday Night Live," most notably, and the comedy hit film, *Bridesmaids*.

Robert and I found the greatest challenge to our relationship was our work schedules. The nature of his job as a motion picture hair stylist meant he had to go where the work was and very often it was not in Los Angeles. We missed each other, so we were always trying to figure out how to keep our relationship alive. I made set visits as much as I could. What I didn't realize was I was also building solid relationships with stars and filmmakers on the film locations, which would serve me well when I became a publicist a few years later.

Visiting Robert on locations had always been an exciting treat for me throughout our marriage. He never knew where he would be going next, so it was an adventure, a star-studded and a wonderful time to re-connect with one another.

Robert always had an incredible work ethic. He was duty focused, while I, on the other hand, was interested in new adventures. He would go to and from work every day without really enjoying the sights of the area until I came to visit. I would research the location and when I arrived, he would join me in seeing the sites in the latest spot. Sometimes I would visit him alone, other times I would bring the kids. Jason, Damon, Kendra and Teron still talk about their fun adventures on movie locations. As time went on, Robert began to check out the newest location before I came. When I arrived, he would know the best restaurants, shopping and sites to see.

It wasn't easy with school-age children and my demanding work schedule to plan a visit. One example of the difficulty I encountered happened when I was working on "Good Times." The kids were out of school, Robert was working in Acapulco and I was determined to go. Being dishonest was never my practice, but on this occasion, I lied to my boss, so I could go. And here's what happened...

It was 1976 and Robert was the hair stylist on Sammy Davis Jr.'s variety TV show, "Sammy & Company," which was taping five shows for several weeks on location in Acapulco, Mexico. I was determined to go, mainly because I had never been to Acapulco. There were stars galore scheduled to be on the show and it would be an amazing, free vacation. I told my boss I was subpoenaed to court regarding my ex-husband's case. I wanted to say something where they wouldn't try to call me at home. I arranged my flight and planned to miss a week of work using sick pay.

Everything went well. I got to Acapulco and had the time of my life. The five shows in Mexico were staged poolside at the Continental Acapulco Hotel. When Robert wasn't working, we hung out at the sandy beach, dining on Mexican cuisine, drinking margaritas and enjoying time with the stars and the film crew. We partied at local discos every night and sunbathed during the day. We even took a hot air balloon ride one day.

When the tapings started, I was given a seat in front with Sammy's wife, Altovise, who I had become friendly with. In my excitement, I had forgotten it was being televised and I would be seen on camera. Once I realized what a predicament I was in, I kept trying to turn my face away when the cameras were pointed in our direction. I couldn't even enjoy myself for worrying I would be found out. What was I thinking? As it turned out, I was never seen, but it haunted me for weeks.

Even worse, when I got back to work, "Montezuma's Revenge" attacked me. I had a horrible case of diarrhea, which commonly affects travelers who visited Mexico. In my case, I had no symptom when I left Acapulco. I guess the amoeba laid dormant until I returned to work. I was at my desk when severe cramps started rumbling in my stomach. I knew I had to find a bathroom far from the office, fast. I grabbed a bottle of cologne out of my purse and ran to a distant bathroom to relieve myself. This went on three or four more times that day and I was miserable. I couldn't say a word to anyone. That day couldn't end fast enough. I made a beeline for the drugstore where I bought a big bottle of Kaopectate to ease my violent symptoms. The situations subsided, but the problem still went on for several more days. In utter silence, I earned the sick pay I had taken as I sat there with my unsuspecting co-workers. God was punishing me. I lied and I had to pay the consequences.

Was it worth it? Of course, I had the time of my life. It was romantic, fun and filled with opportunities to meet stars up close and personal, who I had admired for years. In addition to hanging out with the legendary Sammy Davis Jr., there was his band director George Rhodes, his wife Shirley Rhodes, who was also Sammy's manager, and stars like Billy Dee Williams, Ben Vereen, Lola Falana, Tony Bennett, Sarah Vaughan, comedian Franklyn Ajaye, Freda Payne, Carmen McCrae, our buddy Richard Pryor and many more.

Once again, I never thought to thank God for the incredible life I was having.

My next adventure was in Georgia where Robert was the hair stylist for a television movie called "Just an Old Sweet Song," which starred Robert Hooks, who had the distinction of starring in "NYPD" as the first African American lead on a television drama. He was also one of the founders of the famous Negro Ensemble Company in New York. "Just an Old Sweet Song's" female leads were Cicely Tyson and Beah Richards, two of the most highly revered black actresses of my lifetime. As quick as I could, I made arrangements to visit him for a weeklong visit. Most importantly, on this film production Robert would meet someone who would have a monumental impact on his career for many, many years. And it wasn't one of the stars… it was in God's plan, but we had no idea.

By the time I met Beah in 1976, she had been nominated for an Oscar in 1968 for Best Supporting Actress as Sidney Poitier's mother in the groundbreaking film, *Guess Who's Coming to Dinner.* She also had given memorable performances in *Hurry Sundown* and *The Great White Hope.* I had been a fan of her work since I saw her in the Los Angeles stage production of *The Amen Corner* when I was just a teenager.

Cicely had also been nominated for an Academy Award for Best Actress for her performance as Rebecca Morgan in *Sounder,* one of my all-time favorite films. She also had received two Emmys for her unforgettable performance in "The Autobiography of Miss Jane

Pittman," playing a one hundred ten-year-old former slave. She received an Emmy for Best Actress in a TV Drama, and a second special Emmy for Best Actress of the Year, which had rarely been given.

When Robert arrived on the location for "Just an Old Sweet Song," he quickly learned that Cicely was a temperamental and demanding artist. She first instructed him on the proper care of her expensive handmade wigs. He respectfully listened to what she had to say, even though he was very familiar with how to care for them. Before coming to Georgia, he had discussed her look with the filmmakers. Based on their discussion and reading the script, he had already prepared multiple wigs for her to select from, which were appropriate for the time-period of the film. Nevertheless, he styled her wigs to her specifications. When he returned them to her, he showed her the selections he had, as well. Ultimately, she went with the ones he already had. From that time forward, she always showed great respect for Robert and his work.

A few weeks later, out of the blue, she said, "Robert, do you have a suit?" He said yes; then she instructed him to wear it that evening. To his surprise, he was invited to go as one of her special guests to a birthday dinner being held in her honor. The filmmakers and some of the stars attended; however, Robert was the only crew member invited. The restaurant was closed to the public and the chef prepared a sumptuous spread just for Cicely and her select group of friends. Robert ate, drank, made small talk and was pleased that he was deemed worthy of an invitation. No mention of that evening was ever made again.

When I arrived on the set, she was cordial, but appeared preoccupied with her work. I had hoped to get to know her, but that would not happen until we met again years later.

I spent my time with Beah, who was idle many days, since she only worked occasionally in the film playing Cicely's mother. I was doing my regular tourist trips, so she wanted to hang out with me. Most importantly, she wanted to visit the gravesite of Dr. Martin Luther King, Jr. with its eternal flame. She was thrilled beyond words when we got there, and she began a long commune with Martin. I remember getting antsy as she sat at his grave "talking to him," which felt like well over an hour to me. However, what could I say? She was in a deep emotional state, crying and sharing thoughts with him. So, I waited patiently. As we were leaving, she gathered up some smooth rocks from the grave to keep as souvenirs. When she got back to the hotel, she painted his name beautifully on one and the location and time on the others. She put them together with glue on a small board she decorated.

Beah joined Robert and me one Sunday afternoon for a dinner party at the home of one of the crew members. On location, home-cooked meals are always a highly sought-after commodity for the out-of-town crew. While at dinner Beah surprised us with her zest and vitality. Since she was famous for playing matriarch roles, we thought she was older than she really was. As a matter of fact, she was just three years older than Sidney Poitier; however, she had convincingly played his mother in *Guess Who's Coming to Dinner.* The two were believable in their roles, because he looked extremely young for his age and she sounded and carried herself like a much older woman.

At dinner I was also surprised to learn that Beah was a smoker. We also found out she had been a professional dancer with beautiful legs to prove it. When our dinner hosts played some upbeat R&B music, she was motivated to get up and dance. She was graceful and light on her feet. We watched in utter amazement as she began to prance and twirl all around the room. To be in her presence was inspiring. She had an aura of joyfulness surrounding her. I developed greater admiration and respect for her during that visit.

After she died in 2003, my public relations firm had the privilege of doing the publicity for the documentary on her life, *Beah: A Black Woman Speaks*, directed by actress LisaGay Hamilton ("The Practice"). The two had met when they worked together on Oprah's film *Beloved.* After the film was completed, LisaGay visited with Beah to seek direction for her professional acting career. However, the things Beah spoke about were so rich and full of wisdom that LisaGay asked if she could make a documentary about her inspiring life. Though Beah was suffering from emphysema, she agreed and freely shared details about her phenomenal life and career.

As fate would have it, Beah passed away during the filming, which LisaGay also documented. *Beah: A Black Woman Speaks* is one of the most moving and powerful documentaries on the life of a black actress that I have ever seen. Beah left us a cherished gift, which still gives me chills when I watch it.

We were proud when the documentary won the Grand Jury Prize at the AFI Film Festival. It debuted on HBO in 2004 and continued to air each February during Black History Month for many years. The project meant so much to me; I would have done it for free.

In 1976 during the production of "Just an Old Sweet Song," Robert met a young aspiring actor, who would later impact his professional life in ways he never could have imagined. His named was Samuel L. Jackson and he was the stand-in for the male star, Robert Hooks. Sam was in his final year at Morehouse College. He would chat with Robert everyday about his dream of becoming a professional actor.

"Man, I love this acting thing. I'm going to New York to study my craft and someday you'll see me in Hollywood," he promised with a distinct southern accent.

Years later, Robert was working as the supervising hair stylist on Eddie Murphy's film *Coming to America* and who does he see? Samuel L. Jackson, who was playing the hold-up man of McDowell's, the fast-food restaurant in the movie.

They got re-acquainted and Sam brought him up to speed on what he had been doing. He and his wife, LaTanya Richardson Jackson, were members of the famous New York Negro Ensemble Theater Company. He had had lead roles in various stage productions, like "A Soldier's Story," "Two Trains Running" and "Fences". He was also getting small roles in film and television, however for steady money, he was the stand-in for Bill Cosby on "The Cosby Show." Things were looking up for him.

For fifteen years Sam paid his dues before his career took off. In 1991 he was honored at the Cannes Film Festival for his breakout performance as Gator in Spike Lee's *Jungle Fever.* Soon after that he was nominated for an Academy Award for his supporting role as Jules, the philosophizing killer in *Pulp Fiction.* I still contend it was a lead role, equal to, if not bigger than his co-star, John Travolta, the Best Actor nominee. But that's another story.

In 1996, twenty years after they first met, Robert began to work exclusively for Sam, who had at last emerged as a household name in Hollywood. Their first film together was *The Great White Hype*, directed by Reggie Hudlin, and then it was *A Time to Kill*, which starred a newcomer named Matthew McConaughey. Becoming Sam's personal hair stylist was a wonderful opportunity for Robert. In interviews Sam always praised the wigs Robert created for him. Sam contended that the look of his hair (wig) was very important for the development of the various characters he was playing. Known as "the hardest working man in show business," Sam worked non-stop. For the last fourteen years of Robert's career, he worked exclusively for him. If Sam wore a bald head, Robert would serve as the supervising hair stylist for the film. Together they went all over the world, making movies and swinging golf clubs. Robert retired in 2009 and Sam is still going strong.

CHAPTER 9:
Occupational Hazards

I did all I could…and God did the rest.

After my son Teron was born, I stayed home with him until he was eight months old. Then I made a career change, starting over at MGM Studios in Culver City, which I chose because it was near my home. My goal was to get a position as production coordinator, but first I had to start in the temp pool. According to union rules, I would not be allowed to bid on job postings until I had been a temp on the studio lot for six months.

As I embarked on finding a new career at MGM, I first met Frank Bowe, who was a grand, overly dramatic black executive, the head of human resources. He assured me, "A movie studio is a city within a city, my dear, and there is something for every possible talent." I found that to be true. Finally, I began to pray and soon discovered my true purpose. I was focused and determined to move into a suitable profession. Every day I made it a point to introduce myself and share my resume with whomever might be able to help me advance.

Before that happened, I landed a long-term assignment in the film laboratory for a girl who had gone out on indefinite disability. It didn't take me long to figure out why. I worked at a cold, scratched up metal table, which sat on an even colder cement floor. I was surrounded by rows and rows of film cans from celling to floor. It was dreary.

I knew I was in a strange land when my boss, Bill, came back from lunch with bloody knuckles because he had gotten into a brawl at the

Back Stage Saloon, a bar across the street from the studio. He was from Hattiesburg, Mississippi, and he was proud to let me know that he had Klan newsletters sent to him regularly.

He and the other shift bosses found me very curious. They wanted to know my take on civil rights issues and incidents such as the Watts Riots. When I jokingly admitted I had been a looter, they were horrified. I looked so professional, a wife and a mother, they couldn't believe I would ever have done such a thing. Most of the guys were heavy drinkers, lived reckless lives and were proud of it. One older guy bragged to me saying, "Damn, if I had known I was going to live this long, I would've taken better care of myself!" No one was without their quirks. One of the more unsuspecting, clean-cut, handsome guys regularly dealt marijuana and cocaine through inter-office envelopes.

Pornographic magazines were a mainstay. They got a kick out of showing disgusting magazines to me. OMG! I couldn't wait to get out of there.

However, I had no options. Sadly, for me, it was during the 1980 Screen Actors Guild strike. There were very few jobs on the lot. If someone with seniority was laid off in their department, they could bump a temp like me out of their job. Suffice it to say, nobody was bouncing back to my job. So, I was better off riding out my six months there. The lab was ninety-five percent men and only five percent women. The first time my husband visited, he was shocked at the working conditions and the staff. He said they all looked like they came straight out of the Sam Peckinpah's western, *The Wild Bunch*. Oddly enough, as time went on, I grew fond of that crazy gang. If something was wrong with my car, someone could fix it. If I needed anything, they could get it. However, they had their prejudices, which would rear their ugly heads with no regard or concern for mine or other's feelings.

For instance, there was an older, no non-sense Hungarian woman named Ingrid, who worked as a negative cutter from midday into the night. When she arrived, there would be no parking spaces available on the studio lot. For safety reasons, she didn't want to walk down the dark neighborhood streets when she got off at midnight. During her late afternoon break after many of the top executives had left for the day, she would move her car onto the lot. The breaks were officially only twenty minutes, but you didn't have to clock in and out. However, since they didn't like her, when she left, the afternoon supervisor would document the time she left by putting on a piece of paper in the time clock. When she returned, the supervisor would secretly clock her back in and indicate if she was gone more than allotted twenty minutes. Ingrid was short and round in stature, so she would come back in huffing and puffing with a red face trying to hurry back in time. Sometimes it would be twenty-two or twenty-four minutes. She didn't realize it, but they were building a case against her.

From time to time, I would strike up a conversation with her and I learned that she was a single parent, who was proud that she was able to put two sons through college by herself. I knew she would be devastated if she lost her job. So, I put my nose in where it did not belong. I pulled her aside one day and told her she should be very careful about her breaks because they were documenting her time. She was horrified. She wept and said in broken English that they were mean, heartless people. After that she was careful not to go over her break time. I felt I had done a good thing. But, unbeknownst to me, the department had already brought charges against her. Then she countersued.

One day I was called down to the Human Resources Department. Without telling me, Ingrid had filed a harassment suit against her bosses for the pain, suffering and anguish she had endured at their hand and she named me as her witness. The personnel executive asked me to confirm if her charges were true. I told him I had no comment and I didn't want to be involved.

"Look, this is just between you and me. It won't go any further than this room. Please let me know if this is true," he said.

Finally, I told him, "Yes."

He thanked me and I went back to the lab. As I was approaching the door, I heard the supervisor say, "The personnel chief just told me he had a witness that could confirm Ingrid's claims. Who in the hell could it be?"

Damn! Ingrid and the personnel chief had both double-crossed me. Confidentiality meant nothing to them. Nothing was sacred. I walked in nonchalantly, and for some reason, it did not occur to them that I was the snitch. They surmised it was Phil, a religious guy in the department, who none of them liked. I played dumb, like I was shocked by everything they were saying.

Occupational Hazards

From that day forward, I never let myself get into a position like that again. I realized it was survival of the fittest in the workplace. They didn't care about me, so I didn't care about them. I had to have my own back, because none of them cared about taking me down. If I went down, "Oh well," I was just another person they didn't really care about. That was a hard lesson. It hurt, but it was a reality I carried with me. I made it clear to Ingrid that if it became necessary, I had no intention of testifying for her. I don't really know how the case was resolved, because the strike was over, and I left the department as soon as I could. I was more determined than ever to get out of there and move forward.

In 1981 I came to a major crossroad that would determine the rest of my career path. Finally, I was out of the lab. On a Monday morning I was sent on a temporary assignment in the Publicity Department for the new Director of Publicity, Phyllis Gardner. When I arrived, she had a mountain of papers stacked on her desk. She explained this was her first day and everything that was on her desk needed to be organized chronically and put by film in a file. Actually, I was an expert at organizing files, because on a job I had years ago at the Watts Health Center, I had to work with an efficiency expert to set up a standardizing filing system for the entire center. Now that knowledge came in handy. That day I came to realize that all experiences could be beneficial, and do not begrudge any chance to learn.

Phyllis left for a two-day staff retreat and I proceeded to access the list of films she would be responsible for. I set up the file folders in alphabetical order. I set the folders on the floor and began to deal out the stack of papers to the appropriate file. I then arranged each film's files chronologically, punched on the top of a manila folder and also on the top of each sheet and fastened them with a bracket. I put each file inside a Pendaflex folder with alphabetized label tabs in her cabinet and dropped them in her cabinet. When Phyllis returned two days later, she was stunned and thrilled beyond belief.

When I started at MGM, my plan was to get in the Production Department as a production coordinator. While I was on the publicity assignment, a position had come up in production. The following Monday I had an appointment. The person I would be interviewing with required me to bring my current resume.

That weekend I began to tweak my resume. I said to Robert, "I have lots of television production experience, but this is for motion pictures and I don't have any film experience." Robert thought about it and said, "Why don't you add the film I worked on last year called *Sunnyside*." It was a little-known movie that starred Joey Travolta, John's brother. It sounded like a good idea to me, so I added it. It was a little white lie that seemed harmless.

However, when I arrived at the interview, I gave the interviewer my resume. She took one look at it and without hesitation she said, "*Sunnyside?* You didn't work on *Sunnyside*." As fate would have it, she had been the production coordinator on the project. I was stunned and humiliated. I thought quickly and I said, "You're right, I didn't really. I was allowed to observe on the set when the film went to San Francisco. My husband was working on the film, and he asked the production manager if I could shadow him." My heart was pounding, and I thought I was going to pass out.

"Who is your husband?" she asked. I said, "Robert Stevenson. He was the hair stylist on the project." Thank goodness she knew Robert and liked him. But now I was sitting there, a big fat liar. I acted calm as we completed the interview, but I could have crawled under the rug. I couldn't get out of there fast enough.

I was still on the temp publicity assignment with Phyllis, who was singing my praises for organizing her life. I had seen the secretarial position to work for her on the job postings, but I ignored it because it had stated, "previous publicity experience required." When she suggested I apply for the job and I told her what it said about previous experience. She said, "If you want the job, you've got it!" So, I called the union and applied. Curiously enough, only five people could apply for union positions. When I called, four people had applied. I was the fifth person. Whew!

Next thing I knew, the lady from the Production Department called and she said, "If you want the job, you can have it. I know you don't really have film experience, but I like your determination." I was at a crossroad. What should I do? Do I take the job I had been hoping for, or do I take the job in publicity?

As I pondered the situation, I realized I couldn't honestly hold my head up in the production department. It would always haunt me that

Occupational Hazards

I lied on my resume. I had never considered working in publicity because I never knew about it as a career. I was going into new territory, but I also knew that Phyllis appreciated the work I had done for her, so far. In the end, it was a no brainer. I took the publicity job.

Since I had no idea what a publicist was when this job opportunity came my way, I was surprised to learn God had already given me all the qualities needed to be great at it. I was a self-starter, organized, a good writer, very personable, able to multi-task and detail oriented. As an added bonus, I was a walking, talking encyclopedia of Hollywood life. When I arrived in the Publicity Department at MGM in 1981, God put me among people just like me. While I was a novelty among my friends, in the Publicity Department, I was among kindred souls. Just like me, they were avid movie-lovers, who could quote long passages of dialogue from their favorite films. I thought to myself, "Hello, my people! Where have you been all my life?" Calmness and peace came over me. At last, I was at home. I thought about what mama always told me, "Do all you can, and God will do the rest." This was just the first of many miracles God did for me many times in my publicity career. He began moving me to professional heights I never could have ever imagined.

One of Phyllis' good friends, who I came to know, was Cheryl Boone Isaacs, a young African American, who began her career in marketing in 1977. She was the sister of Ashley Boone, who was one of the top-ranking marketing executives at 20th Century Fox, best known for launching the *Star Wars* films. Over the years, I have felt immense pride in Cheryl's remarkable rise in motion picture marketing. When I first met her, she was a publicist at Melvin Simon Productions. She then went on to Paramount Studios as the director of publicity in 1984 and over time, she rose to become the Executive VP of Worldwide Marketing. Her next move was as President of Marketing at Newline Cinema. However, she will forever be remembered as the first African American and third woman elected president of the Academy of Motion Picture Arts and Sciences from 2013-2017.

Phyllis' reported to Al Newman, who was the President of Worldwide Marketing. He was a genius at strategizing movie campaigns. He was a no non-sense type of guy, who was difficult to work for. He adored me, thank goodness. The filing challenge preceded me and had given me a great reputation in the department. As a matter of fact, whenever Al was having a meeting and needed a specific film file, he wouldn't ask his secretary, he would call me.

I learned to lean toward the people who were in my corner. After working and continuing to do a good job in the department for a while, I realized I had found my calling. I definitely wanted to become a publicist! Through the Human Resources' Department, I learned that MGM had a higher education incentive program, which would pay for me to go to school. There was a PR Designation Program at UCLA Extension, in which I wanted to enroll. I needed the approval of the department head, so I went to Al Newman and told him about my desire to become a publicist.

"And how do you propose to do that?" he said, flatly. I replied, "I already have good writing skills but not specific to journalism. With your approval, the studio will pay for me to take the PR program at UCLA." He seemed surprised and said, "You are the only person who ever came to me with a plan. So, if you want to enroll in the UCLA program, I will gladly sign."

I began to attend UCLA two nights a week for the next year. I did outstanding work, which I would send to Al from time to time to thank him for believing in me. Once I completed the course, I gave myself a party and invited everyone in the department. Yes, I had learned to speak up for myself. Additionally, I learned to have a plan and to execute it and show my gratitude. Finally, I learned that sometimes you have to toot your own horn. At this point, I was forty years old. It was time — at long last — to get my professional career on the road.

Everything seemed to be going my way, but then there was another major bump in the road. When the new fiscal year rolled around, I was supposed to become an apprentice publicist. But before that could happen, Phyllis was let go. Another staff publicist, Marsha Robertson, was put in her position. I was very sad to see Phyllis go, and Marsha assumed I wouldn't want to work for her. Unbeknownst to me, she intended to get an assistant of her choosing.

While I was attending a funeral, Marsha moved Carla to my desk to be her secretary. I knew Carla, who was a clerk in the department. When I came back, Marsha informed me I would be taking Carla's old job, which was taking RSVPs for screenings and premieres. I was stunned and angry. I harshly told Carla she had to leave my desk until this got straightened out. As she ran out, I sat down and called the union. I was a high-level secretary, and Carla was a clerk. According to the union's requirements, she didn't even qualify for my position.

I was summoned to Al's office. He explained that he was trying to make Marsha happy because "she wanted to start with a clean slate." I said respectfully, but firmly, "I'm sorry, Mr. Newman, I don't want to do Carla's old job. If that's my only choice, I will go home."

I also mentioned that I had spoken to the union and Carla didn't qualify to sit at my desk. I turned and walked back to my office. I sat at my desk while the fireworks started. Marsha wouldn't speak to me. She charged out and ran down to Deanna, who was the office manager. One of my friends was temping for Deanna and she relayed to me that Marsha was in there raising hell. Deanna got on the phone with the union and they told her exactly what I had said to Al; Carla did not qualify for my position. Marsha was pissed and she screamed, "Damn it! I will take her, if I have to, but I don't want to!"

Now I had to work for someone who didn't want me. Since Phyllis had been out of the office quite a bit, I made sure I kept track of where we stood on every project. I was able to be helpful and answer all of Marsha's questions. After several weeks, she went to Al and admitted, "Roz is amazing. I hope you make her a publicist." Not long after that I became an apprentice publicist. God is good, all the time!

In the apprentice position I was assigned to help the broadcast publicist. She desperately needed help because she was very distracted. She was going through a nasty divorce and she had two young daughters. She made the bulk of her work my responsibility. I could have made a stink about it, but I learned so much. I learned how to arrange personal appearance tours for the stars and filmmakers. I negotiated all bookings with their personal publicists and the top national TV shows. Logistically, one of the hardest things I organized was a five-part series on "Good Morning America" for *Moonraker*, the latest James Bond film, starring Roger Moore and Maud Adams. For that booking, some interviews were done live in-studio, while others were by satellite from London. It was a huge undertaking, which turned out perfect.

When the publicist I was working for abruptly resigned her position, our boss began to interview outside publicists for her position. I could have pouted, because he didn't even consider me. However, I knew the stellar job I had done, but I wasn't sure my boss knew. Therefore, I prepared a thorough report detailing everything I had done in the last year. He appreciated my report and agreed to speak with me about the position. After all was said and done, I got the job. That's how I became the publicist in charge of national broadcast publicity. Something had changed. At last, I was walking in my purpose. How had this transformation come about?

Melvin and Roz Woodruff on
our wedding day at Bel-Vue
Presbyterian Church.
Roz Stevenson personal photo.
All rights reserved.

Shown in 1968, my mother
Clara (seated) holds my neph-
ew Ricky Steverson. Standing
(l. to r.) are my sister-in-law
Patricia Steverson, sister
Cathy Steverson, husband
Melvin Woodruff, father
Roscoe. I am holding my son
Jason Woodruff, next to my
brother Richard Steverson
and sister Carol Steverson.
Roz Stevenson personal photo.
All rights reserved.

The Woodruff family is shown in 1970 with first husband Melvin, and our sons Jason, four years old, and Damon, seven months old.

My second husband, Robert Stevenson, holds a drum in 1972. He was one of the coolest guys I ever met.

My acting head shot in 1972.

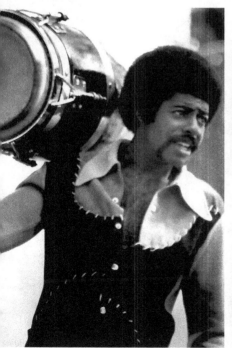

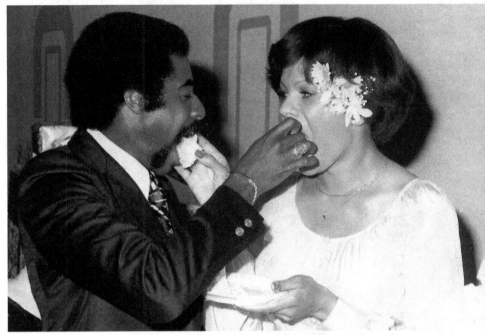

Robert and I got married in 1977. Here we're sharing the wedding cake.

I am being admired by Robert in 1976 when I wore this vintage dress in *Greased Lightnin'*. I played a family member during the home-coming party for Wendell Scott, played by Richard Pryor

Robert and I had a son, Teron. This is us in 1979.

Comedian and actor Richard Pryor greets Julie McCall of Baton Rouge, Louisiana, on the set of *The Toy* in 1982. Robert was Pryor's longtime hair stylist and did this movie.
Roz Stevenson personal photo.

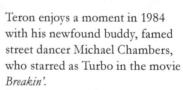

Teron enjoys a moment in 1984 with his newfound buddy, famed street dancer Michael Chambers, who starred as Turbo in the movie *Breakin'*.
Roz Stevenson personal photo.

Hanging out in 1984 on *The Color Purple* movie set with Margaret Avery (l), who played Suge, and Oprah Winfrey, who made her film debut as Sophia. Robert served as the supervising hair stylist on the set.
Roz Stevenson personal photo.

Greeting actress/rock diva
Grace Jones and my boss,
Ed Pine, at the 1985 press
day for the movie *A View
to a Kill* in Los Angeles.
*Roz Stevenson personal photo.
All rights reserved.*

Rock and roll pioneer Chuck Berry gives me his seal of approval during 1987 press
events for *Hail, Hail Rock & Roll*, the documentary on his career.
Roz Stevenson personal photo. All rights reserved.

Iconic Motown Records founder and songwriter Berry Gordy and I share a happy moment in 1987 at a Motown event when I was head of publicity at the legendary label.

Just before daddy succumbed to cancer, the Steverson Family came together for a tribute banquet, "That's What Friends Are For," given by the members of Travelaires to thank mom and dad for arranging their many adventures around the world. Seated in front, (l. to r.) Carol "Cookie" Tucker, Roscoe Steverson, Middle (l. to r.) Michael Bush, Cathy Bush, Louise Donaldson, Jerry Tucker, Cynthia Tucker, Clara Steverson. Back (l. to r.) Doris Epps, Jason Woodruff, Damon Woodruff, Richard Steverson, me and Robert Stevenson.

Autographed picture from Sidney Poitier after I had an opportunity to work as a publicist on *Ghost Dad*, the film he was directing, in 1988.
Roz Stevenson personal photo.

This 1998 photo is of my assistant Ellen Sommers when she had an opportunity to work with Patrick Swayze during the press activities for *Black Dog* in Las Vegas, Nevada. She was his biggest fan.
Roz Stevenson personal photo.

During the 2001 filming Robert touches up Samuel L. Jackson's cornrows during the filming of *51st State* in Liverpool.

We enjoyed our 25th wedding anniversary in 2002 with 125 friends aboard "The Celebration" in Marina del Rey, California. Here we are with our children. Front row (l. to r.) Robert, Kendra Ruffin and me. Second row (l. to r.) Damon Woodruff, Jason Woodruff and Teron Stevenson.

Jesus is the Reason for the Season

This was our 2005 Christmas card with the theme "Jesus is the Reason for the Season," featuring our grandchildren. In the center is Nellon Johnson as the Baby Jesus. Surrounded by (l. to r.) Aman Stevenson as Joseph, Dayna Woodruff as Mary, Valentino "Peanut" Martinez as the shepherd; and Shantel Martinez, Kambria Ruffin and Sage Woodruff as The Wise People.

This is a photo of all our grandkids in 2017 taken at our 40th wedding anniversary party. Front row (l. to r.) Aman Stevenson, Nellon Johnson, Delaney Woodruff; back row (l. to r.) Kambria Ruffin, Sage Woodruff, Dayna Woodruff.

Since Robert and I have retired, we enjoy traveling. Here we are in 2009 aboard the Tom Joyner Cruise.

ACT III:

RETURNING TO THE LORD

CHAPTER 10:
Jesus Takes Center Stage

This was the beginning of forever.

One afternoon in the early eighties, I was jolted by the sight of my fourteen-year-old son Jason searching through the family Bible, while glued to the teaching of an outlandish fire-and-brimstone televangelist. It was upsetting and it caused me to seriously examine my role as a parent. I had failed to give my children a spiritual foundation and he was searching for understanding with the help of a televangelist. I knew that now was the time to make it a priority to find a church home for my family and me.

I had grown up in church, but I had completely stopped going when I got married and moved away from home. Like so many young people who were forced to go to church all the time, once I was on my own, I couldn't wait to let that go. So, on the day I saw my son searching for spiritual knowledge, my heart ached, and I was filled with immense guilt. I felt like I was a terrible parent. I had not provided for my children that basic need for spirituality and values that my parents had given me.

To make things worse, my older boys were feeling lots of anxiety because their father and I had gone through a bitter divorce. After we split up, because he refused to pay child support, I was angry with him all the time and I was very vocal about his shortcomings. My sons dearly loved him, so it broke their hearts when I would rant and rave about their "no good" daddy. As time went on, I learned to deal with the situation in a more civil and positive manner. But up to that point in time, I'm embarrassed to admit, I was one bitchin', moanin' and groanin' sistah!

At one point, my son Damon defended his dad saying, "Mom, we are doing okay. We don't need his money. You should leave daddy alone, because he's just different." Wow! That gave me pause. He was right, my new husband Robert and I were doing okay. Honestly, I was ruining my health and jeopardizing my new relationship by trying to get my sons' father to do something that he simply was not going to do. I thought somehow his sense of responsibility would be different as it pertained to his children because he loved them dearly, but the support situation never changed. He loved them until the day he died, but he rarely provided money for them. Nevertheless, we made it. It was one of those lessons I learned the hard way through trial and error.

My mother also made me see how annoying I had gotten when I constantly complained about my ex. One day I was carrying on, telling her yet another story of his irresponsibility and she cut me off in the middle of my sentence and bluntly said, "Why don't you just shut up about him! He's not the first dog and he won't be the last!" That was it! She didn't say another word, but I finally got it. I realized how much I was irritating my family and friends with all my issues. I had to stop it.

More importantly, once I stopped stressing out about what he was doing against the boys and me, I was able to focus on being all that I could be. My professional growth was moving in the right direction, finally.

I thought back to when Mother Nellie had asked me if Robert and I had a church home. I told her we couldn't agree on one, so we kept putting it off. She said, "Honey, you find a church for your family and, trust me, he will follow." So, that's what I did, and that's exactly what happened. I was learning to heed to the wisdom of my elders.

Grace United Methodist was a church in my neighborhood, which two of my long-time friends attended. It seemed like a good choice. I had grown up in a conservative Presbyterian church and Robert had gone to a lively Baptist church. Grace United Methodist Church was somewhere "in the middle." It wasn't as stiff as the Presbyterian church and it had enough excitement to satisfy the Baptist in Robert. However, he didn't immediately share my enthusiasm about finding a church home. He made it clear that he didn't want me deciding on a church for him. Traditionally, Sunday was his tennis day.

Another problem cropped up. Even though my son had been my catalyst for finding a church, to my surprise, I had a hard time getting the two older boys, fourteen-year old Jason and eleven-year-old Damon, to go. They grumbled but I insisted. Their objection wasn't really about going to church; it was more about the fact that they didn't want to get up, get dressed up and go somewhere on Sunday morning. Sunday had been a lazy day in our house when the boys watched sports, played video games and beat up on one another. My new baby boy, Teron, was only two-years old, I wanted to start him in church while he was still young. Even though the older boys grumbled and complained, we all went, and Robert would join us on occasion.

On one particular Sunday, the boys and I were sitting on the very last pew of the church. At the end of the service, they "opened the doors to the church" and extended the traditional invitation to accept or re-dedicate your life to Christ and join church. Jason nudged me and said, "Mommy, we should go." It touched my heart and as the pastor continued to make the appeal, I felt compelled to answer the call. I got up and walked down the aisle to the altar and beckoned for the boys to follow me. Damon came right behind me, but Jason, who is extremely shy, froze. I didn't notice he did not move.

Once I reached the altar, I felt a warm sensation fill my body from the top of my head to the bottom of my feet. It was amazing that at the very moment I said "yes" to the Lord, the Holy Spirit filled my entire being. I can still remember that feeling like it was yesterday. I was so surprised by the emotional surge that filled me. Instantly, cleansing tears streamed down my face and it felt wonderful. From that moment on, I wanted to be closer to the Lord. I felt like the prodigal son, who had been lost but was now found. I am so grateful for my Sunday morning miracle of salvation. It was a defining moment that changed my life in ways unimaginable. And just to think, He was there all the time, just waiting for me to welcome Him back in.

I went through the required new members classes at the church. I also began sitting with my two-year old in his pre-school class. It didn't take me long to realize that the young teenage teacher was having difficulty just keeping the kids in their chairs, so I stepped in to help. After a few weeks, Sally Bell, the Sunday School superintendent was urging me to become the teacher. I resisted, telling her I didn't know what to teach. She wouldn't take "no" for an answer. She said she could provide me with an easy-to-follow handbook with lesson plans. Just like that, I was the Sunday School teacher for the two to five-year old children.

As it turned out, teaching Sunday School was one of the most rewarding experiences of my life. I taught for five years, long after Teron had left my class. In addition to teaching young innocent minds about the Lord, the experience gave me a chance to create exciting holiday programs at Christmas and Easter. For some programs I made the costumes and for others I got costumes on loan from the studio. They called me "The Hollywood Sunday-School Teacher," an embarrassing and accurate title.

Since I worked long hours at the studio during the week, teaching Sunday-School turned out to be my very special time with Teron. At first, he was very possessive and didn't want to share me with the other kids. He would sit in my lap, hugging me and scowled at the other children muttering, "My mommy... This is my mommy!" When I would ask one of the children to collect the offering, he would snatch the basket before I could hand it to the child. His sense of entitlement and unbecoming behavior became a major topic of discussion with his dad each Sunday after church. However, in my heart, his possessiveness tickled me.

The concept of insisting that children should share had always been a bone of contention with me. Call me unorthodox, but when my two older sons fought over toys constantly saying, "He won't share," I announced to them: "If you really love something, you don't have to share." That stopped the bickering on the spot.

Young Damon, who was always a fast learner, would creep up to Jason when he was playing with a certain toy that he desired and he would ask him, "Jason, do you really, really love it?" If Jason said "yes," he would cry and walk away sad, and he never asked him again about sharing the toy. If nothing else, it stopped a lot of unnecessary fighting and arguments.

One fateful Sunday, a year or so after I had joined, Robert went to church with us. Reverend Hubbard had given a particularly moving sermon that seemed to be directed right towards him. I felt in my spirit that the message had touched his heart. I felt he was going to accept the invitation that day. Sure enough, without saying a word, he stood up and walked to the front of the church, as I cried for joy. Since that day, in that instance, he became dedicated to the word of God, as well. Today he continues to be an avid reader of the Bible, a serious student of the word, a solid prayer warrior and serves as an Ambassador and Deacon at our current church. That day our life together changed, and we wouldn't have it any other way.

Sundays continue to be our favorite day of the week. We look forward to the opportunity to worship and serve the Lord. Over the years, we have changed churches several times, but our fundamental need for a strong Christian lifestyle is still intact. It is the foundation for our marriage. Once we made God the head of our lives, everything got better; our love for each other deepened, our career goals and all of our relationships grew, especially our personal relationship with our Heavenly Father. I came to understand I needed God's blessing and covering over me. This is a prayer someone sent me. I read it every day as I entered my office:

Prayer for the Working Christian Woman

Lord Jesus, as I enter this workplace, I bring your presence with me. I speak Your peace, Your grace and Your perfect order into the atmosphere of this office. I acknowledge your Lordship over all that will be spoken, thought, decided and accomplished within these walls.

Lord Jesus, I thank You for the gifts you have deposited in me. I do not take them lightly but commit to using them responsibly and well. Give me a fresh supply of truth and beauty on which to draw as I do my job. Anoint my creativity, my ideas, my energy, so that even my smallest task may bring You honor.

Lord, when I am confused, guide me. When I am weary, energize me. Lord, when I am burned out, infuse me with the light of the Holy Spirit. May the work that I do and the way I do it, bring hope, life and courage to all that I come in contact with me today. And, Oh Lord, even in this day's most stressful moments, may I rest in You. In the mighty Name that is above all Names, in the Matchless Name of my Lord and Savior Jesus, I pray.

Amen

Jesus Takes Center Stage

My family has a long, rich history as leaders in the Christian church. My maternal great-grandfather, Elijah Russell, started Mt. Moriah Baptist Church in the 1860s, a small rural church which still stands today on cement blocks across from the cotton — now soy — fields in Glen Allen, Mississippi. My mother's father, my grandfather, Reverend Granville Reed, began his ministry in the Baptist church in the Central California area. He eventually founded Reed's College of Religion in South Central Los Angeles, where he prepared men to go into the ministry. My mom's brother, my uncle, Reverend Granville Reed, Jr., was a prominent AME pastor in Chicago, and two of his sons, my cousins the late Reverends Granville Reed, III and Rodger Hall Reed were AME pastors, as well. We are proud that two of my cousin Rodger's children, Pastor Christina Reed and Rev. Granville Reed, IV, have taken up the mantle and are continuing our family's long legacy as Christian pastors. Their mother, Dr. Shirley Cason Reed, just completed two terms as the international president of the Women's Missionary Society of the AME Church. Other family members work in service to God's people as business administrators, politicians, educators, therapists and social workers. However, this call that I had upon my life is different. Previously, no one had the burning desire to go into the world of entertainment.

CHAPTER 11:
The Lion Roars at MGM

When I move, God moves.

In 1984 hip-hop had just become a national phenomenon. So, when MGM picked up an obscure hip-hop dance film called *Breakin'*, no one in the Publicity Department believed in it, except me. My handling of this movie put me on the film marketing map. It was a low budget film, thrown together in just 21 days. However, it featured the latest craze sweeping the nation, break dancing. As a mother of teenage boys, I had my finger on the pulse of this popular dance craze. It was all my kids talked about and attempted to do. I knew it could succeed with teenagers.

Breakin' was the story of a struggling young jazz dancer, Kelly "Special K" Bennett, played by Lucinda Dickey, who meets up with two break-dancers, Ozone played by Adolfo Quinones and Turbo played by Michael Chambers. Together they become the sensation of the street crowds. The film also features Ice-T in his film debut as a club MC. I convinced my bosses to set up an advance screening with my boys and a group of their friends so the marketing staff could see their reaction. As I knew it would, their response went through the roof. The kids didn't care about the bad plot and corny dialog, which were the things that concerned our jaded marketing executives. The film was popping with a hot, soulful soundtrack, featuring the songs, "Breakin' There's No Stopping Us" and "Freak Show on the Dance Floor." The best thing about it was the dancers were real street dancers, not actors trying to dance. Their phenomenal break dance moves were keys to the film being widely received. After witnessing how my boys and their teenager friends reacted, my bosses were starting to feel that the film would be a money-maker.

However, there was one big issue: if it was going to have a chance at the box office, *Breakin'* had to open before Harry Belafonte's highly anticipated film, *Beat Street*, which was scheduled for release in the summer of 1984. MGM scrambled and released *Breakin'* on May 4, when lots of kids were out of school for spring break, and the move paid off. *Breakin'* was the top box office movie for several weeks, topping out at $38.7 million dollars. It only cost $1.2 million to make, so the profit margin was astounding. It became a cult classic and took all of the wind out of *Beat Street,* which only earned $16 million when it came out.

After the opening week, the studio quickly put together an across country personal appearance tour for the two lead dancers, Adolfo, better known as Shabba Doo, a popular member of the dance group The Lockers. Black teens also knew him as the good-looking dancer on the ever-popular Saturday morning TV show "Soul Train." Michael was a famous teenage street dancer, who went by the nickname of Boogaloo Shrimp. I was assigned to take these two sudden stars on the road.

I took them to San Francisco and their first appearance was on "Good Morning San Francisco." By the time the show ended, the television studio was surrounded by hundreds of teenage fans on spring break. Even though the film had just come out on Friday, there were screaming teens outside, who had already seen the film multiple times. Throughout the week, we went to other the large urban cities: Dallas, Chicago, D.C. and New York. It was my first time witnessing, firsthand, a phenomenon explode before my eyes.

The guys' egos blew up, too, especially Shabba Doo's. Newly married, he brought his eighteen-year-old bride, Lela Rochon, along. At that time, she was recognized as the lead dancer in the hit Lionel Richie music video, "All Night Long," which her husband choreographed. As time went on, They eventually divorced, and she has worked successfully as an actress in films. Lela is best known for playing Sunshine in *Harlem Nights* and Robin Stokes in *Waiting to Exhale.* Later she married the highly respected film director Antoine Fuqua *(Training Day)* and they have two beautiful children. We are still friends.

Breakin' is still a cult favorite today and influenced many artists and launched the hip-hop culture onto the world stage.

Grace Under Fire

One of my major tests in my career as a publicist at MGM came in 1985 when I was assigned to supervise the appearances for model/disco diva Grace Jones. She starred in the James Bond film, *A View to a Kill,* as May Day, who was bodyguard and lover to the film's villain, Zorin, played by Christopher Walken. When Zorin betrays her, she joins forces with Bond to save Silicon Valley.

Grace was notorious for being late and marching to the tune of a different drummer. It was my job to get her on our beat, so our publicity campaign could be fulfilled. We first met when she was scheduled to do an interview at her home with her friend Maria Shriver for CBS Morning News. Grace had become friends with Maria and her then-fiancée, Arnold Schwarzenegger, when Grace starred with him as Zola in his film *Conan the Destroyer* several years before.

Despite my urging, Grace kept the crew, her friend Maria, the studio's photo director Steve Newman and me waiting for more than two hours. As I assessed the situation that day, I saw the problem; she was a late riser. It took her forever to put on her make-up and get dressed. Maria was trying to be a great sport about it. Even though she knew how Grace was, Maria got antsy after the waiting time dragged out longer and longer. After that day, I started padding Grace's itinerary with fake start times scheduled long before they actually were. Otherwise, her tardiness was going to jeopardize our interviews and drive everyone crazy.

Interestingly enough, long-lasting friendships developed from that first meeting for several of us. Grace and I bonded over our children. Her son, Paulo, was five years old and so was my youngest son, Teron. By the time I left that day, we agreed to schedule a playdate for our boys. Eventually, Paulo would spend weekends with us, and he would attend my Sunday School class.

Paulo attended a prestigious French school where he had not formed relationships with many of the children and he longed for someone to play with. Grace had a young man working for her, who was responsible for Paulo; getting him up and ready for school, feeding him and driving him to and from school.

Grace also had a young, gorgeous, giant of a boyfriend named Dolph Lundgren. The story was that he had been the bouncer in a club in Australia where Grace had recently performed. He shared with her his aspiration to be an actor. Grace ended up bringing him to the United States, determined to jumpstart his career. Dolph had a minor role in *A View to a Kill*. With Grace's help, he launched his career as an action hero in *Rocky IV,* as the Russian boxer Ivan Drago. His star continued to rise after that. He became an action star in *Master of the Universe, Universal Soldier* and more than thirty other films.

Grace and Dolph's relationship was volatile. She was about ten years his senior, and she was always worried that her boy-toy would leave her. After a stormy four-year relationship, they went their separate ways.

The other lasting friendship that was forged that day as we did publicity for *A View to a Kill* was between MGM's photo director Steve Newman, Dolph and Grace. The friendship that developed that afternoon resulted in Steve leaving his job at the studio to work on Dolph's movies as the unit publicist for the next ten years. He also became a trusted friend/manager to Grace for a number of years, as well.

Grace's entourage also included makeup artist Toni Green, who I recognized as a popular transgender, who had worked in a trendy hair salon in West Hollywood. She was now living in New York and working undetected as a female, which was surprising to me since she was way over six feet tall with huge feet. She pulled me aside and asked me where I got my shoes, since I was five-foot-eleven with size twelve feet. She said she needed some tips on where to get shoes in larger sizes. I chatted with her about shoes and treated her like any other girlfriend.

Somehow Toni and I got on the subject of Compton, which led to talking about my alma mater, Centennial High. She was excited to tell me her cousins went there, Linda and Glorious Griggs. I knew them well because the sisters were on the drill team with me. As a matter fact, Glorious was breathtakingly beautiful and the leader of the Centennettes, our popular drill team. Toni talked endlessly and lovingly about Glorious' good looks and long, flowing hair. She clearly idolized her gorgeous cousin.

Grace's house was on Cherokee, nestled in the Hollywood Hills. As you entered, the patio and pool area were first, and then the house. We usually had the TV crews set up poolside. Once Grace was ready, she always gave amazing interviews. Her slow to start, fabulous interview pattern continued throughout the publicity campaign. It was hard as hell to get her going, but when she appeared, she was incredible. We got to be good friends; me, the conservative publicist, and her, the wild disco diva! We were an odd sight.

Opening week of the movie, I went to pick her up for an appearance on "The Tonight Show with Jay Leno." To my dismay, once again, Grace threw me a monkey wrench. She had decided to dye her hair purple to match the outfit she was wearing for the appearance. When I arrived, she was laying on a chaise lounge with purple dye on her head, which was also running down her neck. She laughed as she saw the horrified look on my face. "Relax, Roz, everything is going to be wonderful, darling," she purred.

I was concerned. I began putting fire under her glam squad to get things moving as quickly as possible. I also enlisted the help of her publicist, John Carmen, who was visiting from New York. She knew we couldn't be late for a live appearance; however, she seemed to get a kick out of driving things to the edge. When she was finally ready to go, we all jumped in the limousine and headed top speed towards Burbank.

Along the way she insisted she needed her favorite Cristal champagne to drink. Her publicist opened the bottle and poured her a drink; however, before she took it, she insisted he stir out the bubbles. Yes, the diva loved champagne, but she hated the bubbles. John stirred them out with the back of his ballpoint pen. Then she drank it down in one gulp and wanted another. This continued until we entered the gate at NBC. She was happy, but we were all wiped out. She got there just as it was time for her to go on the air. She walked confidently out on stage and, as usual, she was fabulous. The only thing that didn't go her way was her hair. After all the effort, her purple hair still looked black on TV.

The most challenging time I had was in New York, because I had to juggle her interviews with Roger Moore's interviews. By contrast, he was an early bird and very punctual, and you already know how she was. For someone like Roger, I made it a point to be early. Thank God! As I approached the Plaza Hotel to take him to the morning show, he was already standing impatiently in the street, looking at his watch. We knew better than to schedule any of their interviews together.

After the morning show appearance, the remainder of Roger's interviews were scheduled to take place in his huge three-bedroom suite at the hotel. We set up TV interviews in his living room, dining room and extra bedrooms. For his part, he wore the same gray suit, but for each new interview, he changed to a new tie and pocket square for a fresh, new look. This way he could move quickly from one interview to the next.

That day Grace only had one late afternoon interview, an industry screening and a party at a private room at a luxury hotel. All went well. I did not attend the party, thank goodness. Guests included Bianca Jagger, Andy Warhol, and members of Duran Duran. The next day it was reported that Grace and her guests shot up the room with water guns filled with liquor, which were replicas of the long, silver, shiny gun she shot in the film.

The world premiere of *A View to a Kill* took place in San Francisco on May 22, 1985. It was the last time I had to wrestle with Grace and her entourage. A long day was scheduled with an afternoon event, the premiere and Grace's private birthday party. I had to make sure that all her guests were provided for in terms of transportation and premiere tickets. Among the guests were her mother, Marguerite Jones, and brother, well-known Los Angeles pastor, Bishop Noel Jones. Toni, the makeup artist, requested two seats for the premiere, however, Grace only had two tickets left and she needed a ticket for her good friend, the popular Queen of Disco, Sylvester. Grace told Toni her dilemma and asked her to go with Sylvester, who was famous for the disco hit "You Make Me Feel Mighty Real." Neither of the divas was happy to be with the other, but they went, dressed fabulously.

The City of San Francisco was thrilled to host the cast and crew of *A View to a Kill*, unveiling the fourteenth 007 adventure to the world as a thank you for shooting the James Bond movie in the city.

Earlier in the afternoon, J. Worth, the skydiving stuntman who had doubled as James Bond since 1979, made a leap from a helicopter, touching down outside City Hall, the building seen in the opening of the epic firetruck chase. Roger Moore delivered a speech, thanking the city for their cooperation. Mayor Dianne Feinstein, who made possible the 007 shoot on location in the iconic city, named May 22 "James Bond Day." And she personally hosted a champagne reception with over a thousand guests.

The celebration then moved to the Palace of Fine Arts on Lyon Street. Grace, wearing an Azzedine Alaia designer gown, joined Roger Moore, Christopher Walken, Tanya Roberts, director John Glen and musicians Duran Duran, who did the movie's title song, in walking the red carpet to the delight of hundreds of fans. They were joined by screenwriter Richard Maibaum, Michael G. Wilson and producer Albert R. Broccoli, and Walter Gotel, well known for playing General Gogol, M's opposite number in the KGB.

Grace and the boys from Duran Duran were wildly welcomed with their groupies almost outnumbering Bond fans. After the stars emerged from the screening, they headed over to Grace's invite-only birthday party.

Once I got Grace's group to the Hard Rock for her celebration, I returned, wearily, to the hotel. I soaked my aching body and feet in a long leisurely bath, then collapsed in the warmth and softness of the bed. The next day, I made sure everyone got on their flights and I celebrated the fact that I was done. I had survived the most challenging personal appearance tour of my career. I gave a deep sigh of relief and patted myself on the back.

Crisis: Set-up for a Break-Through

By June of 1986 I had established myself as a respected and valued member of MGM's Marketing team. Then the unthinkable happened. Media mogul Ted Turner bought the studio. At that time, he was best known for creating a twenty-four-hour news station called Cable News Network. Today CNN is a mainstay, but at that time we wondered who would care to access news around the clock, twenty-four/seven. Soon after Turner bought the studio, it was rumored that the studio was going to be streamlined and many of us would lose our jobs. Everyone had feelings of doom, yet I remained hopeful.

Nevertheless, soon I learned that I was one of the executives whose job would be eliminated. My boss was heartbroken as he explained that the staff members with the most seniority would remain and the rest of us would be let go in six weeks. I officially got depressed, because I didn't have many options. Who could I reach out to?

The first person I called was my former boss, Al Newman, who was now working at an established PR agency. Without hesitation, he offered me a job, however it would be corporate public relations, not entertainment. Hmmm… The offer was unappealing. If nothing else came up, I made up in my mind, I would take it. Entertainment PR was still very exciting to me.

I was also recommended for a position at ABC Television. I went on an interview and was told that the right candidate would be in-charge of mini-series and soap operas. I smiled, but in my mind, I was wondering how could one person do two very distinctly different jobs. More importantly, many of the mini-series were done out of the country, which would require me to travel. I knew that I couldn't do that. Robert traveled, I needed to be at home with my three sons.

Lastly, I was also interviewed by a guy named Brian, who was the Director of Publicity at Universal Studios, for a senior publicist position in the Motion Picture Department. The interview had gone okay. I could tell there was no real connection between the two of us. He was courteous and said I was the first candidate he had interviewed, and he would get back to me with a final decision. I was sad because that was the job I really wanted.

All my penned-up emotions came tumbling down when I went to church that Sunday. Before the church service started, I went up to the altar, knelt on my knees and the dam broke. I started sobbing and could not stop. "God help me. Please help me," I kept repeating. After church I went home and got in my bed and pulled the covers over my head. My behavior was deplorable, but I couldn't help it. God had been so good to me. Now, I was falling apart as I faced losing my dream job. When I spoke to my husband, who was out-of-town on a film location, he tried to be encouraging. However, nothing could get me out of the funk I was in. This is where faith in God is put to the test and I was failing miserably.

The next day I was sitting in my office and Robert called, again, to check up on me. I had been told I was scheduled to be out of my office in ten days. "Have you cleaned out your office?" It seemed like a stupid question, but he insisted I stop feeling sorry for myself and start packing my boxes. Reluctantly, I took his advice and began filling boxes and praying. I separated my important files and papers and put them in file boxes. I called a messenger to take them to my home. I put the rest of my paperwork in trash bags and I had them taken to a dumpster. My office was clean! Surprisingly, the process did relieve my tension. And it gets better. After my office was thoroughly cleaned out, a miracle happened.

For the first time since I had worked at MGM, I got a call from Greg Morrison, who was president of our marketing division. What could he want? He explained that since my immediate boss, Ed Pine, was on vacation, it was his legal responsibility to let me know I would be officially terminated in ten business days.

He said rather dramatically, "I would rather slit my wrist than to tell you this." I explained to him that I had already been told a month before. He was genuinely concerned, and he inquired how my job search was going. I went over my three options and told him how much I wanted the position at Universal Studios.

"Who did you talk to?" he asked.

I said, "Brian, who was the director of publicity."

"I don't know who that is. If you want that job, I will call Barry!" Unbeknownst to me, Barry Lorie was the president of marketing at Universal and one of his dearest friends. Wow! I was in shock. As he promised, they spoke, president to president, and five minutes later, he called me back and told me I had the job! Just like that! I thanked him profusely.

A few minutes later, I received a congratulatory call from Brian, who welcomed me to the staff and asked me when I would like to start. My head was spinning. I told him I would be there in two weeks. All I could say to myself over and over was, "Thank you, Jesus. Thank you, Jesus. You have showed up and showed out beyond my wildest dreams." Through my tears I called Robert to let him know what had transpired. "Guess what? I cleaned my office out and now I have a new job at Universal," I sobbed. We couldn't believe what God had done. And this wouldn't be the only time. There were more miracles awaiting me.

Since that day, every time I am faced with a new dilemma, I start praying and cleaning! Somewhere in the process, I have come to realize when I move, God moves.

CHAPTER 12:
Universal Appeal

Managing people requires something extra.

In 1986 the transition to a new studio with a new staff couldn't have gone smoother. Brian and the staff were quite welcoming. I was given a nice office and an efficient secretary named Judy Martin. In many ways, I was accepted much easier because the people at Universal only knew me as an executive. There was automatically a level of respect that didn't necessarily exist at MGM.

The first publicity campaigns I participated in were Steven Spielberg's first animated film, *An American Tale*, *The Secret of My Success*, starring Michael J. Fox; *Baby Boom*, starring Diane Keaton; *Jaws the Revenge*, starring Mario Van Peebles; *Born in East L.A.*, starring Cheech Marin; *Cry Freedom*, starring Denzel Washington; and *Hail, Hail Rock n Roll*, starring Chuck Berry.

Technological changes were coming to business offices across the country. At Universal's Publicity Department two of the top secretaries were beginning to use word processing computers to do publicity reports and press kits. The rest of us were still using our trusty IBM Selectric typewriters, which I used confidently at top speed. A deep-seated fear swept over me at the mention of using a computer. I knew it would just be a matter of time, but I wasn't looking forward to it. Nevertheless, when we finally did get word processors, it wasn't as hard as I had imagined. However, since all the work we do in publicity is time sensitive, I used to postpone using the mysterious word processor as much as I could. However, eventually, the computer became second nature.

A year or so later, I took sick leave for six weeks for a surgery and when I came back, my secretary chuckled and said, "There's a mouse in your office."

"A mouse!" I screamed. I was thinking of a little, nasty rodent, but they were talking about the newest PC computer gadget. Everyone in the department laughed about that forever. Of course, today I have conquered the computer and my trusty mouse, but in those days, I was freaked out whenever my screen would turn black and I feared I had lost my documents. The younger secretaries in the department helped me tremendously. They had grown up with computers and video games, so technology was second nature to them. But for older staff members like me, it was a challenge. I started off years ago on manual typewriters. This new high-tech world was and still is a challenge for me.

Another office aid, a facsimile machine, better known as a fax machine, became common place at this time. Publicity is all about getting news out fast, so this machine made it much easier and more efficient. We would dial a phone number, push start and in a matter of seconds, the document was transmitted to the recipient. Of course, today computers and communicating by email have become common place, and the fax machines have now become obsolete.

Other improved forms of communication were coming about as well, like CNN, there was also USA Today and Fed Ex. All were new ways of getting information or items to people faster. I thought, who would be interested in looking at Cable News Network, rather than the network news channels, or read USA Today instead of the Los Angeles Times? Who would pay a high price to get a Federal Express package to someone overnight as oppose to sending it through the U.S. Postal Service? Today they are a part of our world and now we wonder how we ever lived without them.

In 1986 HIV/AIDS was just beginning to be a serious health epidemic in the United States. In Universal's Motion Picture Marketing Department, the majority of the men were gay. During a short period in the late 80s, we had four members on our staff, contract AIDS and die from the deadly disease. There were others on our staff who were HIV-positive and took the experimental drugs AZT and DDL with harsh side effects. Some of those men are healthy and still living today.

Brian, my boss, was gay and his companion had full blown AIDS. Brian wanted to give him something to do, so he wasn't sitting at home all day feeling sorry for himself. When one of our staff publicists went out on vacation, Brian let his companion use her office to work. When she came back, she was horrified. At that time, people didn't know they could or couldn't contract the disease if someone used their telephone, typewriter or desk. We know better today, but at that time no one knew for sure how it was transmitted. It was a scary time.

As Brian's partner got progressively worse, my boss had difficulty coping. He began using drugs and it was hard to be under his supervision. He had irrational behavior. He would hallucinate, talking about things that didn't exist. Soon after, he left Universal when his companion passed away. The epidemic was taking a severe toll on everyone.

My top boss at Universal was Sally Van Slyke. She was a former on-air broadcaster, who was beautiful, but talked loud, direct and cursed like a sailor. She was what some call ballsy. Nobody messed with Sally. Most people were afraid of her, but I wasn't. We got along well.

However, there was an incident that challenged our relationship. One of the clerks in our department was Carlin Smith, a black, single mother of two teenage boys. As a matter of fact, she and I knew one another because her sons and my sons were good friends. She was hard working and quiet. One of the head secretaries gave her a press release to send out. Carlin complied and made over one hundred copies of the release and dutifully folded them, sealed them in envelopes and sent them out via messenger. Later, all hell broke loose, because Sally said the press release should not have gone out because it had not yet been approved by Tom Pollock, who was the president of the studio.

The press release had been written by our staff writer. He gave it to his secretary and told her it would go out later that day. He went to lunch and his assistant thought she would get started on it right away and solicited Carlin's assistance. Sally referred to Carlin as an idiot and fired her on the spot. She gathered their personal belongings and left in tears.

I have a soft spot in my heart for single mothers. So, I went to Sally to speak up on behalf of my friend. She was shocked when I had the nerve to tell her I thought it was unfair. I explained how hard-working Carlin was and she should not lose her job for being helpful. Sally contended that someone needed to be fired because she, Sally, had to report to "that man up in the tower," speaking of studio president Tom Pollock's penthouse office.

"Sally, in good conscious, I have to answer to a man upstairs, too, and it's not Mr. Pollock," I said.

I left there thinking, "Roz, you are the next person to get fired." However, she recognized my sincerity. My defense of Carlin made her re-think her actions. She didn't give her back her job at Universal, but she contacted the union and had her placed at another studio. As for my friend Carlin, the firing and job relocation was a blessing in disguise. She got a job at 20th Century Fox, which was much closer to her Culver City home. She continued to work there for the next 30 years, until she retired in 2016.

Cry Freedom

In 1987 Denzel Washington starred in *Cry Freedom* as Steven Biko, a noted student activist, who led the anti-apartheid movement in South Africa in the 1960s and 1970s. He died in police custody and became a martyr of the movement. The film about Steven Biko's life was based on a book by Donald Woods, a white journalist, who had to escape South Africa and go into exile for his involvement with Biko. The film was directed by Sir Richard Attenborough, best known for *Ghandi*, and released by Universal Pictures.

Because of the film's political importance, the studio conducted four prestigious premieres in the United States, including in Los Angeles, New York, Washington D.C. and Atlanta. I was assigned to accompany the studio executives, the filmmakers, the author and their spouses to the D.C and Atlanta premieres, which took place over a four-day period.

In Washington, D.C., Ethel Kennedy, the widow of Robert Kennedy, hosted the premiere showing, followed by a lavish after-party at her Hickory Hill estate in McLean, Virginia, where she and Robert Kennedy had raised their large family. After his death, Ethel continued to host an array of political, social and human rights notables in her home. I was impressed with the huge opulent mansion, which was on six acres of land. It had eighteen rooms and thirteen bathrooms, twelve fireplaces, two swimming pools, paddocks, a small movie theater and lighted tennis courts.

As we entered the party, each guest was asked to pull a table number from a large glass bowl. Apparently, this was something Mrs. Kennedy enjoyed doing to mix up the guests to encourage them to get to know someone new and exchange in interesting dialogue. Most of the Universal staffers were upset by this, because we only talked movies. The other guests were mostly from the world of politics and we felt we weren't knowledgeable enough to have an intelligent conversation with them. Thank goodness, I ended up at the table with a fellow publicist named Gary Goldstein. We stuck together like glue. More upset than we were was the wife of Tom Pollock, the top studio executive. She was used to being on her husband's arms. Having conversations with the political notables caused her great anxiety. Somehow, we all made it through the evening pretty well.

As far as the Kennedy estate went, I was surprised how casual the home décor was. I remember the couches in the living room being ice blue with pastel floral designs on polished cotton. The entire house was a museum dedicated to the memory of her late husband, Robert Kennedy. Hundreds and hundreds of Bobby Kennedy pictures, awards of merit and letters were framed and covered the walls, top to bottom in each room.

The preparation of the dinner was supervised by a beautiful, older black woman, who was so dear to the family that she was acknowledged and proudly introduced to all of us. When she came out and took a bow, she reminded me of my own nana.

At the end of the meal, Sir Richard Attenborough spoke and finished by bringing a humble Ethel Kennedy to the stage. She acknowledged that she was shy and did not relish public speaking. She spoke about the importance of supporting the anti-apartheid movement and about the visit she and her husband had made to South Africa many years ago. She briefly wished us all a good evening and that was it.

I was very excited to be there, because I felt a special historical connection to Robert Kennedy. I had been among the thousands of supporters at the Ambassador Hotel on the fateful night of June 5,

1968, when he was assassinated. I was twenty-five-years-old at the time. My cousin, Virginia McKean, worked on political campaigns, and she invited me to join her at the victory party to celebrate Kennedy winning the presidential primary election in California. Virginia had previously worked for the governor Jerry Brown, and at that time, she worked for Pierre Salinger, who was campaigning for a California senate seat. Salinger was best known for being the press secretary for John F. Kennedy. So, I tagged along for the Democratic Election Night party that fateful night. However, at midnight shots rang out and he was shot three or four times by Sirhan Sirhan.

Once we heard the shots, I remember seeing football great Rosey Grier sitting on the floor sobbing. We were terrified and we ran back into the lobby area where all hell had broken loose. People were screaming that Kennedy had been shot. In the end, Sirhan Sirhan was wrestled to the ground by Rosey, Pete Hamill, Olympian Rafer Johnson and author George Plimpton.

It was a very sad and insane time in America. Rev. Dr. Martin Luther King, Jr. had died on April 4, 1968. Prior to that, Malcolm X was killed in February 1965; Medgar Evers was killed in June 1963; and John F. Kennedy was killed in November 1963. It was as if anyone who stood up for the rights of African Americans was killed. As a young adult, I agonized over the death of these leaders. I was very depressed, and I began to wonder if we, as a people, would ever get to the mountaintop. It was a dark and shameful time in this country.

For this reason, it was an incredible incredible honor to go to the home of Robert Kennedy almost 20 years after his brutal, untimely death. As we left that evening, the keepsake each of us received was a plexiglass paperweight inscribed with the words Robert Kennedy spoke during an important speech he gave in support of the growing anti-apartheid movement in Cape Town, South Africa, in 1966. The inscription, which meant the world to me, read:

> *Each time a man stands up for an ideal, or acts to improve the lot of others, or strikes out against injustice, he sends forth a tiny ripple of hope, and crossing each other from a million different centers of energy and daring, those ripples build a current that can sweep down the mightiest walls of oppression and resistance.*

The next amazing premiere was in Atlanta, hosted by Coretta Scott King, the widow of Dr. King, on behalf of the King Center for Non-Violence. One day I was in the presence of Mrs. Kennedy and the next day in the presence of Mrs. King. This was the amazing thing about working in the film industry; you never knew where life would take you.

We stayed at the Ritz Carlton in Buckhead, which was the model for all Ritz Carltons around the world. Mrs. King has always been mysterious to me because of her prideful, stoic posture, which never changed. She always had the same hairdo and was conservatively dressed. God knows we all felt for her and all that she'd gone through in the public eye, yet she still seemed hard to penetrate. I wondered if she ever laughed and had fun. Despite my thoughts, I had a great time that evening and met many prominent people.

The warmth I had had with the executives seemed genuine. I was there to assist them, which I did without hesitation. I didn't ever feel that we were going to be forever buddies after this trip, but I did feel we had bonded in a positive way. However, I was in for a surprise. Tom Pollock was the head of the studio and was my age but acted much older. He had wild wiry hair, with a wandering eye and wore thick glasses. Nevertheless, he was highly respected and had a reputation as an outstanding legal mind.

As we headed back to Los Angeles, there was a problem with the seating in first-class, which the airline clerk and I were desperately trying to remedy. Before we could figure out the situation, Tom came to me and said in a nasty tone, "If a seat doesn't become available, you won't be getting on this flight." I looked puzzled and said vaguely, "Of course," because I understood, if it didn't get worked out, I would automatically give up my seat. As I had learned, some people with power are rude and make no apologies for it. You can be "buddy-buddy" one minute, then they'll put you "in your place," the next.

Of course, it did work out, but by this time I was pissed. It paralyzed my ability to make light conversation with the group. He never said another word about it. I thought he might offer an apology, but no, it was not to be. I had to develop thick skin.

Very Merry, Chuck Berry

In 1987 director Taylor Hackford made *Hail, Hail Rock and Roll*, a documentary on the life of music icon Chuck Berry. We had heard that Chuck was hard to deal with from the very beginning of production and throughout the release of the film, which is clearly evident when you watch the documentary.

What was the real problem? It was simple. He mistrusted and disliked most white folks. Like many old-timers, early in his career he had been often cheated, so he took matters into his own hands. He had a white assistant, Jackie, who handled all his business deals. He required to be paid all monies due him before he went on stage. He also realized he was a natural, self-taught talent. Keith Richards and all the white rockers idolized him and wanted to mimic his style but couldn't. He relished when they tried to copy his style to no avail. He took every possible opportunity to tell them they weren't playing his music right. He had a smirk on his face and a "greater than thou" attitude, which they detested. He particularly made Keith's skin crawl. He couldn't stand Chuck's ornery ways.

The stories of his antics on the publicity trail were the talk of our department. So, as he headed to Los Angeles for the premiere, final publicity appearances and to receive a star on the Hollywood Walk of Fame, they called on me, as usual, to coordinate Chuck's schedule for the day.

The publicity schedule started early in the morning with TV interviews via satellite. Soon after I showed up at the satellite studio, Chuck arrived. I reluctantly approached him to introduce myself. I was expecting the worse. The itinerary for the day was on my clipboard and I wanted to go over the details with him.

"Hello, Mr. Berry. I'm Roz Stevenson and I will be coordinating your schedule today."

To my surprise, he was thrilled to see my brown face. Apparently, throughout the publicity campaign he had only encountered white people, so he was delighted to see me. He stood up beaming with a big grin on his face and hugged me warmly. He said, "Sister, whatever you tell me to do, I'm going to do it!" Wow! From that moment on, we had the best day.

Once we completed all the satellite interviews, we headed to the location where he was to get his star on the Hollywood Walk of Fame. All the studio executives were on pins and needles when we arrived. All eyes were upon us as I emerged from of the limo with Chuck close behind me. He smiled and held my hand as I directed him to the star ceremony. Their mouths fell open because Chuck was beyond cooperative and friendly. My boss whispered to me, "What in the hell did you do to him?" But I hadn't done anything, except be who I was – a black woman in charge for the day.

We had a wonderful ceremony followed by a luncheon honoring him at The Hollywood Roosevelt. He gladly did additional TV interviews in a suite at the hotel. Then I got him back to the Beverly Hills Hotel, so he could rest until the premiere. He gave me a big hug and we went our separate ways. I assured him I would meet him when his limo arrived on the red carpet.

We had the premiere party at the newly constructed AMC Theater in the Century City Shopping Mall, which had not yet been opened to the public. The entire lobby was used for the after party. They had a stage built and hoped to have Chuck sing, but there was one problem; no one had asked Chuck. Everything went well on the red carpet and premiere screening. But all hell broke loose at the after party, when he realized what they were up to. He grabbed my hand and demanded, "Get my limo. I'm leaving!" So, I reluctantly began to lead him out of the party. I caught the eye of the director Taylor Hackford and gestured for him. He ran after us as we were walking out.

"Chuck, can I talk to you?"

Chuck answered abruptly, "Nope. I'm going to the hotel." Nevertheless, Taylor rushed up, pulled him aside and they talked. Soon I saw Taylor go into his pocket and pull out a large wad of money, which he stuffed into Chuck's hand. Chuck looked at the money, flashed a big grin and, immediately, made an about-face. He waved to me to come on and we went back to the party.

Taylor understood Chuck. He knew what it would take to get him to sing. Once Chuck got some cash, he went up on the stage and began singing his entire repertoire. People went crazy as he blared out all his most famous songs, including "Sweet Little Sixteen," "Maybelline," "Johnny B. Goode," "Rock'n Roll Music," "Roll Over Beethoven" and others. He was serious about getting some money before he would sing one word. It was clear it wasn't the amount of money. It was a gesture of respect. Chuck had to get paid.

No one came with Chuck except his beautiful daughter, Ingrid, and blues guitarist Robert McCray; both sang with him in the film. He was a loner and marched to the tune of his own drum. As the evening came to a close, he told me his daughter also needed to get a hotel room at the Beverly Hills Hotel where he was staying. She had been at Chuck's home in the Hollywood Hills. Apparently, a water pipe had burst, and the carpets were soaked, so she was unable to stay in the house. I went on to the hotel and put her room on my credit card. I was a little worried that I wouldn't get reimbursed, because I didn't get prior approval. However, my bosses were so delighted about my work with Chuck, that they didn't question the unauthorized expenditure.

I had also been a little concerned about Chuck's reputation as a lady's man. He was known for being racy and had had his share of run-ins with the law for his exploits with young girls. He didn't say anything inappropriate to me. However, he did say that I reminded him of Etta James. He winked and said he had always wanted to sleep with her. I ignored his comment and went on my way, realizing that I had once again defied the odds by dealing admirably with a notoriously tough character. I never saw him again, but I will never forget the merry day I spent with the late, great Chuck Berry.

CHAPTER 13:
The Stevenson's Family Vacations

My life on movie sets.

Juggling my career and family life continued to be a challenge. Everything was dictated by Robert's film projects. Regular family vacations to Disney World and other popular spots weren't possible. Our family vacations were film locations. Looking back, God blessed us with extraordinary, unique experiences.

By this time, Robert was considered one of the top hair stylists in the industry, black or white. As I said earlier, he began the eighties working exclusively with Richard Pryor. So, wherever Richard went, Robert went, and our family would follow, in most cases. When Richard wasn't working, Robert immediately was offered other exciting film projects. Many times, he had to weigh multiple offers and hope for the best outcome. For the most part, he picked films that went on to be landmark projects.

On film locations, the stars, filmmakers and crew developed a close family bond. The friendships are sincere and enduring while filming; however, for the most part, after filming, everyone goes their own way. Nonetheless, although you may rarely see one another, a bond is formed that never diminishes.

When I visited, I also enjoyed developing friendships with the cast members and the crew on the set. The relationships I built also served me well in my dealing with talent in my career over the years. I had the opportunity to work with many of the same talent on film projects, which I was assigned to as a publicist. Every time the staff in the publicity department mentioned a star, I already knew them. It became a long-standing joke that I knew every actor in Hollywood. It is one of those things that has worked to my advantage because the business is all about relationships. It wasn't anything we consciously set out to do; it just happened over time. Now Robert jokes that people only know him because of me. However, I say they know me because of him. Either way, it has been a benefit and a joy for both of us. We were, and still are, both highly respected throughout the film industry.

The Toy – '82.

My then three-year-old son Teron and I visited Robert in Baton Rouge, Louisiana, on the location for the comedy *The Toy*, starring Richard Pryor and Jackie Gleason. The most unforgettable occasion for Teron and me was the day we arrived on the film set just in time for lunch. All the trailers were lined up on an empty lot facing the backyards of homes in a residential neighborhood. The joyful sound of children playing in a backyard immediately caught Teron's attention. There were three young children playing on a swing set with a beautiful, young lady babysitting. She noticed us and offered to let Teron join them. I said, "Sure," and she and I struck up a conversation. Her name was Julie McCall and she was eager to find out all the details about the movie they were making. I shared that it was a film called *The Toy*, starring Richard Pryor.

"Oh, my God, do you think I can meet him?" Richard was always kind about meeting fans, so I asked his buddy, David Banks, who was standing outside of his trailer, if Julie she could meet Richard. He turned and looked her up and down. Once he saw the gorgeous Creole young woman, he smiled and said, "Of course!" He went inside the trailer and the next thing she knew, Richard emerged from his trailer and humbly introduced himself to her with a handshake and a warm, friendly smile.

As the kids played, Julie and I continued our conversation. When she told me that she was in her last year of high school, I was shocked because she looked and acted much older. She was poised and mature beyond her years. Julie had recently won a local beauty pageant and it was easy to see why.

Later that day, Richard invited her into his trailer, a few minutes later she came out and she was stunned, because as she was leaving, he kissed her. I had just witnessed "love at first kiss." It was also the beginning of a friendship between she and I that has lasted almost 40 years.

There have been many stories about the women in Richard's life, but never any mention of Julie. The two of them had a love and respect for one another that was genuine. They fell in love in Baton Rouge and she continued to visit him on film sets, in Illinois and at his home in California for the next few years. She shared with me one of her most memorable trips with him was at Thanksgiving when they went to his hometown of Peoria, Illinois. Meeting Richard's family and seeing where and how he grew up really helped her to understand his complexities. She also had an opportunity to meet and interact with his children, his favorite Aunt Dee and his Uncle Dickey.

Julie credits Richard with teaching her, by example, how a man should treat her. He encouraged her to set standards for herself. She valued his opinions and says she is eternally grateful for the encouragement he gave her to be all that she could be. She says Richard was the most soft-spoken, gentle and kindest person she has ever known. When they were dating, he was always a perfect gentleman; opening doors, pulling out chairs and using his personal security to ensure her safety.

Richard was a generous gift-giver, and he gave her diamond earrings, a Rolex watch and lots of clothing. It was unusual for him to receive from those whom he had given to. However, it wasn't that way with Julie. After he had lavished her with gifts, she simply gifted him with a belt with a unique alligator buckle, symbolic of the Bayou. He was stunned and so appreciative. He loved that belt and wore it all the time. He pointed it out to everyone and wore it like a badge of honor. They shared a bond that was so sweet and special. What she experienced was the good side of Richard, but there were more dark and complicated issues that he didn't want her to be a part of.

As time went on, he began to voice real concerns over their twenty-five-year age difference. She was a brilliant student, who had been accepted into a number of top universities. So, as their visits slowed, he urged her to go to college, and promised to provide financial assistance. With his help, she went to Southern University in Baton Rouge and graduated with a degree in Communications.

However, prior to going to Southern, Julie had come to Los Angeles to visit the colleges where she had been accepted: UCLA, USC and Pepperdine. Her goal then was to also be near Richard. She came with his blessings and knowledge, however, when she arrived, she wasn't able get in touch with him. When she could not reach him, she settled on accommodations at a hotel near the airport and close to us. She knew no one else in Los Angeles, so I agreed to take her to visit the colleges. Robert didn't want Richard to think we were meddling in his business, so we asked her not to tell him of our involvement. But when she finally spoke with him, she said she was visiting with us. We were in a dilemma.

The next day I spoke to Lauren, Richard's assistant, to explain what was going on and asked her to let us know what we should do. Once she relayed the information to Richard, he called Julie's mother and explained that he didn't feel Los Angeles was the right place for her and he wanted her to return home. When Julie's mom told her that she needed to come back home, she cried and cried and cried some more. It broke my heart the day I drove her back to the airport. However, she went home and enrolled at Southern University. I think it was the right decision. It made us respect Richard even more, because he truly wanted nothing but the best for Julie.

Eventually, she felt the need to reconnect with old friends and focus on school. She began dating a popular football star at the college and they eventually married. When her nuptials were reported to Richard, he expressed his hurt. However, they remained good friends as they both went their separate ways.

Looking back today, for my part, I feel God put me in the middle of their situation to sway the relationship into an acceptable outcome. In many ways, I saw my younger self in Julie, but she was dealing with much bigger stakes. She was swept away by a world-famous celebrity. A real concern for me was that Richard was also my husband's employer, and I didn't want to jeopardize that relationship. I was caught on a tightrope in terms of my involvement. Thank God, it all worked out for the best.

I am so happy Julie and I recently reconnected on social media.

We have been able to catch up with one another's lives. She shared that she has been married twice, raised two handsome sons. She is still stunning, confident, currently single and a grandmother. Sadly, Richard passed away in 2005 after a long bout with multiple sclerosis, nevertheless Julie vows that memories of him and his love for her will live in her heart forever.

The greatest times on *The Toy* were the weekends, when Richard would host poolside parties at the hotel on Airline Highway for the cast and crew, which included never-ending food catered by local Cajuns. They cooked Louisiana cuisine outdoors around the pool. The red beans were cooked in an enormous kettle, stirred with a boat paddle. They piled mountains of boiled crawfish on plastic tablecloths on long banquet tables. They gave us big bibs and told us to eat crawfish to our hearts content, and they reminded us in their playful, risqué style to "suck the heads." In addition to crawfish, we indulged on all the unique foods of that region; the melt-in-your-mouth beignets, étouffeé, red beans and rice. You name it. We ate it.

The fun-filled afternoons were complete with Cajun music played by local musicians, featuring R&B, blues, soul, and zydeco, which was played on an accordion, the electric guitar, washboard, and keyboard. The musicians got a kick out of pulling Richard up to the band stand to be a part of the fun. Richard loved mimicking their Cajun dialect. His favorite was to continually ask, "Why for you do that?" instead of "Why did you do that?" These were times of pure joy, just hanging out, eating and getting loose, thanks to the kindness of Richard Pryor.

One Sunday we were part of a group of crew members who were invited to attend the church of a pastor, who had worked as an extra on the film. We were warmly greeted and extended "the right hand of fellowship" by the congregation during the service. But we were in for a big surprise when the good preacher got wound up in his fiery sermon. He pointed his finger in our direction and said, "You Hollywood folks need to stop living in sin. I know what you're doing! You're smoking that weed and sniffing that cocaine. You're gonna have to answer to God himself, one day!" Well, we were stunned. We didn't know where that came from. We concluded that it was an assumption people made about everybody in the film industry. Needless to say, that was the one and only time we went to that church.

Superman III – '83

During the filming of *Superman III*, I took all four kids — Jason, Damon, Kendra and Teron — to Alberta, Calgary, for an unforgettable experience. Robert said when we arrived in a van taxi, he thought there would never be an end to the kids pouring out of the back seats. Robert had gotten us a two-bedroom suite for our large family. Robert was still working with Richard, who was gracious and lots of fun for the kids to be around. Their biggest joy was seeing him, as well as his stunt double, being rigged for the flying sequences with Superman, the late-great Christopher Reeves.

Life in Canada was pleasant, and the natural beauty of the environment was not lost on the children. First of all, they noticed the clearness of the Canadian skies, as opposed to the dense smog we endured every day in Los Angeles. Everywhere you looked there were endless, colorful flower gardens, streams of water and huge green trees spread throughout the landscape of the city. In addition to Alberta, we took the kids on a long bus ride up to the historic Banff Hotel in Whistler, Canada, an incredibly, beautiful ski destination.

Flashdance – '83

We were no strangers to the city of Pittsburgh where Robert had filmed *The Fish Who Saved Pittsburgh* in 1978. This time Robert was working with Jennifer Beals, a first-time actress. He was also working with a first-time producing team that included a former agent, Jerry Bruckheimer, and a former studio head, Don Simpson.

Though the two men had had successful careers previously, there inexperience as filmmakers seemed obvious on the shoot. The script was changing every day, while Jennifer, the neophyte actress they had selected, had trouble remembering her lines. Every day was chaotic throughout the shoot. However, what no one realized while they were making the film was that everything about *Flashdance* was destined to become iconic and impact pop culture in profound ways.

Jennifer became an instant star, while Bruckheimer and Simpson went on to be two of the most highly regarded creative forces in the entertainment industry. Their follow-up blockbusters to *Flashdance* included *Beverly Hills Cop* and *Top Gun*, which propelled the careers of Eddie Murphy and Tom Cruise to international stardom. Bruckheimer is still one of the most prolific producers of our time, while Don Simpson, unfortunately, succumbed to a drug overdose in 1996.

Top honors also went to *Flashdance's* original soundtrack, featuring the song "What A Feeling," which went on to win an Academy Award. The extraordinary dance sequences spawned a national craze. Jennifer's oversized sweatshirt worn with the neck cut out and hanging off her shoulder became an instant fashion craze.

To Robert's surprise, even the curly hairstyle Jennifer wore became a fashion statement. Women everywhere wanted to achieve her curly look. Although Jennifer wore her own naturally curly hair, Robert was swamped with interviews from hair magazines to learn how the look could be achieved on straight or kinky hair. The *Flashdance* experience was an eye-opener. You never know the effect a film can have on the world around you.

The Jesse Owens Story – '84

Ultimately, Robert won an Emmy for his work on the TV movie "The Jesse Owens Story," starring Dorian Harewood and Debbie Morgan. Damon, Teron and I visited the Dallas, Texas, location and had a great time. Five-year old Teron had an opportunity to take ice skating lessons, as well as go on visits to Six Flags Amusement Park and other local sights.

However, my greatest memories about that experience involved Debbie. I had met her when she was just starting her career, playing J.J.'s girlfriend on "Good Times" in 1976. I had no idea that she had gone on to be extremely popular as Dr. Angie Hubbard on the soap opera "All My Children." Little did I realize, Angie and her husband, Jesse Hubbard, played by Darnell Williams, were the first African American super couple on daytime television.

I was in for the surprise of my life when I took her shopping in the Dallas shopping mall where Teron was taking his ice skating lessons. Dallas was like the epicenter for soap opera fans. As soon as we got in the mall, people started screaming in full-on southern twangs, "Angie, Angie!" They started running towards us like a herd of cattle. We had to think quickly. I got to the boutique where she wanted to shop for a dress, and the management agreed to lock their door and put her in a dressing room. Debbie needed a dress to wear that night, and the boutique manager was happy to accommodate her. She was thrilled to have Debbie in the store. Fans gathered outside and waited as we found several dress selections for Debbie to try on. When she finally decided on an outfit, we had to get security guards to get us back to our car safely. Teron was very confused. As the fans screamed, "Angie!" He screamed, "Why don't you leave us alone? Her name is Debbie!" It was unreal!

It even got worse that evening when a group of us went to see actor, singer, dancer Ben Vereen, who was in the film, perform live. One fan came up and rudely said in a Texas accent, "Angie, why in the hell did they give you and Jesse that ugly baby? Y'all know you would have a much prettier baby than that!"

Another lady came up and slapped Debbie because "Angie" had done something on the show that the woman didn't like. The soap opera fans were truly delusional. They honestly felt like they knew Debbie personally, even though they were identifying with her character on the show. As a matter of fact, the characters Jesse and Angie returned to the show after 18 years and they were as popular as ever.

Over the years, Robert has enjoyed working with Debbie on several other memorable projects, including *Eve's Bayou* where she received acclaim for her portrayal of clairvoyant Mozelle Batiste Delacroix. She was part of the all-star cast, which included Samuel L. Jackson and Lynn Whitfield. They worked together, again, in the 2005 film, on *Coach Carter*, where she co-starred, again with Sam, as his girlfriend, Tonya.

Hot Pursuit TV Series – '84

I took the children on TV and film locations whenever possible, which they always enjoyed. However, as Jason, the oldest, became a teenager, he didn't want to go as much. One of his last location experiences with the family was when Robert was working on a TV series in Seattle, Washington, called "Hot Pursuit," starring Kerrie Keane and Eric Pierport. It was a show similar to "The Fugitive;" however, in this case, the woman, Keane, was falsely accused of a murder. She and her husband went on the run to try to find clues to prove her innocence.

That summer I decided we would take a scenic and economical

trip, traveling by train to Seattle, stopping along the way to sightsee in San Francisco for a day. Things didn't work out as planned. First of all, I packed a huge basket of food for the boys to snack on until we got to our stop in Northern California. But Jason and Damon were growing teenagers who never stopped eating. So, once we got on the train, they started eating like they hadn't eaten in days. Before we got to Santa Barbara, not even halfway, the food was totally gone. After that, they continued to say they were hungry. I gave them money to go to the dining car where they devoured everything in sight. They ate pizzas, hot dogs, fries, soda, desserts and all the candy they could find. My budget was already blown.

As nighttime came upon us, fourteen-year-old Damon fell asleep and began to snore so loudly, we were embarrassed. He was sitting next to Jason, who tried to nudge him in hopes he would bring down the volume, but nothing helped. Everyone in our car started making audible sighs and mumbled under their breath to let us know they were irritated. Jason had even tried putting the hood of his sweatshirt over Damon's head, but he just yanked it off and never woke up. Finally, Jason refused to sit with him, and I had to change seats with him.

I figured out if I turned Damon's head to the side and pushed it down, it muffled the sound to a low hum. I was thrilled because I thought I had discovered a solution. But every time I would drift off to sleep, Damon's head would roll back to the center and he would start snoring to high heaven, once again. I would push his head back over to the side and down, but, invariably, his head would roll back, and he would roar like a lion, again. Everyone in our car hated us.

In the morning, Damon woke up and grumbled, "You kept hitting my head and I couldn't sleep." I said in a measured tone, "No, Damon. No one in this car got an ounce of sleep because of your snoring." He was stunned. He was young, and I started thinking, "I have got to get this boy fixed, because no one will marry him snoring like that." However, I never did. Now, he is happily married and sleeps every night with a machine for sleep apnea.

To the relief of the other passengers, we got off the train in San Francisco. We toured the city going on the famous trolley car to Fisherman's Wharf. We slept that night in a hotel room before re-boarding the train. We got to Seattle before bedtime, thank goodness!

Once we got to the location, Jason didn't want to participate in the activities we had planned. He only wanted to lay around in the hotel, watching TV shows that he looked at everyday at home. Oh, and, of course, he and his brother kept calling room service all day to order food. That was one of Jason's last trips with the family. I couldn't afford to feed him. Nevertheless, location vacations were always a great learning experience and fun.

Sweet Dreams – '85

In Nashville, Robert served as the department head hair stylist on *Sweet Dreams*, which was the story of country singer Patsy Cline. Jessica Lange starred as Patsy and Eddie Harris played her husband. Robert's friend Toni-Ann Walker was the personal stylist for Jessica, and Robert was responsible for Eddie and the rest of the cast.

Teron and I visited him during the Thanksgiving week. I was very happy to be in Nashville for several reasons. Two of my long-time friends, who I had grown up with, lived there, David Scott and Juarezetta Bass. It was a great pleasure seeing them and meeting their families.

Teron was getting to be an "old hat" at flying and living in various hotels. He even went to night clubs with us in Nashville when we couldn't find a babysitter. He wasn't a problem at all. He had always been a night owl; he loved music and hanging out with his mom and dad.

The Color Purple – '85

We were surprised when we learned that Steven Spielberg would be directing *The Color Purple*, the film version of Alice Walker's popular book. He cast little known actors to play the main roles: a rising comedienne named Whoopi Goldberg, a local Chicago talk show host Oprah Winfrey, Danny Glover and Margaret Avery. This was another gratifying project for everyone involved. Ultimately, the film received eleven Academy Award nominations.

Robert was the supervising hair stylist, and he was proud to be involved in a Spielberg film project. Spielberg was pulling out all the stops to make the film a big screen success. The southern location was perfect. The costuming and look of the film were authentic. The blues and gospel music were awesome, under the music supervision of the great Quincy Jones.

Teron and I visited the location in Madison, North Carolina, for a two-week stay. The aura around the production was buzzing with excitement, and when our time was up, we didn't want to leave. Right away, we fell in love with Whoopi, her mother Emma, brother Clyde and young daughter Alex, who were all fun to be around.

While we were there, Whoopi hosted a showing of her first HBO comedy special, *Whoopi Goldberg: Live on Broadway*. We watched it with the cast and crew on a big screen in the large banquet room at the Holiday Inn. Prior to that, only New York theater audiences had seen her comedic portrayals. She played five unforgettable characters included Fontaine the Dope Head, The Surfer Chick, The Cripple, The Little Girl and the Jamaican Woman. After the special ended, the celebration continued with a fun party with Willard Pugh, who played Harpo, leading the way. After witnessing her amazing performance, we knew we were in the presence of a person who had a monumental career ahead of her. We had seen first-hand the birth of a star. Little did we know, Oprah Winfrey would also go on to international prominence and become a household name.

Black Widow – '86

All four kids and I took our summer vacation to the film location in Hilo, Hawaii, during the filming of *Black Widow*. We met and hung out with the stars of the film, Debra Winger and Theresa Russell. More than anything, the kids enjoyed jet-skiing, swimming, dodging lizards and learning about the culture of the island. We visited a macadamia nut factory, a sugar plantation, a dormant volcano and an exotic zoo. There we saw colorful birds of every type, but most of all we got a kick out of watching the monkeys fight. One monkey would attack the other from behind and steal his food, then the other monkey would turn around and chase him, knocking him in the head. It went on and on. They kept us laughing for hours. They weren't contained in traditional cages. They put netting over a huge outdoor area to create a natural habitat.

We stayed at a great resort, but the kids were disappointed that there was no white sand on the beach, only large black lava rocks, which was all they had along the beachfront on the big island.

Leonard Part 6 – '87

Robert served as supervising hair stylist on Bill Cosby's film *Leonard Part 6*, which filmed in Northern California in the Oakland area. It was a wild ride.

Teron and I spent our summer vacation there. When we weren't sightseeing and visiting friends and family, we hung out on the set. Right away we came to know that Bill wasn't the lovable Dr. Huxtable we all adored from the popular "Cosby Show." To us, he seemed like a pompous know-it-all, who constantly made cutting and nasty remarks to the cast and crew. The film didn't seem funny and no one could make heads or tails of the bizarre story line.

When the film first started, Bill instructed Robert that he would have to wear a white smock in order to cut his hair. Bill said that was because he wanted to see what Robert was doing to his hair, and if he wore a smock, it would serve as the white backdrop he needed to see what he was doing. So, Robert complied and got the white barber's jacket to wear anytime he had to cut Bill's hair and they had no problems.

Bill had a habit of giving opportunities to Black people who wanted to break into films. Sometimes he lacked the discernment to know if they would be able to withstand the demands of film production. Such was the case with Joey, a fun-loving, proudly gay makeup artist from New York, who was highly regarded in entertainment circles. Two of his high-profile clients included Bill's wife Camille and actress Gloria Foster, who starred in the film.

Joey was a prima donna, who was not used to working the long hours required on a movie set. Once he realized he was close to San Francisco, "the gay capital," he stayed out partying every night in the city's notorious club scene. He complained non-stop about the early morning calls. To cover his blood-shot eyes, he pranced around in dark sunglasses, which made it impossible to see what he was doing to the actors' faces. Joey was like a lot of free-spirited people who think it would be wonderful to work in Hollywood. They quickly learn that it is really hard work, and the long hours, alone, are killers. Normal workdays are 12 hours, but on many film sets, the crew works 14 to

18-hours a day. It is grueling and all consuming. It is impossible to work on a movie set all day and party all night.

Gracie Atherton was one of the other makeup artists. In the beginning, Gracie and Joey began by splitting the cast members on the film. But eventually he was only assigned to Bill and Gloria and he couldn't even do that. On one particular day, Joey left to go shopping. Bill was asking for him and when Joey was nowhere to be found, Gracie jumped in to touch him up and he refused to let her touch up his makeup. When Joey strolled back on the set, Bill cursed him out. After that experience, Joey stayed on duty until the end of the film. However, he never worked on another film. He needed his freedom.

Pat Colbert played Bill's wife in the film. She was an actress, best remembered as Dora Mae, hostess of the Cattlemen's Club in the "Dallas" TV series. During the production of *Leonard*, Bill hosted a dinner at his San Francisco house and invited Pat to attend. Bill asked Robert to come and asked if he would bring her from the hotel, since she didn't have a car. Robert agreed to transport her to the dinner.

Right away, Bill and she locked horns, because she was a know-it-all just like him. According to Robert, she got into an argument with Bill about Wayne Newton, the Las Vegas entertainer, famous for his Arabian horses. Pat claimed to know him very well and made some bold statements about Newton's wealth and power in Las Vegas. Bill, who had worked in Las Vegas for many years, contradicted her statements. When she insisted that what she was saying was true, Bill abruptly got up, got Pat and Robert's coats and told them to get out. Robert was stunned, because he was an innocent bystander in the discussion. However, as her driver, he was kicked out, too. Bill was livid and he didn't apologize or back down. He said, "Roberto, get her out of here!" They were forced to leave in shame.

As previously noted, when you're working on a movie, many times you can't really tell whether the film is good or bad. Some films seem odd, but often times, once edited, they work. Such was not the case with *Leonard Part 6*. It was a dismal failure at the box office and got terrible reviews across the board. Bill Cosby was a huge success on television, but his brand of humor did not work on the big screen. But that didn't stop him from trying.

However, when the film was released, a disappointed Bill told people not to bother going to see it. The film eventually won three dread-ed Golden Raspberry Awards, which is given to movies deemed the most horrible films of the year. When the awards were announced, the "Razzies" declared *Leonard Part 6* as one of the worst films of *all time*s. Wow! Nevertheless, we had a good time on the location.

Pure Luck – '92

Now, this was fun! On this occasion, I was the one who had an opportunity to take my older sister, Carol (a.k.a. Cookie) Tucker with me to Acapulco, Mexico, for the press junket for the film, *Pure Luke*, which was a wild, zany comedy starring Martin Short and Danny Glover. Cookie, who had a career in sales for Scholastic book publishing, was very outgoing and friendly. Before we boarded the airplane, she had made friends with my staff and press members. By the time we touched down in Mexico, everybody knew Cookie. She had already set up dates with various folks for drinks by the pool, spa treatments, sightseeing and meals at the outdoor restaurant, all courtesy of Universal Pictures.

We had accommodations at the Las Brisas Villas nestled in the hills overlooking the breathtaking bay. When we arrived, not only did we have our own villa, we also had a personal swimming pool with rose petals of every color floating on top.

We were giggly as we surveyed our room until a slimy green lizard darted across the ceiling. We screamed bloody murder, ran in the bathroom, slammed the door and called the front desk. I was hysterical as I begged the hotel clerk to send someone to slay the lizard. Two men came and laughed at us, "Senoritas, a gecko brings you good luck!" We weren't buying it. "Get him out!" we insisted, and they did.

We were also warned about drinking the water, but they didn't have to tell me twice. I learned my lesson the hard way years ago in Acapulco. Despite having to dart away from lizards, avoid water and meat, we had the time of our lives for four days. It was mostly work for me and big fun for Cookie. I was assigned to Danny Glover, whom I had known since *The Color Purple* days. I was happy about working with him until I arrived at his room on press day and he wasn't ready to start. Apparently, he came with all his belongings stuffed in a small duffle bag. He said he had asked the front desk if they could have his clothes pressed, however when an attendant came to his room, he simply brought him an iron. So, guess who had to iron his clothes? I knocked out as many wrinkles as I could and got him to the interviews, all the while smiling and muttering under my breath. Overall, all went well. He is a sweetheart, so that was the only issue.

My most fun afternoon with Cookie was walking to the beach when we spotted an iguana sauntering boldly across the street. As long as he wasn't in our room, we could laugh about it. With his head held high, his attitude was like, "This is my world. You're just visiting!" We gave Mr. Ig the utmost respect. We stood back and let him have his way. I told Cookie, "Damn, sis! That's a dinosaur. No way that giant thing is a lizard!" We laughed all the way to the beach. We got in the crystal-clear water and as it washed over us, we had schools of tropical fish of every color dancing around our feet.

When we headed back home, there were members of our staff and the press who didn't heed the food and water warnings. They were so sick they literally had to crawl on the plane in agony. There are beautiful places in this world, but, in the end, there is no place like home. As I think about this trip today, I am especially glad Cookie and I shared this special time together. Over the past few years Cookie has had multiple strokes and she is in a nursing home. When we talk, she enjoys remembering the many fun times we had over the years. And this is a special one to remember. Love you, sis.

Waiting to Exhale – '95

Robert was the personal hair stylist for Angela Bassett on the highly acclaimed film by best-selling author Terry McMillan. He had previously worked with Angela on *Strange Days*, *What's Love Got to Do with It* and the TV mini-series, "The Jacksons: An American Dream."

Waiting to Exhale was made in Phoenix, Arizona. Robert had a nice apartment, and it was close enough to Los Angeles for me to drive. Robert and Angela had a great working relationship. During one of my visits, they were filming the famous "girls' night party" scene. On the set, I had an opportunity to re-acquaint myself with Angela, and my old friend, Lela Rochon, who had long since divorced Shabba Doo of *Breakin'* fame and had begun an impressive acting career of her own. Most notably, she had a long run as the one of the Spud McKenzie girls in the Bud Light Beer commercials.

As Robin, "the dingy one" in *Waiting to Exhale*, one of the guys she was dating was obnoxious. His character was named Troy, played by another old friend, Mykelti Williamson, who Robert had met earlier in his career when he starred in a little known film called *Sunnyside*, co-starring Joey Travolta, John's brother, and an unknown actress named Kelly Preston, who later married John. Most recently, Robert had worked with Mykelti on *How to Make an American Quilt*. At the time of filming *Waiting to Exhale*, Mykelti was receiving high praise for his role as Bubba in the Tom Hanks Oscar-winning film *Forrest Gump*. It has been one of our greatest joys to know actors from the beginning of their careers, seeing them move up in the industry and ascend to the top.

On the set, I was also glad to hang out with my old friend, the late, great Gregory Hines, who I became friendly with during the publicity campaign for a MGM buddy film called *Running Scared*, in which he co-starred with Billy Crystal.

Most of all, I was very excited to meet my favorite singer, the sensational Whitney Houston, who played one of the leading ladies, Savannah. I was a huge fan of her heavenly voice and I was equally impressed with her acting chops. She was surprisingly quiet and humble during the filming. Loretta Divine was fun to be around. At a local nightclub she jumped on stage, singing and jamming with the band. One Sunday, Robert, Loretta and I attended a Baptist church as the guests of one of the local crew members.

Robert also did a remarkable job with Angela's hairdos in the film. Her character, Bernadine, started off with beautiful, long hair. Then, in an angry rage against her cheating husband, she cuts off her hair. Robert styled a beautiful, natural looking short wig for her new look. Other than her Academy Award nominated role as Tina Turner in *What's Love Got to Do with It*, many feel *Exhale* was one of her best performances on film. Who can forget the scene when she walked defiantly away from her husband's BMW after she sets it on fire. The film's director was actor Forest Whitaker, who did an incredible job.

A Time to Kill – '95

This film introduced twenty-six-year-old Matthew McConaughey to the world. The Austin native had been up for another role in the film, however he convinced director Joel Schumacher he was right for the lead. Joel took a secret screen test of Matthew in order to gain writer John Grisham's approval. Joel said he really liked Matthew because of his good looks, coupled with his bad-boy persona.

It was a courtroom crime drama film, based on Grisham's 1989 novel of the same name. The all-star cast included Sandra Bullock, Samuel L. Jackson, Kevin Spacey, Oliver Platt, Ashley Judd, Kiefer and Donald Sutherland, and Patrick McGoohan. Filmed in Canton, Mississippi, it is the story of Carl Lee Hailey (Sam), a black man who avenges the brutal rape of his daughter by shooting the men responsible for the crime when they were on their way to stand trial. Jake Brigance (Matthew), an untested lawyer, is tasked with defending him. Jake struggles to believe that a black man can be acquitted in this small, Southern town. As the case moves forward, the town is thrown into a state of unrest with Jake's life and family put squarely in the path of violence. The film was a critical and commercial success, making $152 million at the worldwide box office.

Sam pushed for Robert to be a hair stylist on the film, after he had successfully worked with him on *The Great White Hype*, their first project together. Two staff assistants on the film, who we would work with on *The Help* fifteen years later, were director Tate Taylor and Best Supporting Actress Oscar-winner, Octavia Spencer. In addition to working as a member of the crew, Octavia made her film debut in *A Time to Kill* with several lines as Ellen Roark's (Sandra Bullock) nurse.

Robert partnered with makeup artist Marietta Carter Narcisse to be Sam's makeup and hair team. It was Marietta's first film since giving birth to her son, Gregoire, who became Robert's godson. She came with her husband, Errol, the new baby and a truck full of every conceivable item she thought she might need to work and take care of her son while they filmed for three months. The drivers, who were responsible for moving all of her things, grumbled like hell. They were overwhelmed by the sheer volume, which became a running joke. Motherhood has always been a serious challenge for women who work in the film industry and particularly those working with jobs on movie sets. In Marietta's case, her husband agreed to come and be the caretaker of their baby boy. Eventually, she gave up working in

Hollywood, moved to Florida and found work more suitable for her family life.

I arranged to visit the location during the time when Joel was hosting a Halloween costume party at a local banquet hall. Robert asked me to bring his favorite vintage red and black, brocaded satin jacket, so he could be a R&B soul singer. He finished off his look with a huge pompadour wig and black and white wing-tip shoes. He pranced around the party all night like he was singer Morris Day. My costume wasn't designed to complement his; I already had a cute Cleopatra costume, so that's what I wore. He fixed me up with a beautiful black pageboy wig that gave me Cleopatra's royal look.

Sandra Bullock and three other cast mates came as "The Village People." She had a full-on Indian headdress and a sexy suede outfit. The group brought the house down with their karaoke rendition of "YMCA," complete with a wild and crazy dance routine of the popular song. After a week of hard work, film crews know how to let their hair down.

The Halloween holiday is a big deal in Mississippi. I was surprised by the elaborate, spooky decorations that lit up homes for blocks and blocks. They put a lot of time and money into displays that out-did the most amazing Christmas displays I have seen in California. Ghost, witches, goblin, headstones and the living dead are big in Mississippi. Wherever I visited, I discovered something new.

The Long Kiss Goodnight – '96

This movie was made in the midst of the freezing, cold winter in Toronto, Canada. The weather was unbearable, and I had never been so cold in my life. Nevertheless, I, foolishly, went along for a night shoot to a mountain ski resort and the temperature was fifteen below zero. I had purchased winter wear in Los Angeles, which proved to be totally useless in the bitter cold of Northeast Canada. The film company provided full-on snow gear for the crew, which was so extensive it took twenty-minutes to put everything on. There were knee-high snow boots with two-inch soles, and were lined with fur, which snapped close with huge buckles. They had triple insulated jackets that kept you so warm, you couldn't put it on until it was time to go outside on the set, otherwise you might overheat and pass out. They had thick ski masks to keep the head, nose and mouth warm. They also gave them double lined gloves with hand heating pads to put inside.

No matter what I did, without the benefit of the proper warm clothing they had, I was freezing. To Robert's embarrassment, when I got chilly in the van, I complained about the cold air that came through the floorboard. When Robert looked at me with an evil eye for asking the driver to turn up the heat, I put my tote bag on the floor and propped my feet up on top of that. I should have stayed at the warm and cozy hotel instead of venturing out with him to the sub-zero Muskoka Lake District in Ontario. I was miserable the entire night. The funny thing, director Renny Harlin, who is from Finland, was standing out there with a lightweight jacket and no hat. He hailed from one of the world's most northern and geographically remote countries, which is subject to severe climates. Nearly two-thirds of Finland is blanketed by thick woodlands, making it the most densely forested country in Europe. So, I guess it depends on how your body is programmed. I wondered how Sam and Geena Davis did the scene where they fell into the icy lake. Robert explained how they did it. To make it bearable, they rigged and submerged a hot tub in the lake, but it could only do so much. When we got back to the hotel that night, I ran a hot bath and stayed in the tub until I completely thawed out.

We did have a wonderful weekend trip to Niagara Falls, which was an incredible sight to see. Robert is a very safe driver, which I appreciated, because the roads were slippery in spots with black ice after a snow fall. Other than that, I spent the rest of the time as a *mole*, which is what they call the Canadian people who hang out and shop in the underground world during the winter. To get there we would run out of the hotel, then rush down two flights of stairs and enter a world where you could walk around for miles protected from the freezing temperatures in the winter. That is where we went to the movies, department stores and grocery shopping. Needless to say, if Robert worked where it was snowing and cold weather, I passed. I was such a grump during that visit. I don't think he cared.

Flipper – '96

If I could, I also tried to figure out a way to include my family in my out-of-town work adventures. The food and accommodations were provided, so the only thing to arrange was the airfare. I always wanted someone to enjoy the experiences. Here's an example of one, I will never forget.

I was scheduled to do an out-of-town press junket for *Flipper* at the Universal Tour in Orlando, Florida. It began on April 25, 1996, which was my stepdaughter Kendra's twenty seventh birthday, so I invited her to go with me. *Flipper* was a remake of the 1963 adventure film of the same title, which in turn began a TV series that ran from 1964 to 1967. The film starred Paul Hogan as Porter Ricks, the hippie uncle of an embittered nephew, Sandy, played by Elijah Wood. He was sent to spend the summer with Porter on the Florida Gold Coast. I was assigned to work with Elijah, who was just fifteen-years old at that time. This is way before his fame in *The Lord of the Rings* trilogy.

We were excited about the great accommodations of luxury cottages located on a golf course. However, to our horror no one mentioned that alligators routinely strolled around on the grounds. Although we never saw one, the thought of running into a gator never left our minds. Every day on the news there were alligator sightings in neighborhoods where they strolled boldly on the sidewalks. To make matters worse, mosquitos were swarming all around us, as well, making for a frustrating stay.

Every morning we oiled down with Skin So Soft from Avon as a repellant. The limousine came to get us first, then we would pick up Elijah, his mom and his agent. Elijah was a dream. At the end of each hot and humid day, his group just wanted to go back to their cottage, leaving the car available for our use. One night we ventured out to celebrate Kendra's birthday at a popular restaurant that was suggested to us. When we arrived, curious eyes of patrons inside the restaurant were upon our limo. I emerged first, then Kendra. I said loudly, "C'mon, Sade." Kendra had often been told that she looks just like the famous British singer. She couldn't stop laughing from embarrassment, but I kept the ruse going.

Getting back into our cottage had to be carefully coordinated, because the mosquitoes were swarming under the bright porch light. Before we ventured out of the limo, I would get the key out and make a mad dash to the door, quickly opening and slamming it behind us.

We were sleeping soundly when we were startled by the phone ringing well after midnight. It was my son Jason, announcing that in my absence, Nikki, had given birth early to their baby boy, Sage Christian Ross Woodruff, born April 27. He joined Jason and Nikki's family, which already included Nikki's daughter, Brittany. I had been waiting with great anticipation for the birth of my first grandson, and I missed it. I couldn't wait to get back to see him. The great love we instantly felt for him continues to this day. He is the first grandson, who joined Kendra and Willie's daughter, our two-year old granddaughter, Kambria Monet Ruffin, as the center of our world. Today they have both completed college and we are proud to see them grow into God-fearing, responsible, kind and positive contributors to society.

Being a grandparent is a badge I wear proudly. Our family continued to grow as Damon married Liz and her two children, Shantel and Valentino, became family, too. Together they had Dayna, born on my birthday, May 11, 2004, and Delaney, three years younger, born on May 17, 2007. Teron and Adei, gave birth to Aman, on September 22, 2003. I love every one of my grandchildren from the bottom of my heart.

As Bria said, "Grandpa and Grammie, your house is the center of everything!" I love having my family over. Over the years, I have organized costume parties for Halloween, Christmas productions, Easter egg hunts and summer swim parties. Robert jokingly says I will celebrate "the opening of an envelope."

Thanksgiving is a huge production, which is now planned and beautifully executed by my son Damon and his family. He is a chip off the old block. His daughters, Dayna and Delaney, enjoy making cakes, desserts and decorating the house with their parents. Delaney, in particular, has enjoyed creating the invitations, coordinating the guests list and planning games since she was eight years old. She is good, and they jokingly call her "Little Roz." Hey, I ain't mad!

Rules of Engagement, The Mummy and Notting Hill – '99

In April 1999 Universal Pictures was releasing two movies in London, *The Mummy* and *Notting Hill*. We conducted the press activities for both films and the premiere of *Notting Hill* in the U.K., an unprecedented turn of events. Our staff, along with a contingency of U.S. entertainment press, flew on the prestigious airline Virgin Atlantic.

141

It was particularly exciting for me. Though Robert's job took him all over the world, I rarely went anywhere outside the United States, Mexico and Canada.

The cool thing was Robert was working in Morocco with Samuel L. Jackson on a film called *Rules of Engagement*. As it turned out, they were wrapping their movie as we were beginning our events. Robert coordinated with his production office to get his ticket routed through London so he could get off and hang out with me for a couple of days, then resume his return flight aboard the same Virgin Atlantic flight I was on, so we could fly home together.

We stayed at the Dorchester Hotel, hung out in neighborhood pubs, shopped at Harrod's and went to a curious spot called Speakers' Corner, an area where open-air public speaking, debate and discussions were spirited and a sight to see. We visited on a Sunday morning and were surprised to see how many people stood on soap boxes to raise hell about whatever concerned them about the ills of the world.

We joined the press on a tour of Notting Hill, the affluent West London area where the film was made. Most unique to us were the lush community gardens on each block where the residents planted, grew, maintained and shared the flowers, herbs, fruits and vegetables. The gardens also included sitting areas where participating neighbors had a key to enter and found a peaceful place to interact and/or reflect.

Robert especially enjoyed the star-studded movie premiere of *Notting Hill*, a romantic comedy starring Julia Roberts and Hugh Grant, at the historic Leicester Cinema, which is located in the famous Picadilly Circus area. Hugh had model Elizabeth Hurley, then-long-time girlfriend, on his arm.

When Robert boarded the plane with me to return to Los Angeles, I can't tell you how curious everyone was. It was an extraordinary treat for all of us, so the staff was wondering how my husband got on the same flight and who was paying for him. Virgin Atlantic flights are top of the line, and they pamper the passengers like royalty. On the eleven-hour flight we were served endless gourmet meal selections, exotic desserts and ever-flowing liquor. After a while we had to stop them from bringing anything more, because we couldn't eat or drink anymore. Most of our staff was drunk and slept soundly the rest of the flight. To top things off, if we wanted, there was a massage therapist onboard to rub and dub all our anxieties away. By the time we got back to Los Angeles, we were spoiled rotten. It was an unforgettable way to celebrate our twenty-second wedding anniversary.

Snakes on the Plane – '05

A few years later, before Robert and I retired, we were also able to share set visit experiences with our two oldest grandchildren. I took our twelve-year-old granddaughter, Kambria, who we simply call Bria, to Vancouver, British Columbia, where Robert was working on the film called *Snakes on the Plane*, starring, of course, Samuel L. Jackson.

Robert had a beautiful two-bedroom, hi-rise apartment, so Bria was able to have her own room, which she loved. We also made it a point to take her on sightseeing tours to get a sense of how different life was in the Canadian Northwest. The highlight of our visit was the three of us having an adventurous river-rafting trip one Sunday afternoon.

Most of all, Bria enjoyed going to the set and hanging out with her grandfather, Sam, the other stars of the film and seeing the fake snakes. Neither of us ever had the nerve to look at the real snakes.

Black Snake Moan – '05

We shared another set visit with our nine-year old grandson, Sage, in Memphis, Tennessee, where Robert was working on the film *Black Snake Moan*, also starring Samuel L. Jackson. Sage and I have lots of relatives in Memphis, so it was a great time to visit with them. It also gave some of our family members an opportunity to come on a movie set. Sam was gracious to them and they were excited beyond belief. Sam also let Sage hang out with him in his sprawling personal trailer. Sage ate everything in sight, just like his dad, Jason, used to do.

We also saw the famous "march of the ducks" at the Peabody Hotel, went on Beale Street for barbeque and visited the Civil Rights Museum and the Lorraine Motel where Martin Luther King was assassinated. One of the highlights of the trip was touring Graceland. Sage and I are both huge Elvis fans.

CHAPTER 14:
Motown's My Town

Delight yourself in the Lord, and He will give you the desires of your heart. Psalm 37:4 (ESV)

In the Fall 1987, I joined Motown Records as the head of publicity. It was a position that had formerly been held by veteran publicist Bob Jones, who had left to be in charge of marketing for Michael Jackson's MJJ Productions. For months I had been courted for the Motown position by the president Skip Miller, who was married to my good friend from "Good Times," K.C. Miller. After my initial interviews, I was assured I would be starting right away. However, I didn't hear a word. I was working at Universal's Publicity Department, so I was nervous about leaving, giving the proper notice or wondering if I was doing the right thing. I spoke to a few friends about it, and they suggested that if Motown was that slow in making decisions, I needed to be skeptical about leaving Universal to go there. But I was a huge fan of the record label, so a position at Motown would be a dream-come-true for me.

Part of my decision-making process was to step out on faith, inspired by the untimely death of my father, Roscoe Steverson, on March 15, 1987. Daddy had always encouraged me to follow my dreams. With his passing at only sixty-eight years old, I realized how short life could be. I felt confident that he would want me to take advantage of the opportunity.

We learned that daddy had liver cancer about four months before the disease took him from us. During that time, he often reflected on his life. He had left rural Millington, Tennessee, at age seventeen and came to Los Angeles, where he had only a handful of friends and no family. He was so proud of the life he created and what he had achieved. To most, it may not seem like much, but for him it was everything. He had a devoted wife and raised decent kids, had hundreds of friends and the love and respect of his church and community, where he lived and served admirably. He took great pride in his home in Compton, which he maintained beautifully and filled with all the things that mattered to him.

One of the things that my parents were most proud of was becoming travel agents after they retired from their civil service jobs. They organized The Travelaires, a group of friends, all from South Central Los Angeles, who travelled with them all over the world. Just before daddy passed, the group organized a tribute event called "That's What Friends Are For." It was an appreciation banquet to express their love for the many extraordinary experiences they had shared around the world with my parents, Roscoe and Clara.

Not long after that, daddy passed away. Over six hundred friends and family attended my father's funeral at Bel-Vue Church. We still grieve his loss today.

Finally, the Motown job offer came. I accepted it and gave Universal notice without hesitation. I was so excited I was doing "The Temptation Walk" out of there. Goodbye, white folks! I'm going to be a part of a worldwide phenomenon, Motown Records. In my mind, publicity was the same whether it was film or music. However, as it turned out, I learned it was quite different. Motown operated business very different from the corporate structure I was used to. Minor concerns arose immediately. Getting simple office supplies was a huge task. The first week I gave my list to the mail guy, who promised to fill my requests. The end of the week came, and I hadn't received one thing.

I inquired, "When can I get some supplies?" He said, "Oh, I only do that on Thursday." I said, "Well, this is Friday." He replied, "Well, not every Thursday." What? They were making me crazy from the very first week. But the bottom line was I had made a major career move and I was determined to make the best of it. Honestly, there were days when I so frustrated, I would stand by the window on the seventeenth floor and thought I should just jump.

Don't get me wrong. Motown was fun and people worked hard.

Their administrative style was unlike the studios, so it was a big adjustment. I was used to preparing detailed written reports. Motown wasn't like that. Most things were talked about endlessly, then acted upon once people finally came to an agreement.

I encountered some power struggles with old-timers, who were routinely suspicious of new people. However, over my years in the work force, I was starting to understand how to lay low, do good work and slowly endear myself to people. Today I am still good friends with people from my short stay at Motown.

My first project was for a new artist named Georgio, Motown's answer to Prince. Georgio had an album due out in a few months. I developed a marketing strategy for his album release. Once completed, I sent all top executives the strategy report, however I didn't get one response. I began to think they didn't read it. Then Georgio pops up in my office one day and he said, "Yo, I like what you did."

Apparently, someone thought it was good, and instead of responding to me, they passed it on to the artist. That was strange. I was the only female executive on the creative side and the guys didn't seem to know how to deal with me, so they ignored me. Georgio was talented and good-looking. He scored several dance tracks, notably "Tina Cherry" and "Lovers Lane." To this day, I have no idea what happened to him or his career. After that, he had three more Motown albums, and he disappeared.

One of the other things that concerned me about working at Motown was I was there for well over a month and I had never met the founder and chairman, Berry Gordy. I said to one of the girls on staff, "I really want to meet Berry!" She was stunned. "Oh, my God, don't you dare refer to him as Berry. Out of respect, you must always refer to him as Mr. Gordy or The Chairman. You'll be out of here fast, if you call him by his first name." Okay, well, I assured her I wanted to meet Mr. Gordy, The Chairman. Whatever! I just wanted to meet him. Thank God she told me the proper way to address him, because a few days later I ran into him with his bodyguard on the elevator.

"Hello, Mr. Gordy. I am Roz Stevenson, the new head of Publicity. I've been looking forward to meeting you." He gave me a blank stare and a lukewarm greeting. Soon after that I was called to his office. At that time, we were planning a listening party for Stevie Wonder's

Characters album at the Hollywood Palace. The big problem for me was we had no Stevie Wonder for the launch party. He was working in Japan, so we were going to have him speak via satellite on a big screen. Mr. Gordy wanted to know how I was going to make this event successful.

"I plan to call on the Motown family to celebrate Stevie Wonder," I said. I added that I would like to have him, Mr. Gordy, and as many Motown talent as possible available to talk to the press. He liked that I referred to it as "The Motown Family," which is how he always described his successful label.

He also said he normally never gives press interviews, but because I understood his family concept for Motown, he would help me. He instructed me to write down all the possible questions the press might ask him and write out the responses I thought he should give. He told me he would only speak in a press conference format for fifteen minutes. I did as he asked, and on the evening of the event, he began speaking and we couldn't shut him up. He spoke for forty-five minutes! The press was thrilled because they rarely had access to him. In addition, Smokey, Lionel and other Motown stars came out. The event was a great success.

The Motown staff loved to party. At the end of the week, they were notorious for hosting TGIF parties, usually held in Miller London's office. He was the fun-loving Vice President of Field Promotions, who hailed from Detroit. He had a boyish, youthful face, so he looked much younger than he actually was. Someone would order the champagne and have Vendome, a deluxe wine and liquor store, to deliver it to the seventeenth floor. Once everyone started having some bubbly, Miller would put on obscure Motown recordings and challenge everyone to "name that tune."

"You don't know nothin' about no Motown. Name this song. Name this artist."

I remember him stumping everyone when he played a song called "Buttered Popcorn," which was a single with the late Florence Ballard singing lead for the Supremes. Everyone would dance around the office and have a grand time. If they put on a Temptations song, a group would jump up and start doing the Temps choreography. It was beyond fun!

Just when I was getting in the groove at the record empire, the hammer dropped. Motown was sold to Universal Records for $61 million, three months after I arrived. For several years there had been rumors that they were selling the company and it was one of my big concerns when I was first offered the job. I was assured that wasn't happening. Now, just like that, my life had suddenly changed, again!

Most of the staff was let go and depending on their years of service, they were given a lucrative severance package. Since many of the people started with Motown in Detroit, it was a handsome deal. However, no amount of money could soothe the dark shadow of sadness that hovered over the Motown family. Some staff members were needed at Universal Records to maintain the Motown deals. Then there was the staff, who stayed on to work at the publishing company, Jobete, which wasn't a part of the sale. They remained on the sixteenth floor. I was among the staff members who were asked to stay with The Gordy Company, Mr. Gordy's executive offices on the eighteenth floor. The unsettling aspect for many who were asked to stay is the others got a nice lump sum of money. So, there were those who wished they had been let go and got the severance package, so they could move forward and look for a new job. Since I had only been there less than a year, I didn't expect anything and had nothing to say about it.

At the Gordy Company, I had a huge new, modern office, which included a private bathroom, a bar and conference table along with my chrome and glass desk. The décor was laid with silver and gray stylish furnishings. I loved it. My office connected to Al Bell's, who was the former head of Stax Records; he stayed on with a decent number of great acts. Most recently, he had been co-president of Motown with Skip Miller, who had left and landed at RCA as the head of Black Music.

Unbeknownst to me, the rumbling about no severance package for the remaining staff members was still in effect and had been resolved. Imagine my surprise when someone from the Accounting Department came into my office and gave me a bonus check for five thousand dollars. I had never been given anything before, so I was thrilled beyond belief.

One of my first assignments was serving as a researcher for Berry Gordy's life story. He asked me to read as many books as I could find on black music or black music stars. He wanted me to give him my evaluation and recommendations on each author. Since I am a student of black entertainment, I had already read most of the books on his list. I particularly enjoyed the writings of David Ritz, who had been the biographer for Ray Charles, Marvin Gaye and Smokey Robinson. Mr. Gordy knocked down that idea. In the end, he tried a young writer who wasn't even born when Motown started. He said he wanted someone who was familiar with entrepreneurship, business and mergers. He tried the young man and soon realized he was not at all what he needed.

Next, he decided to write his book himself. Before he did, he wanted me to write down anything that was written about him in all the other Motown books. He would then take what others had concluded and dispute it or expand on it. It was a negative approach, but that is how he chose to do it. Thank goodness, one afternoon he invited civil rights activist Jesse Jackson over for a friendly chat. He began telling him about his writing method and Jesse told him he thought it was absurd. He suggested that Berry outline his book, then tell his own story from beginning to end as he truly remembered it. In the end, Berry agreed.

Soon after that I went to work as a production executive for Suzanne de Passe, the head of Motown Productions with offices in Beverly Hills. After I left, Berry brought in a long-time, trusted Motown colleague, Brenda Boyce, to help him with the biography. He finally released *To Be Loved* in 1994. Since he nixed all my ideas and efforts, I wasn't surprised that there was no mention of my contribution in his book.

One of the most memorable times I spent with Berry Gordy was when I wrote a speech for him. He had been asked to present Suzanne, who was being honored as Woman of the Year by the Women in Film organization. He instructed me to be at his mansion early on the morning of the event, which I did. Apparently, I arrived before he got out of bed. I sat in his living room and was taken aback by the dark green velvet furniture on huge carved dark, mahogany wood. It was not as lavish as I had imagined.

Finally, he came downstairs ready to work. He had on a robe and under shorts. He was totally focused on the speech and trying to put the words on his dinosaur of a computer. I jumped in to help and we finally got it perfect. He studied each and every word to be sure he was effective in conveying his sentiments. Finally, he jumped into his grey suit, then he insisted I ride in the limo with him and his security guy, Roger, as he continued to go over and over his speech all the way to the hotel. His unwavering focus and attention to detail made me realize why Motown had been such a success. He was a perfectionist, who was willing to put in as much hard work as necessary. Once we arrived at the Century Plaza, he was pumped up, confident and excited about making the speech. When he did it, it was very well received. Most importantly, Suzanne was extremely pleased, somewhat surprised and proud of his heartfelt statements.

I was now a member of Suzanne's staff at Motown Productions. The idea was that I would have a dual function; I would do publicity for her upcoming TV-mini-series, "Lonesome Dove", as well as have an opportunity to bring in project ideas as a production executive. I thought it was a wonderful opportunity. Suzanne was best known as co-writer of the *Lady Sings the Blues* and for her amazing specials "Motown 25" and "Motown Returns to the Apollo".

The opportunity to work with Berry and now to work with Suzanne was amazing! I wasn't mad. This was a good thing. For my production deal, I knew right away what I wanted to do. My friend Judi Ann Mason had written a project about Doug Williams, the first black quarterback in the NFL to win the Super Bowl for the Washington Redskins in 1986. Judi Ann had known Doug since they both attended Grambling University in Louisiana. We got a commitment from Blair Underwood to play Doug. Apparently, it was better to have a bankable actor's name already attached to a project in order to get it green lit.

I first witnessed Suzanne's extraordinary persuasiveness when she accompanied me to the CAA Agency for my first pitch meeting on the project. We rode in her chauffeur-driven town car, which was how she always traveled. She considered time spent driving a waste. Because she had been pre-occupied with other pending projects, we had had very little time to discussion the Doug Williams project. On our way to the meeting, I brought her up to speed, giving her as many details as I could about Doug's story, Judi Ann and Grambling. When we got into the meeting, she took over and painted a picture so vivid, I sat in amazement. Every time I was ready to jump in and add my two cents, I couldn't get a word in edgewise. She was incredible. When we left the meeting, I was walking on Cloud Nine and felt certain that it was just a matter of time before we got the green light from one of the networks!

Soon, two events happened that changed the situation. First of all, Doug started to back pedal because he thought his story should be a motion picture, not a TV movie. At that time, *Lean on Me*, starring Morgan Freeman, was a big hit at the box office. Someone Doug was associated with knew one of the producers of the film and he said they were interested in doing his story. He told Judi Ann, "I would rather my story be a motion picture than a TV movie." She begged, "Doug, I am your sister. Don't you want to give a black person the opportunity to do your project?" He said, "It's not a matter of black and white, Judi Ann. It's all about the green." Nevertheless, since we didn't know how serious the offer was from the other producer, we kept moving forward.

Then we ran into another major roadblock that brought the project to its knees. Doug's wife left him, emptied his bank account and went to the media charging him with spousal abuse. It was a big national story. At that point our story deal fizzled. It was a big disappointment. Doug eventually got back with his wife, but to this day, nothing has ever been done about his historic accomplishment.

Back at square one, I began to weigh my options. Did I really like being a production executive? Yes. However, I saw how many hours could be spent negotiating a deal that might crumble in a matter of seconds. I remained focused and tried to see where I would go from there. Then God answered my prayers greater than I could have ever imagined. I was asked to return to Universal Pictures.

CHAPTER 15:
Guess Who Came into My Life

God's timing is always perfect.

From out of nowhere, I got a call from Alan Sutton, a former colleague at Universal. He was looking for a publicist to work on Bill Cosby's upcoming film, *Ghost Dad*, which was being directed by Sidney Poitier! Did he say Sidney Poitier? He didn't have to say it twice. I was headed back to Universal. I left Suzanne's company with the intention of taking a temporary leave from Motown, promising to attend her Tuesday staff meetings. However, once I got back to Universal on that very first Monday, I felt so at home. I realized how much I had missed film publicity. I realized that was what I did best. That day I called Suzanne to say I wouldn't be coming back.

Most importantly, serving as the publicist on *Ghost Dad* was an opportunity to fulfill my dream of working with my hero, Sidney Poitier. In addition, Bill Cosby had been my favorite comedian since college. I knew every word of his two most popular comedy albums, *Wonderfulness* and *To My Brother, Russell, Whom I Slept With*.

I was so caught up with the career opportunity that it took me a minute to realize that God had allowed three of my biggest dreams to come true. In 1988 I had the chance to work intimately with every one of my entertainment heroes: Berry Gordy, Jr., Bill Cosby and Sidney Poitier. Since I was twelve years old, I had dreamed of working with Sidney; now, after thirty-three years, it happened.

First, I had a successful interview with Bill Cosby, who knew me well through my husband. That was a breeze. However, I was a bundle of nerves about interviewing with Sidney. As I entered his office, my heart was jumping out of my chest. He had no clue how momentous the occasion was for me. He asked me a lot of routine questions about my publicity experience. I answered as calmly and professionally as I could as the sound of his dignified, distinctive voice washed over me. As the interview came to an end, he spoke very sternly as he told me he had only one requirement; he wanted absolutely no press interviews on the set while he was directing. He said if I could fulfill my responsibilities without press disruption, I was hired. I shook my head and kept saying, "Of course, Mr. Poitier." "No problem, Mr. Poitier." He didn't have to worry. I would kill a gorilla with my bare hands, if it was headed his way.

Finally, he stood up and extended his hand to me and said, "Welcome aboard." I stood up slowly and said as calmly as I could, "Mr. Poitier, I have admired you for so long; if you don't mind, could I get a hug?"

"Of course," he kindly opened his arms and I thought I had died and had gone to heaven.

Ghost Dad ended up being the last movie that Sidney would direct. It was clear to me during the production that he was getting older and the daily responsibilities and the grueling, long hours took a toll on him. His nerves were on edge every day. Bill didn't make it any easier. He was so full of himself from the unprecedented success of "The Cosby Show." He proved to be hard for his old friend to direct. Sidney had lots of pride and dignity, and I observed how agitated he became as Bill challenged and second guessed him. He was clearly the main source of Sidney's frustration. He couldn't control him. Bill had his hand in everything. Sidney would tell the cast how he wanted a scene done and Bill would say, "No, let's do it this way." Sidney was literally spitting nails every time Bill contradicted him. The film also involved extensive special effects of Bill flying, which involved "green screen," a new technique for Sidney, so he had a lot on his plate.

Sidney was constantly on the lookout for strangers on his set. My boss had asked me to bring select press on the set to discreetly observe the filming. Even though Sidney nor any of the cast were asked to do on-set interviews, he still did not want the press there. The stars who wanted press were willing to do interviews in their trailers. I tried to stay out of his sight, but he still got agitated anytime he saw me on the set. Sidney was also advised that the electronic press kit camera crew needed access to the film set on a few specified days. This was needed by the marketing department to create a behind-the-scene reel to use in promoting the film at the time of release. That did not matter to Sidney. This was particularly distressing to me, given my respect for him for so many years. It was a real balancing act for me, because Bill had the opposite attitude about publicity.

No, Bill certainly wasn't the caring, lovable Dr. Cliff Huxtable we all knew and loved from TV. He was a man who was very proud of his success, which made him boastful and he carried himself as if he was God. Although I found him to be all-knowing, demanding and preachy; he was also generous, a jokester and fun with a surprisingly dirty mouth.

Bill had made a concerted effort to make sure there were as many African Americans working on the film as possible. So, when he learned that Eddie Murphy's film, *Harlem Nights*, had started three weeks before we had and they had an even larger number of black crew members, including my husband, he said jokingly, "Oh, everybody is over there, and I got all the left-over negroes!"

He wanted the blacks on our crew to be beholding to him for being hired. If he saw one of them sleeping on the set, he would have his long-time friend, still photographer, Howard Bingham, take his or her picture. He created a "Hall of Shame," on a huge poster board where he had a montage of the sleeping crew members displayed for all to see.

To his credit, Bill was also always looking for a way to show his love to the film crew. One late afternoon he sent his driver to Pink's Hot Dogs, a historic spot in West Hollywood to buy a surprise snack for the crew. He got hundreds of plain hot dogs, plus all the fixings on the side, including chili, onions, cheese, coleslaw, sauerkraut, bacon and guacamole. The crew devoured those hot dogs like there was no tomorrow.

Bill particularly loved to have tasty desserts, so on another occasion when someone told him about Harriet's, a black-owned bakery in

Inglewood that made delicious cheesecakes, he had me call ahead and order up one of every kind of cheesecake they made. He sent his driver to pick up the cheesecakes so he could share them with the crew.

One of the fun lunches I coordinated for Bill was a surprise Italian meal for the crew, which he hosted on the empty sound stage next to where we were shooting. We had the stage decorated in Italian colors with green artificial turf on the floor, round tables with red and white checkered tablecloths, centerpieces created using loaves of sour dough bread and bouquets of red, yellow and green bell peppers. We had the tables set with white dishes, silverware and red napkins. The food was catered by Matteo's Restaurant in West Los Angeles, Bill's favorite Italian eatery. We had a huge spread that included appetizers, chopped salad, Caesar salad, pastas of every kind, veal and chicken. For dessert we had Tiramisu, Italian tarts and cannoli stuffed with ricotta cheese.

Imagine the film cast and crews amazement when lunch was called and we told them to report to the next sound stage for their meal, courtesy of Mr. Cosby. It was a huge surprise that was truly appreciated by everyone. Bill also loved music, so he provided background music played on a boom box, which blasted all his hand-picked jazz selections throughout the lunch hour. It was hard for everybody to get back to work after that relaxing experience topped with a tasty, hearty lunch. He sat back with his signature cigar in his hand, chuckling and grinning from ear to ear.

Bill complimented my smooth and efficient coordination of the event. He was especially happy that I was assisted in the endeavor by a recent Spelman College graduate, Solombra Tucker, who was working on the film as a production assistant. He drilled her all the time about her goals and aspirations. He wanted to be sure she was going to be successful in her pursuits. Spelman was important to him, because he supported Historically Black Colleges and Universities. His show, "A Different World," was inspired by Spelman.

Everyday Bill cornered me to find out what was happening with the stars on *Harlem Nights*, especially Eddie Murphy, Richard Pryor and Redd Foxx. He loved to gossip and he wanted to know how the three were getting along.

Finally, one day he came up with a grand idea to have a baseball game between the two film crews. Because of the caliber of talent, it wasn't the kind of event we could just say we'll meet at a public park and play. What started out as a baseball game became a huge media event, which we arranged to have on the campus of Loyola Marymount University in Westchester, California.

In order to make it happen, I had contacted Eddie's publicist, Terrie Williams, to see if *Harlem Nights'* filmmakers and stars would be interested in participating. Their production agreed. Then we each had to go to our studios – Universal and Paramount – and ask for money. Without much resistance, we got each studio to put up $25,000 to cover the use of the university, security, t-shirts, audio video equipment, buses and trailers, plus catering for fifteen hundred people, which included the stars, the filmmakers and the crews with their family members.

Although Eddie had famously mimicked Bill on his *Raw* comedy film, the two had never actually met. The photo opportunity of the day was their first meeting during the coin toss on the pitcher's mound. It became a huge news story, which was covered in USA Today, wired nationwide by Associated Press, aired on CNN, Entertainment Tonight and all the local news channels. In addition to the two lead stars, there were a number of other stars in the two casts. *Harlem Nights* had Pryor, Foxx, Della Reese, Arsenio Hall, Jasmine Guy, Lela Rochon and *Ghost Dad* had Cosby, Poitier, Denise Nicholas, Kimberly Russell and Omar Gooding.

Prior to the event, I had asked Sidney to do a few interviews for the occasion, and he said he wasn't interested. However, once he got there and saw everyone else doing it, he decided to join in the fun.

Popular comedian Sinbad was the commentator and he had everyone in stitches, making non-stop jokes during the baseball game. He made it funny, as some of the biggest stars struck out, struggled to get around the bases and generally hammed it up. Richard was not in good health, so he did not play, but he never stopped talking mess and laughing from the sideline. In the end, *Ghost Dad* won the game, which was irrelevant, because the entire day was unforgettable. Never before had the crew members and their entire families been given an opportunity to hang out, up close and personal, with that many stars.

Each movie company had t-shirts made for all and their family members. For *Ghost Dad*, we had white baseball shirts with red sleeves. Bill had a friend who designed the shirts with caricatures of Sidney and Bill on the back, and the film's title was on the front. *Harlem Nights* cast, crew and family members wore gray t-shirts with a Harlem skyline and the name of the movie on the front. Two caterers provided an abundance of picnic delights and soul food throughout the afternoon.

To top off the fun-filled day, we had a wild James Brown dance contest. The winners were actress Lela Rochon, who played Sunshine in *Harlem Nights* and had been the lead dancer in Lionel Richie's "All Night Long" video. She danced with an unknown, aspiring actor, Cuba Gooding Jr., who was the break-dancing brother of young actor Omar Gooding from our film. I had come to know their mother, Shirley Gooding. She shared with me that her older son was an actor, too. She said he's getting ready to make a movie called *Boyz 'N the Hood*, with a young filmmaker from USC. I brushed it off, assuming it was a student film, and I really thought they needed to change that corny title. Later, I had to admit I was wrong about it when the landmark film, *Boyz 'N the Hood*, propelled twenty-five-year-old John Singleton's career to be the youngest and first African American director and screenwriter to be nominated for an Academy Award. He won the Oscar for Best Original Screenplay. Needless to say, it also launched the film career of Cuba Gooding Jr., who later won an Oscar for Best Supporting Actor in *Jerry Maguire* with the catch phrase, "Show me the money!"

The baseball event was a lot of hard work, but both studios were thrilled to see everyone having so much fun, as well as generating mountains of positive press coverage for both upcoming films. The thing that made me happiest was to see Sidney off the set, relaxed and having the time of his life. Finally, I made the man I dearly respected, happy, if only for one day.

After I finished the project, I was faced with a career dilemma. I had no job. I had truly enjoyed being a unit publicist, which means you are the publicity person on a film while it is in production. Nothing could top that experience. However, since most films are shot on location and my kids were still in school, I couldn't continue to do unit publicity as a regular gig.

It was a blessing when I was asked to stay on as the film's project publicist. That meant I would implement all publicity strategies for the film until it was released a year later. I was asked to come back into the department by the top boss, senior vice president Sally Van Slyke. She sincerely said, "I want you to come back. Honestly, I really admired you for standing up for that girl I let go." She was referring to the Carlin Smith incident. I was shocked. And I was back in the department. Thank you, Jesus! However, the National Director of Publicity and my direct boss was a brilliant marketing man named Roger Armstrong, who let it be known that he was annoyed that Sally asked me back without consulting him. I don't think it was about me; it was a matter of respect.

Throughout my assignment as the *Ghost Dad* project publicist, I had the adventure of a lifetime. Surprisingly, it was not with Sidney, who was pre-occupied editing the film. I essentially worked for Universal Pictures and Bill.

We were looking for a unique way to kick-off the opening of the film. At that time, Universal Studios Tour in Orlando was just opening. They asked if Bill would serve as the grand marshal for the opening event. He informed me that he was willing to do it, but there was one problem. The weekend of the opening, he was already scheduled to host the Harlem Junior Tennis Tournament. He told me, "Watch how I do this." He then said, if the studio was willing to give the Harlem tennis tournament a $10,000 charity donation, he would agree to be the grand marshal for the grand opening. Without hesitation, the studio agreed. He was so proud of what he was able to do for the kids in Harlem, and he giggled about having that kind of clout. However, I doubt he could have gotten it a year later after our movie bombed, big time.

Leading up to the grand opening event, we created a Whistle Stop Train Tour, starting in New York City down the eastern seaboard to the Grand Opening in Orlando, introducing "Cosby's Other Family." The other stops on the tour included Philadelphia, Pennsylvania; Washington D.C.; Columbia, South Carolina; and, finally, Orlando, Florida. Along for the ride were the *Ghost Dad* kids – Kimberly Russell with her sister, Salim Grant with his parents and sister, and young Brooke Fontaine with her parents and brother. My husband Robert and our son, Teron, were able to go, as well. It was an amazing vacation for us.

The neon lights and energy of New York City absolutely mesmerized my son, Teron, who was twelve at the time. The sights and sounds of the city resonated with him in a special way, and he has had a love for New York City ever since. The highlight of our visit was an opportunity for our group to attend the Broadway show, *Black and Blue*, a musical revue celebrating the black culture of dance and music in Paris between World War I and World War II. The production featured the music of W.C. Handy, Duke Ellington, Louis Armstrong, Eubie Blake and others. The outstanding musical talent included two of my rhythm and blues favorites, the late Linda Hopkins and the late Ruth Brown, who belted out songs like "St. Louis Blues," "Stompin' at the Savoy," "I Can't Give You Anything but Love" and more. Even more exciting, it was our first opportunity to witness the incomparable talent of Savion Glover, the phenomenal, young tap dancer, who at age fifteen went on the be the youngest person ever nominated for a Tony for his role in the production.

The next morning, we visited the Statue of Liberty and the Empire State Building before heading south on the tour. Once we got to Orlando, we stayed at the luxurious Grand Hyatt Resort. There was a lavish kick-off party for all the celebrities who were participating in the event, which included Sylvester Stallone, Michael J. Fox, Henry Thomas and Steven Spielberg. Early the next morning, Bill arrived via his private plane, *The Camille*, just in time for the grand opening event. For the festivities, he rode in a car down Main Street to the stage ceremony, participated in a VIP breakfast, rode on the King Kong Ride before heading back to his private plane. Before he left, he asked me to get him two hot dogs smothered with onions, chili and cheese. His wife had him on a strict diet, so this was his chance to cheat. Though I resisted, in the end I complied with his wish. He didn't take "no" for an answer.

Spike's Might

When I returned to Universal from Motown in 1989, I was introduced to the newest black filmmaker Spike Lee, who would go on to make six pictures for Universal Studios -- *Do the Right Thing, Mo' Better Blues, Jungle Fever, Crooklyn, Clockers* and later *Inside Man*. I was no stranger to his work. I was a big fan of his debut film *She's Gotta Have It* and I loved *School Daze*, his follow-up film, dealing with social issues facing

160

black college students.

From the onset, I found Spike to be a cantankerous character, who didn't mind speaking his mind. He stayed on the marketing department's case with his hands-on approach regarding the publicizing and advertising of his films, because he recognized how vital it was to the film's success. Spike would unnerve white folks as he moved throughout our department. He would ask people point blank what they were doing for his film. To his credit, he also insisted on having an African American publicity agency on board to handle his projects. During that time, he used the Tobin Agency, headed by my dear friend, the late Pat Tobin. Jackie Bazan's agency in New York has been his PR firm for many years.

When I came back on staff at Universal, they rushed to introduce me to him, so he would know they had an African American publicist on staff. As a matter of fact, he later told a reporter that after he complained that there were no blacks on staff, they hired me. He had no idea I was returning, not newly hired. My position had nothing to do with him. I had been working in publicity when he was still in high school.

On our first day working together, Spike continually questioned my plans and the day's agenda. He expressed negative opinions about the work ethic of black folks, convinced we wouldn't do things right. I was offended, because I prided myself on being very organized and I was an expert at setting up press itineraries. However, he had to learn that out for himself.

We were scheduled to do our press interviews at the famous Chateau Marmont Hotel in West Hollywood, built in 1929 to resemble a Gothic chateau built along the Loire River in France. The hotel is best known as the place where John Belushi died.

As we always did, my assistant, Ellen Sommers, and I arrived early and got Spike's holding suite set-up with refreshments, the hospitality suite for the press, as well as providing the necessary press kits and video tapes for the television crews. As each crew arrived, we set them up in separate suites. Once they were set up, we provided breakfast for the TV crews. Then we went to wait for Spike's arrival. He stepped out of the car with a scowl on his face.

"Good morning, Spike," I said warmly. He just grunted. I let him know we were ready for him.

"Here's our schedule and you can follow me to your suite. If you would like to eat, we have a variety of items already set-up for you. The hair and makeup people are here, too," I continued.

"Let's get started. What's first?" he said. So, we then bypassed his suite and went directly to the interview.

"Okay, come with me," I said, as I led him to the first TV crew.

Before we started, he barked, "What's next?" I told him and then he wanted to know if they were ready. I assured him they were. This went on throughout the entire day.

"What's next?" "Are they ready?"

"Yes, yes, yes!" I wanted to scream, *I got this, brother, I got this!* But I was cool. Finally, he relaxed when he recognized I had it together. Once we did all the interviews like clockwork that day, I was never challenged by Spike again.

He continued to make it known to the marketing executives that he was dissatisfied with the number of theaters in which the Distribution Department planned to open his movie.

"You are only opening *Jungle Fever* in less than seven hundred theaters. You don't do that to the white boys! What kind of shit is that?" he grumbled.

He did his homework. At that time, most mainstream films opened in twelve hundred, two thousand or more theaters. He said he would never be as competitive at the box office because he opened in far less theaters. The studio's theory was the film would build momentum, but Spike didn't buy that because it very rarely happened. To make his point, one day in 1991 I was driving Spike to the backlot to do a photo shoot, when he spotted the billboard on Lankershim Boulevard for *A Kiss Before Dying*, starring Matt Dillon, which Universal had recently released and it flopped.

"Look at that shit, Roz. That movie died before he even got a kiss," he complained. "How many theaters did they open that piece of shit in?"

I checked it out. Universal had opened *A Kiss Before Dying* in 1500 theaters and it made only $4.3 million opening week, a mere $2,855 per screen. On the other hand, the following week Spike's film *Jungle Fever* opened in only 636 theaters and earned $5.3 million the first weekend, an impressive $8.4 million per screen. Spike's point was well taken. If he had had an opportunity to have as many screens as the Matt Dillon film, it could have made more money when the iron was hot over the opening weekend. More importantly, the film may have possibly been one of the top three movies at the box office.

As unorthodox and negative as Spike's approach was, his constant complaints actually made the studio executives re-think their release pattern for "urban" films. Soon they began to open black films in more theaters, not just in the black community.

In 1992 Spike went with Warner Brothers to make *Malcolm X*, his highest budgeted movie at that time. *Malcolm X* opened in twice the number of theaters than Spike's previous films had. Still not wide, but double was much better than they had been doing. When he returned to Universal, the theater release numbers equaled *Malcolm X's*.

Towards the end of my career, my company shared publicity duties with Universal and Jackie Bazan's New York P.R. agency on Spike's film *Inside Man*, which became his highest grossing film to date. Starring Denzel Washington, Jody Foster and Clive Owen, *Inside Man* opened Number One with $28 million in over twenty-eight hundred theaters. The movie ended by making $88 million domestically. Surprising to me, it was the biggest opener for Denzel, too.

I had the pleasure of serving as the consulting producer for a personal and insightful thirty-minute special for the film called *"Inside Men: An Intimate Conversation with Denzel and Spike,"* which was produced by my friend, Stephanie Frederic of FGW Productions, and aired on both BET and TV One to promote the opening of the film.

Cicely, pronounced Sicily –

It had been over ten years since I first met Cicely Tyson on the set of "Just an Old Sweet Song." Our next encounter was in 1987 during the marketing phase of *Cry Freedom*, starring Denzel Washington. Although she wasn't in the film, she loved the book, *Cry Freedom*, and had asked the filmmakers to be involved somehow. To that end, she had made special arrangements with Ebony magazine to be their guest photographer for the film in South Africa.

I oversaw the first screening of the *Cry Freedom* for the filmmakers, cast and studio executives, and she was among the people invited.

Everyone arrived on time, except Cicely. I checked on her limousine and received word that she would be arriving in a few minutes. The director Sir Richard Attenborough and I waited in front of the Alfred Hitchcock Theater on the Universal Studios lot to greet her.

When she arrived, we were in for a surprise as she stepped out of the limo wearing a platinum blond Dutch Boy wig and ice blue contact lens. Throughout her long career, Cicely has always been a trendsetter, willing to try out various daring hairdos, so this was an example of her creatively expressing herself. Sir Richard was particularly stunned, because he said she had been so natural and authentic on the location, wearing no makeup and a head wrap. So, when she "went Hollywood" on him, he didn't know what to say. We simply ushered her in and got the movie started.

She was so moved by the film that she sat in the theater softly weeping for quite a long time after it ended. She cried so much I was sure she must have washed out those blue contact lens. After everyone had left, she and Sir Richard sat in the empty theater for an in-depth conversation about the film, which meant so much to her.

I worked with her, again, in 1991 when we were preparing for weekend press interviews of *Fried Green Tomatoes*, followed by the premiere on Monday night. I went to the Century Plaza Hotel at 10 p.m. on Friday night to greet the grand dame. I remember mispronouncing her name, "I am so delighted to see you, again, "Cess-sa-lee." She quickly corrected me, "My name in Cicely, pronounced like the Italian city, Sicily." Well, I could never forget that. I got it right from then on.

She had arrived from New York. At her request, we had provided her with a suite with a connecting room set up for her assistant, Lois. When she examined the suite and Lois' room, she snapped, "This is unacceptable! Lois needs better accommodations."

I explained that Lois had what they called a parlor suite, but she wouldn't accept it. I went to the front desk and begged them to find a connecting room that was more suitable, and they did. I finally got her settled in and I got home around midnight.

Cicely had a small but important role in the film. Everyone kept saying she could possibly get an Oscar nomination for her supporting role. "From your lips to God's ear," she would chime each time with a giggle. However, when Oscar time rolled around there was no mention of the film, her performance or anyone else in it.

During the press roundtables that Saturday morning, one of the press members made the mistake of asking Cicely about the passing of her ex-husband, the late great Miles Davis, who had died three months earlier. Apparently, it was the first time she had been asked about him publicly. Her voice quivered as she began to get choked up. Before we knew it, she was weeping uncontrollably.

She turned to me crying and declared, "I can't go on." I looked to Lois to help console her and she was crying harder than Cicely! I got her up and led her out of the room. Once I got her in her suite, it got worse. I wasn't sure what to do and weeping Lois was no help at all. I continued to comfort her as she shared how hard it was to speak about him. They had divorced three years prior and it was unpleasant, so even she was surprised that she had those deep emotions bottled up inside her.

Slowly she began to pull herself back together. I got her ice water and, after a time, asked her if she could continue. She said she could, however insisted I could not allow anyone to mention his name again. I left her so she could regain her composure. I ran back to let the press know we would resume, but for goodness sake, please don't bring up Miles Davis.

Once she came back, we finished the press interviews with no further disruptions. I was on pins and needles the entire time. When we finished everything, including the premiere, she gave me a note card with her name printed on top. Lois had typed, "Mrs. Stevenson, You were quite competent." Then Cicely signed her name. I was proud of that note and held on to it for many years.

Cruise Control

In 1992 I was assigned to coordinate the press day for Tom Cruise, who was promoting Universal's upcoming film *Far and Away*, in which he starred with a new, little-known actress, his young wife, Nicole Kidman. Tom was the new superstar client of one of the industry's most prominent publicist. Tom had a reputation for being very, very demanding to his team. She wanted to make sure things went well for her maiden voyage. I quickly learned that the warm and friendly smiling face Tom puts on in interviews wasn't the same for those who worked with him. He was very controlling. He'd put on a huge smile in a reporter's face and mutter comment about the person as he or she left the room.

Tom had enacted another unique requirement; members of the press had to sign a waiver, which stated that their interview with him would only be used for the approved media outlet they were listed for. This was a very unsettling situation for many of the press, because once they had an interview with a star, they commonly went about offering it to as many other outlets as possible. That is how they made their money. But that wasn't happening with Tom. The press complained among themselves about it, but they had no choice but to sign and accept his terms.

To say I was feeling uneasy about working with him was an understatement. However, you would not have known based on my demeanor. His publicist laid the ground rules for me when I arrived. She said forcefully, "Tom will only work from 9:00 a.m. until 5:00 p.m. That's it. No exceptions. You will need to stay on time and keep the interviews going." From the onset, that was a problem because he was ending his day one hour before we normally end. Each interview was five minutes, plus we allotted two minutes turn-around time. This was where I could pick up needed time. I'd make the interviews a little shorter and shorten the turn-around time. As the press people arrived for their interviews, I kindly explained the tight schedule and asked for their help in making a quick exit once the interview ended. That meant once it concluded, I couldn't allow idle chit-chat, no autographs or photos. Just, "Wham-bam, thank you, ma'am. Next!" I figured if I cut the interviews by one-minute and used only one minute or less to turn around the interviews, I would pick up the needed sixty minutes by the end of the day.

As the day began, my plan was working well. I would have the next reporter enter the room with me as I said "thank you" at the conclusion of the previous reporter's interview. I was moving them in and out of the suite in record time. Tom was pleased and his publicist just watched as the day progressed smoothly. Lunch time came and we all went our separate ways; Tom went to his personal suite with Nicole and his sister/assistant, Lee Anne. His publicist went to the hospitality suite for lunch and so did I.

She engaged me in a brief conversation about wanting to do something to help in the black community. This was during the time of the Rodney King uprising and white folks felt compelled to help the poor, mistreated black folks. She asked me about First AME Church, which she heard I attended. Actually, I was a member at Brookins AME Church. AME stands for the African Methodist Episcopal Church denomination. Somehow when white folks hear the church mentioned on television, they only hear "AME." I didn't correct her. I had long gotten used to going along with the program. I got the phone number for the church and told her the name of the pastor, Reverend Cecil "Chip" Murray, who the media constantly sought out to speak about situations in the black community. She thanked me and seemed genuinely sincere about wanting to help.

As the lunch hour was drawing to an end, I hurried back to the interview suite to make sure the crew would be ready to start on time. I got the next reporter in the seat and I had another reporter on deck. I went to Tom's suite, knocked on the door and his sister answered. She told me that it was his publicist's birthday, and they had a surprise cake that they wanted to give her. A wonderful gesture, but that destroyed my timetable. Once they lured the publicist into their suite, they had the birthday celebration, which extended the lunch period by fifteen or more minutes. Ending on time was now going to be a problem.

We started back and I tried even harder than before to get the reporters in and out without skipping a beat. I was proud of myself. Finally, it was 4:57 p.m. and we had only one reporter left, Sam Rubin of the local station, KTLA - Channel 5. As the interview ended with Pam Thompson, a beautiful local reporter for KABC – Channel 7, I got her out of the seat and turned to get Sam. When I turned back around, to my utter surprise, the room was pitch black. His publicist had pulled the plug! Sam moved into the dark room and said, "Hey, Tom, I'm your last guy. Aren't you going to speak with me, pal?" Tom smiled and said, "Of course, please turn on the lights," which they did.

However, as Tom began to speak with Sam, his publicist pushed me out of the room into the hallway. She started ranting, raving and shaking her finger in my face. "Don't you ever, as long as you live, do this to Tom Cruise. Do you hear me? Never!" I was shocked and humiliated that she spoke to me loudly in front of my colleagues like

I was an insubordinate child. As I stood there frozen with disbelief, I was seething on the inside.

The Compton in me wanted to kick that bitch's ass, but I caught myself and I took the high road. However, my voice was shaking as I reminded her, "I am sorry. I did everything I could to make this day work and we were only going to be a minute or two past 5 o'clock. If we went over, it was because of your birthday celebration, which had nothing to do with me."

Her face was red and her eyes were bulging out of her head. Before I slugged her, I quickly turned away from her. I did not want to do something that would ruin my career. I stormed down the hallway so fast that I was knocking down press chairs as I headed to the hospitality suite. I didn't look at anyone, nor did I say a word. I snatched my purse from the closet and left as fast as I could. I was so pissed off I was shaking and pacing back and forth as I waited for the valet to bring my car. I sped out of the hotel on two wheels and headed home at top speed.

Once I got home, I couldn't stop seeing visions of her long, boney finger shaking in my face. My head was pounding as I climbed in my bed. The phone rang and it was my boss, Alan Sutton. He said he heard about what happened and he was pleased with the work I had done. He paused. Then he said on the next day, the final day of interviews, he wanted to assign someone else to work with Tom. I told him, "No! I don't want her to think she ran me off. I didn't do anything wrong." So, he reluctantly agreed that I could continue to work with Tom.

The next morning when I arrived at the front of the Four Seasons Hotel, there was an unusual sight; Tom's publicist and his sister Lee Anne were standing there. I thought, "What the hell are they doing out here?" I got out of my car and tried to walk pass them, but his publicist stopped me and awkwardly threw her arms around me. She began apologizing profusely, as Lee Anne looked on with arms folded. The look on my face said, "What the hell?" Finally, Lee Anne spoke. She said Tom really appreciated my work, and he would be honored to have me work with him today. Wow! I couldn't believe my ears.

I glanced at his publicist, who looked pale and meek as a lamb. Then she said she didn't know what had come over her yesterday. Her excuse was that she had a pinched nerve in her neck, which had her in severe pain and it affected her judgment. She was really laying it on thick and asked me to forgive her. I accepted her apology, and we went up the elevator to the suite where Tom waited. He had kind words for me, too, and, as a cool gesture, he autographed a picture for me from the film's press kit. And, so began a very pleasant and unusual day. The interviews ran smoothly as my co-workers looked on with curiosity. I often wonder what Tom had said to his publicist. I have never seen such an about-face. I went home that day feeling redeemed. Little did I realize that wasn't the end of it.

On the Monday morning, reporter Sam Rubin broadcast a story about the entire incident on the air. He started off explaining to TV viewers how press junkets work and how TV reporters line up to speak with the stars. He told of being the last reporter and how shocked he was when a well-known Hollywood publicist pulled the plug before he could get his interview. He said, "I won't call her name, but you know who you are!" Anyway, he said Tom Cruise couldn't have been kinder. He had the lights turned back on and granted him the interview. He ended by playing his complete interview with Tom.

Well, the next day the news story was the talk of the marketing department. The studio always ordered tapes of the interviews that air on TV from a monitoring service, and this was no exception. However, when I went to our weekly staff meeting, to my surprise, the playing of the tape was the first order of business. I had to re-tell the story for the entire executive marketing staff. The marketing department always had a love/hate relationship with the talents' personal publicists. Often their demands regarding their "A-list clients" caused the studio so much grief as we tried to conduct a successful campaign. The story was hilarious to them, especially the part about the publicist having to humble herself and apologize to me in front of Tom's sister. I told them how his publicist kept holding an ice pack on her neck throughout the day to ease the pain of her supposed pinched nerve. It was fun to talk about it with the staff, however that wasn't the end of it.

Next, Tom Pollock, the head of the studio, called me to get a copy of the tape so he could play it at his meeting with all the studio heads. Again, the story was re-told, and they all got a big laugh out of it. For me, I still had my job and I learned a big lesson: Don't worry about getting back at someone, leave that to God. He can work it out in ways you never ever imagined.

CHAPTER 16:
Unforgettable Stars

Shine bright like a diamond.

A Double Scoop of Patrick Swayze

My long-time assistant at Universal, Ellen Sommers, was the biggest Patrick Swayze fan ever! When I learned about a premiere event celebrating the tenth anniversary of *Dirty Dancing*, I arranged to get tickets and took her for her birthday gift. To top the evening off, after the screening, I arranged for Ellen to meet Patrick. The excitement of that evening was enough to keep her happy for the rest of her life.

However, as fate would have it, not long after that Patrick also starred in a film for Universal called *Black Dog*. I was responsible for doing press interviews for the film in Las Vegas. Though assistants do not usually go out-of-town, I asked my boss if we could make an exception, because I wanted Ellen to have an opportunity to work with Patrick. He agreed and she was beyond thrilled. She went with me to Las Vegas and she was with Patrick, of course. It was her responsibility to make sure he stayed on schedule and to help navigate his day for Universal. Ellen took her job very seriously. Too seriously!

At one point, I knocked on the door of his suite to see if he was ready to do the next round of interviews. She cracked open the door ever so slightly and whispered, "Not now! He's on the phone with his manager. Come back later." Then she abruptly slammed the door in my face. I stood there stunned. I guess she forgot she was working for the studio; now she was working for Patrick. Eventually we completed the day and it made me feel good to add that day as the icing on her Patrick Swayze cake.

We laughed about that incident for years. After I left Universal, Ellen and I didn't see each other often. Throughout Patrick's illness and his eventual passing, I thought about her and how sad she must be. I reached out to her and, as I thought, she was grief stricken. After that, she and I got together for lunch and she talked for hours about meeting him and what a delight he was to work with. He had no greater fan than my former assistant Ellen Sommers. He died too young and will always live in our hearts.

Eddie Murphy's Law

I became an expert at breaking the ice with the most difficult stars. When I was assigned to work with Eddie Murphy on *The Nutty Professor,* it was a no-brainer. While he was cordial, right away I mentioned to him that we had met before when my husband, Robert, served as the hair stylist on his iconic films, *Coming to America, Harlem Nights* and *Another 48 Hours.* He had great experiences with Robert, so it made my bonding with him quick and easy.

Eddie's first comment was about my husband's youthful look. "Robert always looked so good for his age. How old is he now, eighty?" he said followed by that legendary chuckle. With Eddie and many other stars, their familiarity with my husband always made my job easier. It was always smooth sailing after they made that positive connection. I was "good people," if Robert was my husband, they felt.

I enjoyed working with Eddie and his team. His assistant Charisse Hewitt was particularly efficient and helpful. She saw to it that all his special quirks and demands were met. "Eddie is a superstar, and he should be treated that way," she would often say.

One of the special events I escorted Eddie and his family to the grand opening of the "Islands of Adventure" theme park at Universal Studios in Orlando, Florida, in 1997, when the studio invited stars to bring their families. It was a three-day event and the studio only required me to arrange one national television interview for Eddie. It was an easy assignment and a fun get-away for me. We stayed at the Portofino Bay Resort Hotel, where Eddie's family was given the entire top floor with every suite going to him, his then-wife Nicole, their five children, his friends and the members of his large entourage.

The entourage and I arrived a day before Eddie and his family. One of the things that Eddie enjoyed was having his room set up with his personal library of movies. One assistant had the responsibility of setting up Eddie's film collection alphabetically for the stay, so the nocturnal performer could easily watch any movie he wanted at any time of the day or night.

His team and I had our biggest fun the day before Eddie arrived, because once he came, we would all be at his beck and call twenty-four/seven. That night we dined, laughed and drank margaritas non-stop at Tommy Bahamas.

On the opening night, I escorted Eddie and his group to the outdoor gala under the stars on the resort's waterfront. No expense was spared, as we dined on a magnificent feast with entertainment provided by the Orlando Philharmonic Orchestra. They performed musical selections with fireworks exploding and dancing across the sky. Other entertainment icons and their families who were taking part in the magical evening included Steven Spielberg, Edgar Bronfman, Ron Howard, Brian Grazer, Whitney Houston and many others.

The next night there were two private musical concerts scheduled at the theme park for the celebrity guests. The first was an outdoor concert by R&B legend Smokey Robinson; the second was a Sheryl Crow concert across the way in a nearby club in the park. Smokey's show was great fun, because the VIPs and stars seemed to know every word to his many classic hits, like "Shop Around," "Oh Baby, Baby," "Mickey's Money," "Tears of a Clown," "I Second That Emotion" and "You Really Got a Hold on Me." Everyone sang along at the top of their lungs.

Just as the concert was coming to an end, suddenly there was a loud boom. Thunder had erupted, lightning lit up the sky and a heavy torrential rain came pouring down. Luckily, for the guests, we were protected under a huge canopy. However, Smokey, the band and their instruments were instantly drenched.

Some of the guests began to run from under the canopy and head for the club across the park. That didn't make any sense to me, because within seconds the water was already six inches high. It covered people's shoes when they stepped into the unprotected area. Eddie looked at

173

me and said, "We are not going anywhere, right, Roz?" He was right. Then, as quickly as the rain started, it stopped. When we saw there was a break in the rain, we made a run for the resort van parked backstage, which safely took us across the way to the Sheryl Crow concert.

The next day the park opened early for the celebrity families. Eddie made it clear he didn't want to get up in the morning. His wife, Nicole, took their five kids with the help of the assistants. Eddie, his buddy singer, Johnny Gill, and I arranged to meet them for lunch. We hooked up with the family in one of the restaurants at the appointed time. After we ate, I had scheduled an interview with "Access Hollywood" to speak with Eddie, his wife and kids at the "Cat in the Hat" attraction. We taped the interview with no problems. After that, Nicole and the children continued to the enjoy the park attractions.

Eddie and Johnny got into the back of our waiting limo, and a security guy grabbed my arm as I followed right behind them. Stunned, I said, "Excuse me?" The guy said, "Where do you think you're going?"

"I'm with Eddie, sir." Eddie leaned out and said, "Hey, fella, she's with us." The security guard reluctantly let me get in the car. Eddie thought that was hilarious, and he and Johnny laughed about it all the way back to the resort. Once we got back, Eddie and Johnny went their way and I went my way. My job was done. I had the rest of the day to splurge on relaxing spa treatments. What a great life!

The next afternoon we were all scheduled to leave. However, before I headed back to Los Angeles, Eddie's assistant said the family was requesting to stay a few more days so the kids could go to Disney World. The resort was kind enough to extend their complimentary accommodations for a few more days. Following their Orlando stay, the Murphy clan had scheduled to take a vacation on a private island in the Bahamas.

The Rise of Bernie Mac

Once again, I had a successful working relationship with Eddie on the comedy-drama *Life* at Universal in 1999. Eddie co-starred as Ray Gibson with Martin Lawrence as Claude Banks in what I felt was one of their funniest performances. To top it off, the ensemble of actors was hilarious, the stand-out being Bernie Mac as Jangle Leg. Others included in the film were Michael Taliferro as Goldmouth, Miguel Nunez as Biscuit, Bokeem Woodbine as Can't-Get-Right, Guy Torry as Radio, Obba Babatunde as Willie Long, Anthony Anderson as Cookie and Brent Jennings as Hoppin' Bob.

Life is one of my all-time favorite comedy films. Though the subject matter of blacks wrongfully accused of crimes is a serious issue, this movie was done with two of the top comedians of our times and it was hilarious. In the end, they got revenge on the bad cop and out slicked the prison system to gain their freedom. The comedic dialogue continues to make me laugh every time I see it. One scene that stands out is when Superintendent Abernathy holds up his white daughter's beautiful chocolate baby girl to the inmates and asks, "Who is the pappy of this here baby?" one inmate after another takes responsibility. However, when Bernie Mac says, "I's that baby's pappy," it cracks me up every time.

As a key component to the marketing campaign, I was producing a BET special for *Life*. We needed one of the stars to narrate the special, however Eddie and Martin were on to other projects, so neither was available. In our staff meeting I suggested Bernie Mac, who none of the white executives were familiar with at that time. As I often did, I explained that Bernie Mac was extremely popular in the African American community and he consistently sold out 5000-seat venues throughout the country. This was 1999, a year before he came to national prominence in *The Kings of Comedy*. After that, Bernie blew up and got his own TV-series and went on to appear in the *Ocean's* franchise with George Clooney, Brad Pitt, Matt Damon and Don Cheadle, and other films.

After some convincing, it was agreed that Bernie Mac was a good choice to narrate the special. He did it and the special was a big success with the BET viewers. *Life* opened Number One at the box office with $20 million and grossed $63 million during the domestic run. *Life's* soundtrack had even greater success. It was produced by R. Kelly and Wyclef Jean with selections by various urban soul and hip-hop artists. Most memorable was the heart wrenching soul ballad, "Life," sung by K-Ci and JoJo, which played over the closing credits. The album had already garnered platinum status prior to the opening of the film.

Over the next few years, I worked with Bernie through my company, RSPR, on three more film; *Head of State* (2003, DreamWorks),

Charlie's Angels (2003, Sony) and *Guess Who* (2005, Sony). My husband, Robert, had an opportunity to get to know him, as well, when Bernie starred with Samuel L. Jackson in *Soul Men*, his last motion picture. Bernie's spirits never wavered, and he gave it his all; however, in between scenes he was on oxygen. Most people did not know that he had suffered for many years with sarcoidosis, which is an inflammatory lung disease that contributed to the decline of his health.

Bernie's career was on a roll with multiple movie roles and his successful sitcom that ran for five seasons. It was a sad day when Bernie Mac died from pneumonia at the young age of fifty-one years old on August 9, 2008. After he passed, Bernie had the rare distinction of being in two movies that opened on the same day, *Madagascar: Escape 2 Africa* and *Soul Men*, on November 7, 2008.

Bernie was a hilarious, extraordinary talent and I feel blessed to have had several opportunities to work with him before he left us too soon.

CHAPTER 17:
Honoring Ancestors, Gold Rush Pioneers

We are family.

In addition to my star-studded career as a publicist in the entertainment industry, I always valued my family. One of the proudest moments for me is captured in the following headline from June 19, 1999 in the Record Newspaper in Stockton, California's read:

THE HALLS AND THE QUIVERS
African American Gold Rush Pioneer Families Receive Monuments and Grave Markers from Their Descendants

For this moving and unforgettable event, Robert and I joined my entire family in Stockton, California, for a historic reunion honoring our descendants who came to California for the Gold Rush.

Among the family members were my mother, our matriarch seventy-nine-year old Clara Reed Steverson of Compton, California; our family historian Viola Baecher with her family of Chicago, Illinois; my cousins Councilman Philip Hall Reed and his twin sister Elinor Reed of New York; Ted Carter and wife Marsha of Stockton, California; Reverend Rodger Hall Reed and wife Shirley of Washington D.C.; Reverend Granville Reed and wife Ida of Jacksonville, Florida; Professor Richard Earl Reed of Chicago, Illinois; Carol Tucker of Los Angeles, California; Richard Steverson and wife Marianne of Manhattan Beach, California; Norma Halston and Alexis Mansion of Antioch,

California; and Catherine and Michael Bush of Concord, California. Additionally, all of our children, my nieces, nephews and grandchildren came for the deeply moving, meaningful three-day celebration.

The reunion started with a dedication service honoring our Gold Rush pioneers, Henry Hall and Emanuel Quivers. Family members came from all over the country to provide grave markers for eighteen relatives buried in the family plot, who had unmarked graves in the Stockton Rural Cemetery. We also erected two monuments stating our family's historical contributions. One read: *The Halls - California Pioneers since 1849*, the other read: *The Quivers - Trailblazers for Education and Equality Since 1877*. The program was held in the cemetery chapel and included biographical sketches of each of our pioneering ancestors, who made significant marks in the early days of the new and developing State of California.

The event was spearheaded by my cousin Viola. She is one of the great-grandchildren of Henry Hall and one of the great-great grandchildren of Emanuel Quivers. Viola was a social worker and amateur genealogist from Park Forest, Illinois, who began research on the family and uncovered our family's rich history in California since the Gold Rush in 1849. The family patriarch, Henry Hall, came to California in 1849 on horseback at age fourteen from Texas. He was an excellent horseman and had a thriving business as a teamster, hauling to and from the mines for twenty-five years. He died at age fifty-nine, leaving a sprawling ranch on Waterloo Road to his family. He was one of only two blacks to be inducted into the San Joaquin Society of Pioneers.

Henry's wife, Mary Ann Quivers Hall, came from another prominent family. Her father, Emanuel Quivers, had been a skilled slave ironworker in Richmond, Virginia. He purchased freedom for himself and his family from the owner of the Tredegar Ironworks and left for California in 1849. Among the artifacts in Viola's genealogical search are the manumission (freedom) papers for his wife, Frances Quivers, and her five children, as well as a copy of the emancipation document for Emanuel. My great-grandparents were Henry and Mary Ann Hall, who had four children - Oswald Hall, Herbert Hall, Artemissa Hall Potts and my grandmother Susie Hall Reed. Susie married my grandfather Granville Reed in 1910. They had three sons, Granville, Theodore and Arnold. Their one daughter was my mother, Clara Ann

Reed Steverson, born April 23, 1920.

Emanuel Quivers, Sr. was a successful blacksmith, who sought an education for all his children. When his son, Emanuel Quivers, Jr., was refused admission to Stockton's high school because of his race, he was educated in San Francisco at great expense to the City of Stockton. After reviewing his case, the school board voted in 1877 to discontinue the color line for public education in Stockton.

Another of Emanuel's children, Sarah, married Moses Rodgers, who was one of the top mining engineers during the Gold Rush. A wealthy and respected businessman, Moses was a former slave who gained an education and became a respected metallurgist. He acquired early ownership of a group of mines in Hornitos, Mariposa County and was superintendent of the Mt. Gaines Mine. In 1898 he built a home in Stockton at 921 San Joaquin Avenue, which was declared Stockton Historical Landmark No. 22 by the Stockton City Council in 1978, listed in the national register of historic places.

Viola's search was speeded up because each of our family members are prominently mentioned in history books on blacks in the Gold Rush; Delilah Beasley's *The Negro Trailblazers in California*, Professor Rudolph Lapp's *Blacks in Gold Rush California*, Virginia Strubaker's *Stockton's Black Pioneers*, Sue Bailey Thurman's *Pioneers of Negro Origin in California*. Other significant discoveries were made at Stockton's Haggin Museum, Bancroft Library, San Joaquin Historical Society and the archives at the University of the Pacific.

For my part as the publicist in the family, I organized the three-day event that included the dedication service at the Stockton Rural Cemetery, a family picnic, and a closing family church service at Ebenezer African Methodist Episcopal Church. Our family members had lodging accommodations at Stockton's Marriott Residential Inn, which had kitchens and allowed us to prepare breakfasts, lunches and snacks onsite. More importantly, it was a beautiful opportunity for family members, young and old, to get to know one another, relax and fellowship at a time that was very meaningful. As we recognized our ancestors rich past and accomplishments, it informed our family members in a way that allowed them to look to the future knowing we had a history to be proud and to be shared with generations to come.

We recognized how impactful the Stockton reunion had been when our late cousin Councilman Philip Reed of New York succumbed to cancer in 2008. It was his wish to have his ashes buried with our ancestors, who had been laid to rest in the Stockton Rural Cemetery so many years ago. After his official funeral service in New York City, according to his wishes, we conducted a graveside service for him where we committed his ashes to the ground in Stockton as his final resting place.

For cousin Phil's great work in his district in New York, he was honored with a street re-named in his memory. The press release issued on September 10, 2011, by New York State Senator Jose M. Serrano read: The East Harlem community honored Councilmember Philip Reed by naming the intersection of First Avenue and 111th Street "Philip Reed Way."

Philip Reed was a member of the New York City Council from 1998 to 2005, where he represented District 8, which encompasses East Harlem, portions of the South Bronx, and Central Park. He was the first openly gay African American Council Member.

"It is an honor to witness this momentous occasion and to pay tribute to a local leader who truly loved serving his community, and who worked diligently to ensure underserved neighborhoods received their fair share. Not only was he a remarkable elected official, he was also a wonderful friend. Through this intersection, future generations will always be reminded of all that he accomplished in this community," stated Senator Serrano.

We were so proud of cousin Phil. Growing up, we didn't know where he and his twin sister, Elinor's were after their parents divorced. We are grateful that Philip discovered my mother's letter to his mother from years ago. In 1992 he made contact with my mother and we were able to complete our family tree. My cousins Philip and Elinor Reed have been a welcomed addition and are truly a blessing to the Reed family.

CHAPTER 18:
Roz Stevenson Public Relations

It's true: You do all you can, and God will do the rest.

"Why isn't this your job?" Terry Curtin asked to me. I was puzzled by her question. She was the newly appointed head of Publicity and Promotions at Universal. She was referring to the black press activities I had assisted with on two highly acclaimed African American films we had recently released; *The Best Man* with an ensemble cast that included Taye Diggs, Terrence Howard, Nia Long and Sanaa Latham, and *The Hurricane*, starring Denzel Washington as convicted boxer Ruben "Hurricane" Carter. Both were released in Fall 1999.

For my part, as the broadcast publicist, I had arranged all mainstream national TV and radio press and bookings for the actors in these films. In addition, I always voluntarily did as much as I could for the African American press. I prepared and sent out feature stories and photos to over two hundred and fifty black weekly newspapers nationwide, obtained cover stories in Jet magazine and behind-the-scenes specials on BET or TV One. I also arranged for the black press from around the country to attend the press junkets. Because of my primary broadcast responsibilities, I couldn't do much more. No one else on our staff was specifically seeking out the African American press. That meant we rarely got coverage in black monthly magazines, which are long-lead publications and had to be approached, locked-in with interviews and photo shoots organized at least three to six months before a film was released.

Apparently, every time Terry had asked about the black press campaign, my bosses would tell her, "Roz will do it." They were right. I did it because I did not want my community left out from the information about a good film, especially when it was targeted to our people.

"This is what you should be doing," Terry insisted. I agreed with her and explained that I had often asked, but no one ever saw black press as a singular job. She had come to us from Disney Studios, where they had a VP of Special Markets. She said that is exactly what my job should be. Her words were music to my ears.

In order to advocate for me, Terry said she needed me to give her a detailed report showing every opportunity we missed by not having someone specifically targeting the African American market for *The Best Man* and *The Hurricane*. This was around Thanksgiving time. I was able to prepare and gave her an extensive report right after New Year's.

She said, "This is exactly what I need, however." I tuned her out because it seemed like she was back peddling on her original offer and was telling me why she could not do it. She said the studio was re-engineering the departments and she was forced to eliminate some of the current executive positions. Blah-blah-blah. I did my part and now she was backing down, I thought.

Then I heard her say, "But I really think this is important. What if we start you a business? We would contract you to do all the African American publicity and promotions for Universal films. However, we would give you an open contract, so you can seek other studios. You will provide a much-needed service and you will make a lot of money. What do you think about that?"

I snapped out of my funk. I thought I had died and gone to heaven. Did I hear her right? What? I couldn't believe my ears. I said, "I would definitely do that. I would love it."

She suggested I discuss her offer with my husband, because there was a downside; I would lose my health and pension benefits. I said I would let her know, but I should have told her we could move forward right then and there. Actually, health insurance wasn't an issue with us, because Robert and I were double covered under the Motion Picture Health and Welfare plan. I was ready to move on it. Once again, a miracle had happened when I least expected it. And I muttered the words, again, that my mother always said, "You do all you can, and

God will do the rest." Hallelujah!

It took six months to put the entire business plan and contracts together. By June 2000 I turned on the phones at my home office and I was in business. Roz Stevenson Public Relations (RSPR) began with one employee, journalist Ronda Penrice, whom I had always admired for her textbook knowledge of blacks in entertainment. I turned my kids' former two bedrooms into offices and every day I walked down the hall to work. At fifty-seven years old, I was thrilled.

I gave a launch party for all members of the black entertainment press in Los Angeles, who already knew me. Ronda and I prepared an impressive packet of our upcoming projects and showed them the "Coming Attractions" reel. We talked about our goals and served sumptuous soul food around the pool at my home. They were beyond happy to have me as an advocate for them.

Next Ronda and I took a road trip to visit BET, TV-One and all of the black magazine, newspaper and online publishers and editors in New York, Washington D.C., Atlanta, New York and Chicago.

"How can I better serve you?" I would always ask. One publisher at the largest and oldest magazines, sadly said, "Just take our calls." The black press felt the studios routinely treated them like stepchildren. I listened to one unhappy story after another of mistreatment, real or perceived.

The music industry, on the other hand, apparently, always treated the black press well. They understand how important it was to serve their artists' fan base. But, sadly, once TV and film stars arrive in Hollywood, for some reason they don't feel they need the black press. The most successful black stars are controlled by white managers, agents and publicists, who don't know the black press and don't feel a need to seek them out. Many of the black stars don't fight for our press, either. Apparently, they don't want to rock the boat or, worse, they want to forget where they came from.

During my launch I showed the black press the movie trailer for the upcoming cheerleading film *Bring It On*, starring newcomer Gabrielle Union. They quickly realized it was about a competition of a hip black squad whose routines were stolen by a white school. Immediately, they wanted to know one thing: Did the black squad win? Instantly, I realized how sensitive we, black people, are about things being stolen from us.

"The black squad wins," I told them. Whew! At that point, I realized if the film was going to be accepted by our community, I had to do something you don't ordinarily do; reveal the ending. Without consulting the studio, I decided to have black stars of the film give away the ending during their interviews. By doing this it enabled our community to go and enjoy the movie without worrying about a possible negative outcome. The studio was surprised when the low budget film opened number one, at $17 million and earned $68 million by the end of the domestic run.

We also organized advance screenings with cheerleading squads in top minority communities around the country. The word-of-mouth within the cheerleading sub-culture nationwide was key because they had a vested interest in the film. My bosses never knew about my unusual approach to publicizing the film until Patrick Goldstein of the *Los Angeles Times* interviewed me about my marketing strategies for the unexpected hit.

The Fast and the Furious, another film we publicized during my first year, was a surprise hit, too. The studio was shocked when the film surpassed the number one film, *Tomb Raider*, opening in the top-ranked position with an unbelievable $40 million and a lifetime gross of $144 million.

Here again was a sub-culture, street racing, which was much bigger and stronger than anyone realized. For that film, I took on the responsibility for the Asian campaign, where the racing phenomenon was the strongest. Nobody was doing anything with the Asian press, so I was pro-active and took it on. RSPR was off to an impressive start. The *Fast and Furious* franchise continues to this day. My company headed up the campaigns for the first three: in 2001 *The Fast and Furious*, my friend, the late John Singleton, directed the second film, *2 Fast, 2 Furious* in 2003, and the third, *The Fast and Furious: Tokyo Drift* in 2006.

RSPR was perfect for me. I loved being an advocate for and fighting for the black press. Since I had a good relationship with Universal's marketing staff, they were willing to listen to my pitches. To be honest, once they appointed me, they trusted me and didn't question my judgment on the black press. They gave me the utmost respect and left it all up to me. I would share with them who and what was good and what wasn't. Of course, they were knowledgeable about the major

African American outlets, like BET, Jet, Ebony and Essence, but that's about it. It was my job to inform them of the other media outlets and their significance. However, the struggle never ended. If the studio agreed, then I would have to fight with the actor's personal publicist. They always gave me grief.

My biggest weapon was the facts. I became the eyes and ears of everything black. The primary point is that most white people don't realize how small but powerful the African American community is. We are only eleven percent of the population. Yet, since we are trendsetters and major moviegoers, we seem much larger than we are. I had to know everything about black history, black organizations, black colleges, black movers and shakers, and, of course, blacks in entertainment.

Our mission wasn't just marketing solely for African American films. Sometimes there are popular black actors in a mainstream film, therefore seeing that film would be of interest to our community. Even if the actor is not the lead, if black folks are aware of a favorite black performer being in the film, it is a key factor when deciding whether to go see it or not. There are also some films with no black actors; however, the film has a universal theme, and we had to make our community aware of those films, too.

Fittingly, one of the first film assignments for my company, Roz Stevenson Public Relations, in 2000 was *The Nutty Professor II: The Klumps*. As was my custom, I worked exclusively with Eddie during the publicity campaign. Universal held the press junket for the film in New York. Still requiring star treatment, Eddie started his interviews an hour after the other cast members that day. His love interest in the film was played by Janet Jackson, whom I knew from years ago when she was a child actress playing Penny on "Good Times."

Eddie's first interview was with *Entertainment Tonight*. Next, we went across the hall where Janet was just completing her interview with *Access Hollywood*. As they were switching rooms, she ran up and hugged him. Over his shoulder she saw me.

"Oh, my goodness, Roz?" she said with a huge smile. I was surprised that she remembered me from "Good Times," which had been over twenty years ago. Surprisingly, as the two of us chatted, she remembered all of our "Good Times" staff members, my kids and all kinds of personal trivia. Eddie stood there like, "What the hell is going on?" We had to let him in on how we knew one another.

Janet's manager, Lindsey Scott, stood there in shock, too. He had given me major grief about doing a photo shoot for the cover of a popular new black magazine called Honey, which was geared toward young Black women ages eighteen to twenty-five. Eventually, we got it done, but not before he made disparaging comments about the publication's low circulation. I had to kindly educate him on the fact that African Americans are only eleven percent of the population; therefore, a publication that is targeted at our community will never have the numbers that a mainstream publication has. More importantly, I reminded him that the black community was Janet's core audience, and they should be served.

I had to do this kind of intervention on behalf of black press all the time. Anyway, once Lindsey realized Janet knew and adored me, he said, "Why didn't you tell me you knew Janet?" I thought, "Why should I have to?" To be honest, I didn't mention it because I would never had imagined that she would have remembered me from so long ago. Apparently, the staff at "Good Times" made a huge impression on her young, impressionable mind. She said, "You always had such beautiful nails and wore the prettiest head wraps."

"I did?" How did she remember that?

RSPR, my company, was also requested to do the African American campaign on Eddie's film *Daddy Daycare* for Sony Pictures in 2003. I was delighted when the film had a successful opening and ended up earning over $100 million, as most of Eddie's films had earned over the years.

In 2007 RSPR was hired by Paramount Pictures to do the African American campaign for Eddie's wild comedy *Norbit*, in which he displayed his genius by playing three distinctly different characters that included *Norbit*, a nerd; Rasputia, a fat girl; and Mr. Wong, a Chinese man.

When I saw an advanced screening of the film, I was concerned that Paramount wanted to release it during the awards season, while Eddie was campaigning for Best Supporting Actor for his dramatic performance as soul singer James "Thunder" Early in *Dreamgirls*.

I felt *Norbit* was a comedic film that would taint the opinion of

Academy voters, because, traditionally, the Academy snubs comedy actors. It wouldn't take much for them not to take Eddie seriously. However, he was on a roll. He had already won the Golden Globe, Screen Actors Guild Award and a Broadcast Film Critics Association Award for his performance. This is usually a good indication that he would be a shoo-in to win the Oscar.

Eddie learned he was nominated for the Academy Award for Best Supporting Actor on January 23, 2007. *Norbit* was released on February 9, 2007 and the awards were given out on February 25. Unfortunately, while the Academy ballots were still out, two Los Angeles Times writers, Robert Welkos, and, surprisingly, an African American, Greg Braxton, wrote scathing articles about Eddie's latest film on February 8, just a few days before the votes were due. Most damaging was the picture in the Los Angeles Times of Eddie as the morbidly obese girl Rasputia in *Norbit.* The cruel headline read: *Is This What a Future Oscar Winner Looks Like?*

The article went on to say the following:

Eddie Murphy's on the verge of an awards season trifecta — his charismatic portrayal of a tragic R&B singer in *Dreamgirls* has already nabbed him a Screen Actors Guild award and a Golden Globe, and he's considered a front-runner for a best supporting Oscar. But the most high-profile image of Murphy these days — while Oscar ballots are still out — is on billboards and in movie trailers wearing a fat suit, garish eye shadow and little else.

Sadly, I believe, the article had everything to do with many Academy members, ultimately, changing their votes from Eddie to Alan Arkin for his unremarkable performance in *Little Miss Sunshine.* When Alan won, it was considered an upset. I was concerned when Eddie's management insisted that *Norbit* be released at that time. In their judgment, his amazing talent for playing multiple characters would help him. Sadly, it had the opposite effect.

As for *Norbit,* despite being critically panned, the comedy was a huge box office success. The movie opened to $34.2 million in the United States and was Eddie's 14th No. 1 box-office opener. In the end the film garnered $159.3 million at the box-office worldwide.

One day I pray he receives recognition by the film industry for his unique ability to play multiple characters. There had been discussion at Universal, when he did the first *Nutty Professor*, to have him nominated for Best Supporting Actor for each of the seven roles that he played. In the meantime, the extraordinarily talented Eddie Murphy keeps on keepin' on.

In our first six months, RSPR's projects were a mixed bag and taught us how to deal with various types of films. In addition to working with *Bring It On, The Fast and the Furious* and *Nutty Professor II: The Klumps*, we worked on *American Pie, Dr. Seuss' How the Grinch Stole Xmas, Meet the Parents, The Adventures of Rocky & Bullwinkle* and *The Family Man*. We had our work cut out for us and we did an admirable job.

In the beginning, I found myself up at 5:00 a.m. and sometimes working until 11:00 p.m. I wanted to make sure everything was right. I would get a jump on my East coast calls early in the morning. Then I found myself working late when it was quiet and there were no interruptions. However, after that first year, I was pretty confident about what I was doing, and I began to cutback and work regular hours.

When my contract was renewed, I began to relax and seek work at other studios, as well. Our reputation for outstanding work had preceded us. Eventually, I also had film projects at Sony Pictures, Paramount Studios, Screen Gems, DreamWorks, New Line, HBO, as well as independent projects. As the projects grew, so did my staff. Eventually, my offices spread to all three of my kids' former bedrooms.

CHAPTER 19:
Didn't See It Coming

Another dream comes true.

Of the more than one hundred films RSPR publicized and promoted from 2000 to 2008, my favorite was a movie that was originally called *Unchain My Heart*, later changed to simply *Ray*, with Jamie Foxx starring in the life story of music great Ray Charles.

I will never forget sitting in a Universal staff meeting, bored to death and about to fall asleep when the department head, Michael Moses, said, "Roz, this week we will have a staff screening for a movie you are going to love. The studio just acquired a film about the life of Ray Charles."

I lit up like a Christmas tree. I, instantly, knew I had hit the jackpot. I always got excited when I learned about a project that was going to be a source of pride and curiosity to the African American community. In this case, because I had seen and hear him many times, I knew, so I was about to jump out of my skin. But first I had to see it.

My staff and I attended an afternoon screening on the studio lot. At that time, my staff consisted of my son Teron, my goddaughter Marissa Burton and a former BET staffer, Sharon Pinnix. When I first witnessed Jamie Foxx's performance, it was so phenomenal that I got chills. Right away I felt, "Oh, my God. Jamie Foxx is going to win an Oscar!"

I have always been a huge Ray Charles fan, so I knew Jamie's depiction of him was dead-on. I was curious how my young staff felt about.

As we left the screening room, my twenty-three-year old son said, "Mom, that was one of the best movies I have ever seen!" The others concurred. I was so excited because I knew, then, it wasn't just me.

The campaign we mounted for *Ray* was a dream come true. Jamie Foxx was willing to do everything we needed him to do. He was on the cover of every black publication and was available for all major interviews and screenings. Leading up to the film's opening in October 2004, we began early showings for high profile opinion-makers and communicators who covered every facet of the black community; Congressional Black Caucus, for 1,500 politicians with an introduction from Jamie and the late Julian Bond in Washington D.C.; National Association of Black Journalist for 400 in Washington D.C. with Jamie dancing up the aisle at the film's conclusion; National Black Arts Festival for 500 with a Q&A with Kerry Washington and Regina King in Atlanta, GA; and Gospel Music Workshop of American for four hundred radio gospel broadcasters at the convention in Kansas City, MO.

Jamie was joyful and grateful as he introduced the movie to the audiences at each major event. The movie stood on its own and played beautifully everywhere we went. By the time *Ray* premiered at the Toronto Film Festival, we were the toast of the town.

Throughout the entire marketing campaign, Jamie would welcome audiences; however, he refused to sit and watch the film. He waited until the night of the world premiere in Los Angeles. Once he saw it, he cried. Kerry Washington and Regina King, who played his wife and love interest in the film, comforted him and said, "You knew you were great. What are you crying about?"

Jamie said, "Y'all know I couldn't see what I was doing." Apparently, to assist in playing Ray's blindness authentically, he wore prostetics throughout the filming, which prevented him from seeing clearly.

To be honest, all the cast members saw it at various times, and each one of them cried. *Ray* was a powerful film. Central to the phenomenal success was Jamie's incredible portrayal of Ray Charles. He perfectly emulated his blindness, speaking voice, singing, piano playing and his walk. In the end, he was nominated for and won the 2005 Academy Award for Best Actor in a Motion Picture.

During the campaign I met Sharon Warren, a first-time actress from Alabama, who beautifully played Ray's mother in the film. She had been cast by director Taylor Hackford when he read actors in Atlanta, Georgia. The casting of this role was of particular concern to Ray Charles, who described his mother as a very thin woman who was rural, uneducated, yet strong and determined not to let his blindness cripple him. He didn't want any Hollywood type playing a glossed over version of his mother. Sharon fit the bill. She gave a "stand out" performance that many felt might earn her a Best Supporting Actress nomination.

Since *Ray*, both Regina and Kerry's careers have soared. Regina is the recipient of an Academy Award, a Golden Globe Award, and four Primetime Emmy Awards, the most for an African American performer. She also produces and directs and was named one of Time Magazine's 100 Most Influential People in the World in 2019. While Kerry, who is also a busy actress, producer and director, gained wide public recognition for starring as crisis management expert Olivia Pope in the ABC drama series "Scandal."

My husband Robert has been a voting member of the Motion Picture Academy's Makeup Branch since 1995. We had never tried to attend the Academy Awards, but this time I insisted we try to go. Since there were only three thousand seats and there were more than six thousand Academy members, the attendees are selected by lottery. In January 2005 I put our name in for it and sent in a check for $700 for two orchestra seats. Three weeks later, I got a letter returning my check, telling me, unfortunately, I had not been selected. Not one to give up easily, I called the Academy and said I wanted to change my seating choice to the mezzanine, where I would probably have a better chance. The gentleman kindly explained to me that the lottery was already completely done and the best he could do is put me on the waiting list. I told him fine, please put our name on the list. He advised that if they had seats for us, on the weekend before the Academy Awards, they would call us. He warned that they would not leave a message on the voicemail. If someone did not answer, they would go to the next person. I had my fingers crossed. I already had my dress made, so I had to go!

As luck would have it, the weekend before the awards, I went to spend the three-day holiday with Robert in San Bernardino County at the Morongo Resort. It was President's Day weekend, and he was working on the film *Jarhead*, which starred Jamie Foxx, in nearby El Centro.

In my haste, I forgot to forward our home phone to my cell phone. I was absolutely outdone with myself. When I drove home that Tuesday, it was pouring rain. Robert called to see if I had gotten home safely and while we were talking, the phone clicked. I switched over and a voice said, "This is the Academy. If you still want two orchestra seats, I have them for you!" Oh, my God! I wrote a new check and I sped over to the Motion Picture Academy office in Beverly Hills to get them.

To top it off, on that very same afternoon at the Publicists Guild luncheon, the film was nominated for and won for Best Marketing Campaign of the Year. When my boss Michael Moses went up to accept the award, he said, "Roz Stevenson, please come up here and get this award. You were determined that every African American in this country was going to know about this amazing movie."

Well, I wasn't there. I was so excited to get the Oscar tickets that I rushed to pick them up wearing a warm-up suit. Once I got there, it dawned on me that I was supposed to go to the Publicists Guild event right down the street at the Beverly Hilton Hotel. But it was too late, and I wasn't dressed properly. Oh, well, you can't make everything.

That Sunday Robert and I proudly strolled down the red carpet and sat with anticipation in our orchestra seats. When they finally announced that the winner for Best Actor was Jamie Foxx, I stood up and screamed and applauded like a proud mother, just like I had for Sidney Poitier so many, many years ago. It was a full circle moment!

Jamie Foxx had gone all the way. What I had predicted the very first day I saw his performance had come true. It was the most rewarding campaign I ever experienced. Nothing will ever top *Ray*, the thrilling campaign and, finally, the moment when I saw Jamie Foxx, holding the Oscar in his hand. I thanked God for His faithfulness to me.

CHAPTER 20:
The Black Oscars
Hollywood can be a lonely place.

The "Black Oscars" and the "Black Emmys" are how we all referred to the "Tree of Life Awards," which took place the night before the Oscars and Emmys. It started in 1981 by three black businessmen from the east coast that included Al Nellum, Eugene Jackson and Isaac Sutton.

They came to Los Angeles twice a year and sponsored a black-tie event honoring black actors, filmmakers, and behind-the-scenes talent, who were nominated for the Oscar and the Emmy. Additionally, they honored black films and talent, which they deemed outstanding, even though they had been overlooked by the mainstream. The evening was always very intimate, maybe two hundred people tops, and it was always a "Who's Who" of Black Hollywood.

The event was also always classy and offered much needed encouragement to black stars, who rarely joined together for special events. Everyone was always overjoyed to see one another and thrilled to have an intimate setting where we could break bread and show love and appreciation for one another. Very often the recognized actors were overtaken with emotion and cried, because they were with "family" and could express their true feelings. Blacks in the film industry have a lonely struggle and even the biggest stars always felt delighted to share this special time together. They were happy that someone cared enough to recognize their hard work and bring them together with their African American peers.

The very first event Robert and I attended was a cocktail party at The Brown Derby. However, it quickly elevated to an elegant sit-down dinner at the Regent Beverly Wilshire Hotel. The invitations were very impressive in black with gold, embossed print. On the back it listed the most respected names in Black Hollywood as participants of the event, called "Friends of the Black Nominees." For example, the 1995 "friends" included Maya Angelou, Jheryl Busby, Reuben and Linda Cannon, Bernie Casey, Ivan and Berlie Dixon, Louis Gossett, Jr., Robert and Donna Guillaume, Charles and Anne Johnson, Robert and Sheila Johnson, Quincy Jones, Albert and Velma Nellum, Debbie Allen and Norman Nixon, Sidney and Joanna Poitier and Cicely Tyson.

It was a highly sought-after, strictly invitational event and, initially, there was no cost involved. As years went on, honorees and their guests received complimentary seating; however, the other invited attendees were charged, because the list continually grew. Everybody wanted to be there.

As was the custom, all previous honorees continued to be invited guests for each event twice a year. My husband Robert was nominated for two Emmys in 1985 for Outstanding Hair stylist for "The Jesse Owens Story" and "The Atlanta Child Murder". And he won for "The Jesse Owens Story". From that time on, we attended in February for the pre-Oscar dinner and again in September for the pre-Emmy event. The honorees often said in their acceptance speech that it didn't matter what happened the next night at the actual Academy Awards or the Emmy Awards, because they had already been honored by their own in a very special and respectful way.

One of the biggest challenges the Master of Ceremonies had was getting everyone's attention. Everybody would be meeting, greeting and networking like they were at a family reunion. I remember the year that Whoopi Goldberg attended when *The Color Purple* had eleven Oscar nominations. As was her custom at that time, she was dressed casually, rather than in dressy attire. During the reception she came up to Robert and me and whispered, "Hey, who are these brothers? This is really nice. If I had known it, I might have dressed up more. But you know me, when I get up in the morning, I put on something functional."

The awarded honorees were given the "Tree of Life" statue, which was a treasure. It was a tall, black hand-carved African art object, created by the Makonde tribe of Tanzania and Mozambique. It was an ancient family symbol expressing unity, togetherness and the struggle for survival.

We were there for many memorable evenings, but one that stood out involved Will Smith. When he received the "Tree of Life Award" for his starring role in *Ali*, he dedicated his award to his dad, who was in attendance that night. In giving it to his father, he shared a story about how, as a kid growing up in Philadelphia, his father had a refrigeration repair business. He and his brother always grumbled and complained about the hard work their military-trained dad required them to do. Normally, it entailed assisting with the refrigeration equipment and wiring. However, one summer, his father informed them that they were going to knock down the entire brick wall in front and rebuild his office building.

"What? How are we supposed to do that?!" an exasperated Will asked. The father said, "Son, we are going to tear it down and build it back up brick by brick." With that he gave them sludge hammers and they, begrudgingly, began to demolish the building. Over the next several months, after they tore it down, they dug a new gutter, poured cement and began the long, slow process of re-building the wall. They would lay each brick on the cement and check to be sure it was level before moving on to the next brick. Eventually, by the end of the summer, before their eyes they saw an incredible sight: a new office building.

Will said this was the same patience and tenacity he applied to the overwhelming task of playing Muhammad Ali, executing the role slowly, but surely, brick by brick, he did it. He thanked his father for teaching him how to face a challenge. By the time he finished telling that story, Will, his father and all of us were in tears.

For everyone in attendance, the uniqueness of the event was always appreciated. However, by 2005, all of the original organizers had gone their separate ways, except for Al Nellum, who was having serious health challenges. That was the year that there were two African Americans up for Best Actor: Jamie Foxx for *Ray* and Don Cheadle for *Hotel Rwanda*.

There was so much excitement in the air throughout Black

Hollywood. Despite the rivalry the media tried to create between Jamie and Don, they embraced one another as they traveled through the awards season journey together. That evening was extra special, and, as always, the nominees were so happy to be honored by "their own."

That last "Tree of Life Awards" dinner was held at the Century Plaza Hotel. As the marketing company for *Ray*, I purchased tables for my staff and my family. I wanted everyone to share in the impending victory "up close and personal." I wanted them all to share in this moment attended that special moment in our Hollywood careers. It meant the world to them to have all the nominees come to our table to meet and greet them. In addition, they got an opportunity to be among the "who's who" of Black Hollywood for an elegant, intimate affair. The next night, when Jamie won, it was extra sweet for all of us.

After twenty-four years of honoring Black Hollywood, "The Tree of Life Awards" came to an end. In the opening page of the program, Mr. Nellum printed the Statement of Purpose:

> *We began the practice of coming together to honor Black Emmy and Black Oscar nominees in the hope that this recognition would not only recognize their accomplishments, but also serve to inspire and encourage the rest of us. Throughout this time, we have tried to focus on those values considered important to us and to the future of our people. We have argued the necessity of presenting positive images; the need to open opportunities at every level of the industry and the importance of telling our own stories the way we see them; and the way we know them to be.*
>
> *We have also stressed the need for preparedness and togetherness; the need to study our craft and sharpen our skills; the need to reach out to one another; support one another and to give back to the community.*
>
> *Tonight, we especially applaud those of you who recognize the importance of these principles. We ask those of you who are joining us for the first time to remember that we are your family, here not only to applaud you but to advise, assist and support you whenever you might need it.*

Early, during the marketing campaign for Ray, I said to Essence

Magazine editor Cori Murray, "Your magazine seriously needs to consider having a presence in Hollywood during the awards season, similar to Vanity Fair magazine."

At that time, there was nothing so special and intimate as the "Tree of Life Awards" for African-Americans in the filmmaking community. In recent years Essence has begun to hold an Oscar week event for black women in Hollywood. They are wonderful, but nothing will ever compare to the very special dinners given twice a year by "The Men from the East" who gave us the "Tree of Life Awards".

CHAPTER 21:
Denzel as American Gangster

A time and season for all things.

When I first saw the crime drama *American Gangster*, I felt it had all the makings of another *Ray* experience for my company. However, it wasn't long before I realized we weren't going to be able to duplicate that campaign. While Denzel Washington, the star of the film, was incredible as drug kingpin Frank Lucas, sadly, he wasn't available to us for any advance publicity. At that time, he was busy editing another film, which he had directed and starred in called *The Great Debaters*.

American Gangster was released at the end of the year on November 2, 2007, and the release date for *The Great Debaters* was ten-weeks later, on Christmas Day. Denzel knew our gangster movie could stand on its own, but *The Great Debaters* needed all the help it could get. I was disappointed that both films were being released so close to one another, because I was a huge fan of both projects.

I tried to acquire *The Great Debaters* as a project, but it went to another agency in New York. I had major concerns about its release date. Since it focused on a black college and had a limited audience appeal, I thought it might have a better chance if it was released during the Martin Luther King Holiday weekend when colleges had resumed from Christmas break. As it turned out, when the film didn't meet expectations during its opening weekend, the film company scrambled to do last ditch publicity prior to the King Holiday, but it was too late. *The Great Debaters* was highly acclaimed, yet it opened in eleventh place with $6 million and ended with only $30 million total take.

For the little time we did have with Denzel, he was extremely accommodating during *American Gangster's* two-day press junket and premiere, but that was the only time we had him. We did a special advanced screening, as we had for *Ray* at the National Association of Black Journalists convention in Las Vegas. *American Gangster* was the hottest ticket at the convention and the screening went through the roof. However, the film's subject matter wasn't appropriate for any of the other organizations we had tabbed for *Ray*. We did conduct a well-received screening in New Orleans, Louisiana, at the national convention for an African American police organization called NOBLE (National Association of Black Law Enforcement Executives).

Nevertheless, *American Gangster* was the hottest ticket in town, opened number one with $43 million, ended with $130 million domestically and $266 million worldwide. However, as far as awards attention, it wasn't a contender, except for the late, great Ruby Dee, who was nominated for Best Supporting Actress. She had played Denzel's mother, and amazingly she was nominated for less than twelve-minutes on screen. The clincher scene for her character was when she abruptly slapped her disrespectful son, Frank. That moment always got a huge reaction from audiences.

After *American Gangster*, I considered retiring. I was sixty-five-years old and tasks that had previously been simple were no longer easy. When I would go on press assignments and meet young press people who knew my kids, I felt old. Because I have always wanted to do my best, I felt stressed all the time. I began to yearn for peace, quiet and no drama. God was tapping me on my shoulder letting me know it was time to pack it in. I decided I would make the move when my Universal contract ran out in June of 2008.

At that point, I had two staff members, whom I adored. One was my niece Brandy Stowers, who had recently graduated from Cal State Long Beach with a degree in journalism. I also had hired a professional photographer-turned-publicist Steven Williams, who was also a computer genius. His I.T. skills had proven to be a much-appreciated help to my business. However, at this point, I needed to scale things back to just one person — me. I finished the last eight months by myself. No payroll. No hassles. I didn't take on any new campaigns except for fulfilling my responsibilities for the Universal's films.

Simply put, I was tired. I was tired of waking up each morning with demanding campaigns dancing around in my head. I am naturally task-oriented, so I have always wanted to do everything with excellence. I had had a beautiful career. I couldn't keep going and doing the incredible work I demanded of myself. I knew it was time to wrap things up. My company had been successful, so I wanted to leave on a high.

As I reflected on the film projects I worked on, I realized that great projects come only every now and then. However, the challenging, loser projects that caused me so much grief kept coming. At this point in my life, they weren't worth the time and effort.

I came to realize that no matter how hard you work in marketing films, you cannot fool the moviegoers into seeing a film that is lousy. Pretty much, the public can tell by the movie trailer whether it is worth seeing or not. A successful marketing campaign is measured by the opening and second weeks' box office results. Once the word-of-mouth takes over, it is out of our hands. Today, with texting and cell phones, a film can be deemed a "hit or miss" during an advance screening as audience members begin to notify their friends if a film is worth "the cost of admission" or not. Once the word gets out, there's not much else you can do. Also, with social media platforms like Facebook, Instagram and Twitter, the marketing challenges are even greater.

The members of the African American entertainment press were devastated when I announced my impending retirement. They were my friends and my children. I felt obligated to leave them in good hands. I promised to get someone good to take my place, which I did. Sonya Ede, an African American publicist on staff for many years at Paramount Pictures, turned out to be an excellent choice.

When the time came, June 6, 2008, the African American entertainment press joined forces with my colleagues at Universal Pictures Marketing to host a wonderful retirement party for me at The Grill Restaurant at Universal Studios. To my surprise, press also came from New York, Atlanta, Washington, D.C., Chicago, Oakland and Seattle to wish me well. Wonderful tributes were given, and many media outlets ran stories praising my career and retirement.

With retirement, it was now time for me to relax and enjoy the ride.

Time to try new things and imagine other possibilities. It was time to play and expect adventures. It was time to make new plans, to nap without guilt and take time out just for me. I couldn't wait. For me, it would be a time to pursue that thing in life that meant the most to me – my family.

As I look back over my life and career, I think about one of my favorite spirituals that says:

I have had some good days,
I've had some bad days,
I've had some hill to climb.
But when I look around and I think things over,
God has been good me,
More than this old world has ever been.
I won't complain.

Robert retired six months after me in January 2009 after working forty years non-stop in the industry. Today Robert and I wake up every morning and we reflect on our jobs well done. It doesn't get much better than that.

CHAPTER 22:
Just When We Thought

Our work was not done.

In 2011, three years after I retired, I was hired as a consultant by Stephanie Kluft, a former colleague from Universal, now a VP at Disney. She hired me to supervise the national 12-city publicity tour for *The Help* with actress Octavia Spencer, director Tate Taylor and at some points the filmmakers and all the other cast members.

Since I had the assistance of the local agencies in each city, my responsibility was to get the talent to and from the airports, hotels, screenings, dinners or receptions and interviews. We traveled first-class and had accommodations in five-star luxury hotels. The cities included San Francisco, Chicago, Boston, Miami, New York, Philadelphia, Washington D.C., Atlanta, Jackson, Dallas, Las Vegas and Los Angeles. The great thing was they also enlisted my husband Robert's services to act as hair stylist for Octavia throughout, as well as for Viola Davis, Emma Stone, Jessica Chastain and Allison Janney in some cities. We had the greatest time with Tate and Octavia, because it was exciting to see how their careers had shot up to the top since Robert first met them on *A Time to Kill*, fifteen years ago when they were both staff assistants.

The entire cast of *The Help* came to Jackson for the premiere event, which had an after party, hosted by then governor, Haley Barbour, at the governor's mansion. The Who's Who of Mississippi was there, including Charles Evers, brother of slain civil rights leader, Medgar

Evers. We stayed at the Fairview Inn, which is an antebellum mansion turned into a charming bed and breakfast. We laughed that the ghost of the white masters from the past must have been spooked by black folks like Robert and me enjoying all the amenities at the magnificent inn.

The tour took six weeks to complete and we had many remarkable experiences, however we were exhausted when we got back to Los Angeles. That was when it hit me, no matter how inviting the opportunity, I was too old to roll.

Robert got pulled back to work on films, too. In 2012 director Lee Daniels director Lee Daniels appealed to him to serve as the co-head hair stylist on *The Butler.* He had never met Robert; however, his reputation preceded him. After some resistance, Robert accepted, and ultimately won another award for his work on the film. For me, the biggest joy for me was seeing Lee Daniels again.

I knew him years before as the manager for a young actress, Kimberly Russell *(Head of the Class)*, who starred in *Ghost Dad* as Bill Cosby's oldest daughter. I had spent time with Lee when he wanted to be sure she was included in the publicity efforts and not get lost in Bill's spotlight. He had taken me to dinner on Melrose, and when he had an issue with his credit card, I brushed it off and offered to take care of it on my expense account, and he was grateful.

When I arrived on *The Butler's* film location, they were shooting in a cemetery and it was blistering hot. When Lee saw me, he abruptly stopped production. "Cut!" he screamed. He went on to introduce me to the entire cast and crew. He humbly said that I had been wonderful to him a long, long time ago when, "I didn't have any money."

He then ushered me into a three-sided tent with cold air blowing where I spent the afternoon chatting with the stars Oprah Winfrey and Forest Whitaker. My husband rolled his eyes and sarcastically said, "Aren't you something! I'm running around here like a Hebrew slave, pouring in sweat, and you're sitting in the cool lap of luxury!" It wasn't my fault that Lee adored me. Lee continued to treat me like royalty each and every time I came on the set.

In 2013, Robert was again lured back into another film project when our friend, director Tate Taylor, asked him to style the wigs for Chadwick Boseman, the star of *Get on Up*, the James Brown story. From day one, Robert and Chadwick got along beautifully. Chad was so grateful that Robert came out of retirement to do his wigs. He loved hearing Robert's tales of working in Hollywood "back-in-the day" with stars like Richard Pryor and Eddie Murphy. Chad had a contagious laugh and a smile that would light up the room. The hours were grueling, but Robert loved the creative challenge of doing so many old-school looks, which were much appreciated by Chad and the filmmakers, one being Mick Jagger of the Rolling Stones.

Though Chad was taller than James Brown, he convincingly spoke and sang just like him. Chad had a keen ear and could expertly lip sync James Brown's famous lyrics. Prior to filming, the only thing that concerned Chad was the fact that he wasn't a good dancer. However, he miraculously perfected James' moves with the help of Aakomon Jones, a choreographer, who trained him like an NFL player by first developing his abs and strengthening his legs. They worked together for months prior to the start of production. Once production started, Chad had mastered James Brown's strenuous dance routines, even the splits.

Robert first met Chad when he went to measure him and to discuss the wigs at a dance studio in Burbank where he was deeply immersed in the choreography. The two of them shared admiration for each other from that very first meeting. As I had done so many times before, once production started, I spent lots of time on the locations in Natchez and Jackson, Mississippi. I got to know Chad and meet his parents. The best part was watching Chad's performances as the God-father of Soul. He was amazing as he did the song and dance routines with the same intensity for each and every take. When I saw how convincing he was, it reminded me of Jamie Foxx's turn as Ray Charles.

We were anticipating the release of the film; however, when friends at Universal invited me to an advance screening of it, I was concerned because I found the story confusing and hard to follow, as it jumped around from the past to the present. In the end, the reviews for *Get on Up* were lukewarm, with the exception of rave accolades attributed to the outstanding performances of Chadwick Boseman, Nelsan Ellis, Viola Davis, Octavia Spencer and other fine actors in the film.

In 2016 Robert was excited when he had a chance to speak with his young friend, Chad, prior to the release of the highly anticipated film, *Black Panther.* Robert's youngest sister, Joanetta Stowers, was Chad's makeup artist on *Marshall*, in which he portrayed Thurgood Marshall, the first African American Supreme Court justice. He insisted she get Robert on the phone and she connected them. Robert had an opportunity to express how proud he was of him and his soaring career.

Today we are deeply grieved over the untimely passing of Chadwick Boseman on August 28, 2020, at just forty-three years old. Robert is eternally grateful to have been a part of a career of this young man who has gone down in cinematic history. The fact that Chad starred as the *Black Panther*, the Marvel film which became a worldwide phenomenon, was his supreme gift to us and the universe. Even more unbelievable is that he did it while secretly battling colon cancer. We are amazed by his bravery and deeply saddened over his loss. Chad will never be forgotten.

The last film Robert agreed to work on was a little-known film called *Bolden*. It paid extraordinarily well, but it went on forever. In 2015 when Robert started experiencing serious health challenges, he left before the film ended. It is hard to say goodbye to Hollywood. But at some point, it is time to sit down and call it a wrap.

CHAPTER 23:
Obama, Mama and Me

History in the making.

One of the greatest events for us post-retirement was on November 4, 2008 when Barack Obama was the first African American elected President of the United States. I was, and still am, a huge supporter of his presidency. My home office is a virtually a museum dedicated to *my* President Barack Obama and First Lady Michelle Obama.

After his historic win, I became obsessed with attending the inauguration. I wrote letters to each and every California Congressman and woman trying to secure tickets. Finally, my husband gave me a reality check, "Roz, even if you got tickets, you won't be able to stand that long outdoors in freezing cold weather." He was right. So, eventually I purchased tickets for a brunch viewing party taking place at the historic Willard Hotel on Pennsylvania Avenue, two blocks from the White House. It proved to be ideal, because it was comfortable, warm inside with delicious food. The event was full of people we had never known, but immediately bonded with over the historic event. At the moment when he was declared President, the whole room erupted with cheers and applause. We hugged and cried with complete strangers. Additionally, we bought tickets to attend the inaugural Illinois Ball, a formal dinner and party which took place at the Renaissance Washington Hotel later that night.

Since hotel accommodations had been non-existent or had sky-rocketing prices, I got in touch with my cousin, Rev. Rodger Reed, who lived in Maryland, and he agreed to let us stay at his home. It was great to share time with my cousin, who is a Chicago native, his family and two of his former school buddies who stayed there, too. We enjoyed celebrating the historic time with our family, eating home-made meals, particularly my cousin Shirley's crabcakes, which she is famous for. Another great thing was that their son-in-law had a limo service, so he drove us to and from the key events.

We also took part in activities with "The Calbamas," a group of our Ladera Heights neighbors, which was organized by our friends, Doctors Jeffrey and Jean Clements. We joined them in D.C. for a church service and other events at the National Mall and the Smithsonian Museum. It was definitely a once in a lifetime, proud, joyful moment for African Americans.

The next morning, still walking on Cloud Nine, a group of us went by train to the black-owned, popular Ben's Chili House, just because Obama had eaten there a few days before. We waited in the long line in front of a huge red/white & blue mural of Obama, all the while interacting with other happy, optimistic folks from all over the country. We then took the train to the "Newseum" which is a museum launched by the founder of USA Today, that displays the front-page for that day of newspapers from around the country and the world. The headlines for Obama's Inauguration were varied and magnificent. While there, I was approached by a reporter for the local NBC News, who interviewed me to share my enthusiasm about my inauguration experience. Seeing my interview air several times that day was the icing on the cake.

There were a whirlwind of exciting events going on. One I didn't want to miss took place the day before the inauguration. It was a star-studded special taping of the "Oprah Winfrey Show." My friend and I were among more than two thousand enthusiastic Barack Obama supporters and Oprah Winfrey fans, who packed in the Kennedy Center. The guys dropped us off for the all-female audience event. We had great seats in the orchestra section about six rows from the stage. I waved at celebrity friends Angela Bassett and Debbie Allen, who were sitting near us.

The show featured performances by Seal, Faith Hill and the Black-Eyed Peas', will.i.am, and appearances by such celebrities as Ashton

Kutcher and Demi Moore. The finale of the show was the performance of "America's Song," written by will.i.am and David Foster for Obama's inauguration. Singers Mary J. Blige, Faith Hill and Seal joined them singing, with U2's Bono taking part on video. Vice President-elect Joseph Biden Jr. and wife Jill appeared on the show as well.

The party continued as we flew back to Los Angeles on a flight filled with Obama supporters who were convinced that "Yes, We Can!" do any and all things from that moment on.

Time with Mama

One of the greatest joys of retirement was having more time to spend with my mom, who was eighty-eight years old at the time. I remember signing her up at the senior center near her home in Compton, so she could take part in some of their wonderful group activities and outings.

One of the first events that she and I participated in was a bus trip to see "The Glory of Christmas," an annual holiday stage production at the famous Crystal Cathedral in Anaheim, California. Years before mom and I had seen it and we both loved the incredible staging, elaborate costumes and the traditional songs of Christmas sung with a full orchestration. The afternoon trip also included an early dinner, so we were in for a treat with a full day of fun.

When I got mom to the location, the bus was already filling up. I rolled her up to the bus in her wheelchair, which we always took on outings, so we could move faster once we got to our destination. The courteous bus driver helped get mom to her front row seat on the bus as I folded up her chair and the driver's assistant loaded it under the bus. I rushed on the bus and when I went to sit down with mom, I heard someone ask, "Is that Roz?" Another person shouted, "Yes, that's Roz!" I looked up and the entire bus was filled with many of my former high school classmates. I whispered to my mother, "Oh, my God, mom! I thought this was your bus. This is MY BUS!" Mama couldn't stop laughing.

It was a wonderful reunion with friends, many of whom I hadn't seen in over forty-five years. In case I had any doubts about it being "my bus," the driver put on a CD of Al Green's Greatest Hits and I joined everyone else swaying from side to side, snapping our fingers and singing along to every song. The dinner was great, and the production was outstanding. It was a fabulous trip.

Another one of my favorite outings with mama was going to see a stage production of *The Color Purple* at the Music Center in downtown Los Angeles. Jeanette Bayardelle played Celie, the lead actress in the play, and was a friend of my goddaughter, Solombra Ingram. Jeanette was kind enough to give mama and me orchestra seats, as well as backstage passes to meet the cast afterwards. Mama loved great singing, so when she met the cast after the show, she cried uncontrollably. After the performance she asked me to take her to favorite downtown spot, Philippe's Restaurant, famous for French dipped corn beef sandwiches. It was located at 1001 N. Alameda, just minutes away from her former job at the Los Angeles County Registrar's office, where she had been a supervisor for many years.

When we arrived, we were lucky to get the very first spot in the parking lot. Mama didn't think she needed the wheelchair, so I got her walker out. It was a short, but steep walk to the entrance, and she soon realized she couldn't make it. Luckily, someone who was leaving saw us struggling. I asked if he could assist me by getting her wheelchair out of my car; he agreed, and I popped the trunk with my key. Normally, mama would have too much pride to use the chair, but she was so glad when she was able to sit down. The man put her walker away, as we thanked him profusely. She ordered her favorite, a huge corn beef sandwich, however she could barely eat half. We took the rest home, and it was another good day.

Mama had been a world traveler, so as she got older, she would get antsy and just wanted to go anywhere. Since she and my mother-in-law, Fannie, loved to gamble, I would take the two of them on overnight trips to Pechanga, located south of Los Angeles in Temecula. We would leave home after the evening traffic, have dinner when we arrived, go to relax in the suite, then head out to the casino floor. Mama and Fannie loved the slot machines. They would play until they were ready to drop. We would sleep in late and then order a sumptuous breakfast from room service. They felt as though they had gone to the French Riviera. After gambling some more, we would grab some lunch and head back home. It makes me laugh when I picture those two sitting in the casino, smiling at those "one armed bandits."

We had many more enjoyable experiences however the ultimate was mama's ninetieth birthday celebration. Fifty-five of her best friends joined us for a home-cooked breakfast at her house. Then they boarded the luxury bus waiting outside her home. It swept them away to her favorite spot, Pechanga Resort & Casino, for a day of gambling and a birthday lunch. We had fun games and prizes on the bus as we headed to our destination.

On the way back, we played a Tyler Perry movie, *Madea Goes to Jail*, which the old folks loved. They laughed, cursed and screamed out loud at the screen, as Madea did her wild and crazy deeds. We also arranged for mama to receive a congratulatory birthday letter from President Barack Obama and First Lady Michelle Obama. We could not have made her happier.

Unfortunately, in June 2011, mom was hospitalized for a blood-clot. To our surprise, after four days in the hospital, she peacefully made her transition. It was Father's Day and I had gone to visit her around 8:00 p.m. She was experiencing severe discomfort in her stomach. However, when the male nurse suggested giving her morphine, she waved her finger at him and said emphatically, "No morphine!" By the time I got back home, they called and said she had passed away. I thought, "How can that be? She was still giving orders." We had a remarkable Celebration of Life service for her at her long-time church, Bel-Vue Presbyterian.

My Family and Me

I will always cherish my times with mom, who was all about family. Likewise, I have always been a big lover of my family. One way I show my love is through preparing holiday meals, as they had been done by my parents.

Robert and Roz Stevenson's clan now numbers fourteen; including: Jason with Kai Gordon, his son Sage, his grandson Nellon Johnson; Kendra with husband Willie, their daughter Kambria; Damon with his wife Liz, son Valentino a.k.a Peanut, their daughters Dayna and Delaney; Teron and his son Aman. Just like when I taught Sunday School, I love having my grandchildren perform during the holidays. I create Christmas productions and arrange costumes for them to perform for family and friends. Because, most of all, I want them to understand that "Jesus is the Reason for the Season."

My family is filled with creative energy. Robert is no exception. Four years before he retired, he began drawing on movie sets as a way of passing time during long production days. At the end of the day, he would throw his drawings in the trash. However, when impressed colleagues began to retrieve them, he was pleasantly surprised. To encourage his efforts, co-workers bought him an artist sketch book and art supplies. He tossed out his spiral notebook and began to create his works of art in earnest.

Fueled by the positive responses of an ever-growing group of onlookers, he began drawing everywhere he went – on poorly lit movie sets, on airplanes, in the makeup trailer, in hotel rooms and in the serenity of our home. Before he realized it, he had more than eight hundred drawings. Today his creative juices continue to flow and there seems to be no end to the delightful images he creates. God had given him another gift!

As he embarked on retirement, he had his first art show at the Museum of African American Art, hosted by Samuel L. Jackson. He presented 42 lithography in a show entitled *Head Trips: Art as Seen Through the Eyes of a Hollywood Hairstylist*. His unique collection featured animated portraits of men, women and children with intricately drawn hairstyles and hair accessories. Through his artistic eyes, he recognized very keenly how people use hair designs, hats, wraps and ribbons to adorn themselves, express themselves and, in many cases, identify who they are. Today he continues to draw and most recently created a collection of all-occasion cards.

As for me, after I retired, I was pleased to be honored for my career accomplishments. On January 1, 2014, I received the Trailblazer Award at the annual "Night of Tributes" given by the Pan African Film Festival in collaboration with the African American Film Critics Association, founded by Gil Robertson, one of my former press colleagues.

It took place at the opulent Taglyan Complex in Hollywood where the Grand Ballroom features a stain glass ceiling, so magnificent it takes your breath away.

I was recognized for my groundbreaking role in making films' hits at the box office. The award was presented to me by Sonya Ede, the publicist who had taken over my business, and Sandra Varner, my friend and one of my favorite journalists from Northern California. My family and longtime friends shared the experience with me.

Others who were honored that evening included Jeff Clanagan of Code Black Enterprises, who got the Pioneer Award; veteran actor Charles Dutton, who received the Lifetime Achievement Award; young actor Tequan Richmond, who received the Rising Star Award; and Emayatzy Corinealdi, the female Rising Star Award, as well. The presenters included actor Isaiah Washington, PAFF executive director Ayuko Babu and the late actress Ja'Net DuBois of "Good Times" fame.

I was excited to see publicist-turned-renowned filmmaker Ava DuVernay there to present Ryan Coogler. Both have gone on to have soaring careers in the motion picture industry.

At the event Coogler was receiving high praise for directing the movie *Fruitvale Station* and the upcoming film *Creed*. Not surprisingly, today he surpassed all expectations as the director of the international blockbuster, Marvel's *Black Panther*, with an all-star cast led by the late-great Chadwick Boseman.

Prior to becoming a filmmaker, Ava had been a colleague, who ran a public relations firm similar to mine. However, after winning top prize at the Sundance film festival in 2012 for writing and directing an independent film, *Middle of Nowhere*, she parlayed that success into directing the acclaimed film *Selma* that year, which put her on the map and earned her Oscar nods. She was nominated for an Oscar once again for her next project, the documentary *13th* on privatizing prisons. The documentary won her two Primetime Emmys, including Outstanding Documentary, Nonfiction, and Outstanding Writing for a Nonfiction Program. These days there is no stopping Ava. She has a great TV series on OWN, "Queen Sugar," and was lauded for the Netflix miniseries "When They See Us," about the Central Park Five. Ava has had one amazing accomplishment after another.

EPILOGUE

Even in retirement, Sunday continues to be our favorite day. Robert is glad that he finally has the time to serve. He first signed up to be an Ambassador at our church, West Angeles Church of God in Christ. He loves greeting parishioners at "his door" in the magnificent five thousand seat cathedral. He has also been selected to be a Deacon, a responsibility he takes very seriously. I sing in the Women's Choir and served as Robert's business manager for his all-occasion cards, which have been sold at our church as a successful fundraiser during the holiday season.

Together, we are members of the Married Couples for Christ organization at our church. Each year the group reads a Christian book on marriage and discuss the challenges presented. This year's book is *What Did You Expect? Redeeming the Realities of Marriage* by Paul David Tripp. We have very spirited discussions as we share our opinions among those newly married and "old hats" like Robert and me. In February 2020, we hosted a Valentine's dinner at our home for the group. We had a potluck New Orleans cuisine, featuring all the favorites from that region.

I am also active in "I'm Every Woman" (IEW), which is a Christian book club for women founded by Solombra Ingram. She is "one of my daughters," whom I met on the set of *Ghost Dad* when she was a production assistant, and I was the publicist. She hails from Columbia,

South Carolina, and is a Spelman graduate, who came to California in search of a career in the entertainment business.

Not long after she arrived, she joined Maranatha Community Church. Covered by her Christian walk, she set out to conquer her Hollywood dreams. Over the years, she found employment as an executive assistant for Debbie Allen, Arsenio Hall, Sinbad, Flex Alexander, Toni Braxton and Babyface. However, more importantly, she fell in love with Maranatha's pastor, Dr. Billy G. Ingram, and became the First Lady of Maranatha. After eleven years of marriage and twin boys, sadly Pastor Billy suddenly passed away in his sleep from congenital heart disease on March 8, 2011, at fifty-eight years old. It was a devastating blow to all of us.

We had been members and very active in his unique ministry. He was a brilliant biblical scholar, with had a photographic memory, who had memorized the entire Bible. After his messages, he would routinely sit casually on the steps to answer questions on his message. It was amazing to watch him respond and off the top of his head, deliver passages from the Bible to clarify his message. His untimely passing alarmed the Christian community in Los Angeles. The over-whelming response was so great that his two thousand seat church was not large enough to accommodate the attendees for his homegoing service. Bishop Charles Blake graciously offered his church, the West Angeles Cathedral which seats five thousand. A year later Robert and I joined West Angeles.

After Pastor Billy's passing, Solombra maintained IEW book club by presenting entertainers who have authored books about their careers and Christian beliefs. Some of the authors who have come and shared their books included Phillip Bailey of Earth, Wind & Fire, percussionist Sheila E., filmmaker/producer Devon Franklin, Magic Johnson's wife Cookie Johnson, TV producer Aaron's wife Candy Spelling, former WNBA star Lisa Leslie, actress Vivica Fox and actress Sheryl Lee Ralph. Non-celebrity authors included Dr. Betty Price, Jemeker Thompson Hairston, Maura Gale, Tracy Brooks, Jacquelyn Gouche-Farris, Candace Cole-Kelly, Judge Karen Gauff, and first lady Myesha Chaney.

Finally, since I retired, one of my greatest joys also is participating in Community Bible Study (CBS), which is an international organization.

I attend daytime classes at a church in my neighborhood with women of all ages, races and nationalities from many different churches. We meet once a week and dig deep into the word of God. My heart has been transformed in many ways by being in the classes and feeling God's presence in that place. I am impacted by the women around me, who come together from September through May each year to study from the carefully prepared themed workbooks for in-depth study of one or two books of the Bible each semester.

We study each lesson in three ways: Individually we are required to read our lessons at home and use our Bible to carefully answer the questions. Secondly, when we come together, we break into Core Groups with ten to twelve women to share our responses to the lesson we have studied. The discussions are life-changing from the women who have one common bond, we all love the Lord. Finally, everyone gathers together, around seventy-five women, for an inspiring final message on the lesson delivered by our director.

CBS's mission is simple, to develop disciples of the Lord Jesus Christ in our communities through caring, exhaustive Bible study, which is available to all. To truly study the word has been a desire of mine for years. Having found CBS seven years ago, it has been one of the most gratifying aspects of my life in retirement.

Look at God! He has been good to Robert and me and He continues to be awesome, all the time! Seek God and never give up on your dreams!

FILMOGRAPHY
for Roz Stevenson

Roz Stevenson Public Relations (RSPR) provided African American motion picture publicity and promotional campaigns on the following films:

2011
THE HELP, Walt Disney Studios
(Post retirement: Supervised 12-city national press tour)
2008
THE EXPRESS, Universal
WELCOME HOME ROSCOE JENKINS, Universal
DEFINITELY, MAYBE, Universal
2007
CHARLIE WILSON'S WAR, Universal
AMERICAN GANGSTER, Universal
THE KINGDOM, Universal
WHO'S YOUR CADDY?, Weinstein
TRANSFORMERS, Paramount
TALK TO ME, Universal Focus
EVAN ALMIGHTY, Universal
KNOCKED UP, Universal
GRINDHOUSE, Weinstein
ARE WE DONE YET?, Sony
I THINK I LOVE MY WIFE, Fox Searchlight
NORBIT, Paramount
BREACH, Universal
SMOKIN' ACES, Universal
ALPHA DOG, Universal

2006

CHARLOTTE'S WEB, Paramount
CHILDREN OF MEN, Universal
THE PURSUIT OF HAPPYNESS,
Sony
OPEN SEASON, Sony
IDLEWILD, Universal
GRIDIRON GANG, Sony
MONSTER HOUSE, Sony
THE BLACK DAHLIA, Universal
MIAMI VICE, Universal
THE FAST AND THE FURIOUS 2:
TOKYO DRIFT, Universal
LITTLE MAN, Sony
UNITED 93, Universal
AMERICAN DREAMZ
ICE AGE 2: THE MELTDOWN, Fox
INSIDE MAN, Universal
FREEDOMLAND, Sony
LAST HOLIDAY, Paramount

2005

JARHEAD, Universal
DOOM, Universal
SERENITY, Universal
DOMINO, New Line
THE GOSPEL, Screen Gems
THE MAN, New Line
THE SKELETON KEY, Universal
LAND OF THE DEAD, Universal
KICKING & SCREAMING,
Universal
XXX: STATE OF THE UNION,
Sony
THE INTERPRETER, Universal
KING'S RANSOM, New Line
GUESS WHO, Sony
IN MY COUNTRY, Sony Classics
ARE WE THERE, YET?, Sony
COACH CARTER, Paramount

THE WEDDING DATE, Universal
IN GOOD COMPANY, Universal
WHITE NOISE, Universal

2004

MEET THE FLOCKERS, Universal
RAY, Universal
FRIDAY NIGHT LIGHTS, Universal
WHITE CHICKS, Sony
THE BOURNE SUPREMACY,
Universal
THUNDERBIRDS, Universal
TWO BROTHERS, Universal
CHRONICLES OF RIDDICK,
Universal
VAN HELSING, Universal
BEAH: A BLACK WOMAN
SPEAKS, HBO
YOU GOT SERVED, Screen Gems

2003

HONEY, Universal
LOVE ACTUALLY, Universal
PETER PAN, Universal
RADIO, Sony
CAT IN THE HAT, Universal
S.W.A.T., Sony
THE RUNDOWN, Universal
CHARLIE'S ANGELS: FULL
THROTTLE, Sony
BRUCE ALMIGHTY, Universal
BAD BOYS 2, Sony
HOLLYWOOD HOMICIDE, Sony
DADDY DAY CARE, Sony
HEAD OF STATE, DreamWorks
2 FAST 2 FURIOUS, Universal
INTOLERABLE CRUELTY,
Universal
NATIONAL SECURITY, Sony

2002

EMPIRE, Universal
8 MILE, Universal
BLUE CRUSH, Universal
XXX, Sony
DRAGONFLY, Universal
BIG FAT LIAR, Universal
THE TRUTH ABOUT CHARLIE, Universal
THE BOURNE IDENTITY, Universal
UNDERCOVER BROTHER, Universal
SCORPION KING, Universal
E.T. THE EXTRA TERRESTRIAL, Universal
BET AWARDS, Red Carpet Supervisor

2001

A BEAUTIFUL MIND, Universal
HOW HIGH, Universal
AMERICAN PIE 2, Universal
K-PAX, Universal
JURASSIC PARK III, Universal
THE FAST AND THE FURIOUS, Universal
THE MUSKETEER, Universal
JOSIE AND THE PUSSYCATS, Universal
THE MUMMY RETURNS, Universal
PAN AFRICAN FILM FESTIVAL, Universal
HEAD OVER HEELS, Universal

2000

DR. SEUSS' HOW THE GRINCH STOLE CHRISTMAS, Universal
THE FAMILY MAN, Universal

MEET THE PARENTS, Universal
BOESMAN & LENA, Kino International
THE ADVENTURES OF ROCKY & BULLWINKLE, Universal
BRING IT ON, Universal
NUTTY PROFESSOR II: THE KLUMPS, Universal

FROM 1980 – 1999

Roz Stevenson worked on hundreds of films for Universal Pictures and MGM/UA. Here is a partial list of the most memorable.

UNIVERSAL (ENDING IN 1999; STARTING IN 1987)

APOLLO 13
BABE
BACK TO THE FUTURE II
BEAUTIFUL MINDS
BEETHOVEN
BOWFINGER
CASINO
CLOCKERS
COOL AS ICE
CROOKLYN
DO THE RIGHT THING
ERIN BROCKOVICH
FLIPPER
FRIED GREEN TOMATOES
JUNGLE FEVER
JURASSIC PARK
LIFE
MAJOR PAYNE
MO' BETTER BLUES
NOTTING HILL
PRIMARY COLORS

PURE LUCK
SCENT OF A WOMAN
SCHINDLER'S LIST
THE BEST MAN
THE FLINTSTONES
THE HURRICANE
THE MUMMY
THE NUTTY PROFESSOR
THE SCORPION KING

MGM/UA
(ENDING IN 1986; STARTING IN 1980)

9-1/2 WEEKS
A CHRISTMAS STORY
A VIEW TO A KILL
BRAINSTORM
BREAKIN'
CANNERY ROW
CLASH OF THE TITANS
DINER
ENDANGERED SPECIES
GARBO TALKS
MOONRAKER
POLTERGEIST FRANCHISE
RED SONJA
RICH AND FAMOUS
ROCKY III
ROCKY IV
RUNNING SCARED
SHOOT THE MOON
STRANGE BREW
THE POPE OF GREENWICH VILLAGE
YEAR OF THE DRAGON
YENTL
YES, GIORGIO

FILMOGRAPHY
for Robert Stevenson

Robert Louis Stevenson served as a motion picture hair stylist on the following films, ending in 2019 and beginning in 1969:

FILM/TV CREDITS

2019   BOLDEN (wig consultant)

2015   MILES AHEAD (wig designer)

2014   GET ON UP (wig consultant)

2013   LEE DANIELS' THE BUTLER (co-head hair stylist)

2010   UNTHINKABLE (key hair stylist)

2008   THE SPIRIT (hair stylist: Samuel L. Jackson)

2008   SOUL MEN (department head hair stylist)

2008   LAKEVIEW TERRACE (hair stylist: Samuel L. Jackson)

2008   KNIGHT RIDER (TV Series) (hair department head - 1 episode)

2008   JUMPER (hair stylist: Samuel L. Jackson)

2007   CLEANER (hair stylist: Samuel L. Jackson)

2007   1408 (hair stylist: Mr. Samuel L. Jackson

2007   RESURRECTING THE CHAMP (hair stylist: Samuel L. Jackson)

2006   HOME OF THE BRAVE (hair stylist: Samuel L. Jackson, Spokane)

2006   BLACK SNAKE MOAn (hair stylist: Mr. Samuel L. Jackson)

2006   THE SANTA CLAUSE 3: THE ESCAPE CLAUSE (key hair stylist)

2006   SNAKES ON A PLANE (hair stylist: Mr. Samuel L. Jackson)

2006   FREEDOMLAND (hair stylist: Samuel L. Jackson)

2006   ALPHA DOG (hair stylist: Sharon Stone)

2005   JARHEAD (hair department head)

2005   THE MAN (hair stylist: Samuel L. Jackson)

2005   XXX: STATE OF THE UNION (hair stylist: Mr. Jackson)

2005   COACH CARTER (key hair stylist)

FILMOGRAPHY

2004   Twisted (hair stylist: Samuel L. Jackson)

2004   In My Country (hair stylist: Samuel L. Jackson)

2003   S.W.A.T. (hair stylist: Samuel L. Jackson)

2003   Coaching the Minors (Short) (key hair stylist)

2003   Basic (hair stylist: Samuel L. Jackson)

2003   Biography (TV Series documentary) (hair stylist - 1 episode)

2003   Unchained Memories: Slave Narratives (Doc)
(hair stylist: Samuel L. Jackson)

2002   xXx (hair stylist: Samuel L. Jackson)

2002   ESPY Awards (TV Special) (hair stylist: Samuel L. Jackson) /
(key hair stylist)

2002   No Good Deed (hairdresser: Samuel L. Jackson)

2002   Changing Lanes (hair stylist: Samuel L. Jackson)

2002   The Comeback (Short) (key hair stylist)

2002   Hollywood Salutes Nicolas Cage (TV Special)
(hair stylist: Samuel L. Jackson)

2001   Formula 51 (hair stylist: Samuel L. Jackson)

2001   The Caveman's Valentine (hair stylist: Mr. Samuel L. Jackson)

2000   Unbreakable (hair stylist: Samuel L. Jackson)

2000   Shaft (hair stylist: Samuel L. Jackson)

2000   Rules of Engagement (hair stylist: Mr. Samuel L. Jackson

2000   Any Given Wednesday (Short) (key hair stylist)

2000   Supernova (hair stylist: Angela Bassett)

1999   Three Kings (hair stylist supervisor)

1999   Deep Blue Sea (hair stylist: Samuel L. Jackson)

1999   From Star Wars to Star Wars Industrial Light & Magic
(hair stylist- Samuel L. Jackson)

1998   The Negotiator (supervising hair stylist)

1997   Jackie Brown (key hair stylist)

1997   Amistad (key hair stylist)

1997   Eve's Bayou (supervising hair stylist)

1997   One Eight Seven (hair department head)

1996   The Long Kiss Goodnight (hair stylist: Mr. Samuel L. Jackson

1996   A Time to Kill (hair stylist)

1996   The Great White Hype (key hair stylist)

1995   Waiting to Exhale (hair stylist: Angela Bassett)

1995   How to Make an American Quilt (key hair stylist)

1995   Strange Days (hair department head)

1995   Dangerous Minds (key hair stylist)

FILMOGRAPHY

1995 BAD COMPANY (hair stylist: Laurence Fishburne)

1993 SISTER ACT 2: BACK IN THE HABIT (hair stylist)

1993 WHAT'S LOVE GOT TO DO WITH IT (hair designer)

1992 THE JACKSONS: AN AMERICAN DREAM (TV Mini-Series)
      (hair department head)

1992 MELROSE PLACE (TV Series) (hair stylist - 2 episodes)

1992 CLASS ACT (hair department head)

1992 SISTER ACT (key hair stylist)

1992 JAKE AND THE FATMAN (TV Series) (hair stylist - 1 episode)

1991 TERMINATOR 2: JUDGMENT DAY (hair stylist)

1991 OSCAR (hair department head)

1991 THE MARRYING MAN (hair stylist)

1991 IN THE HEAT OF THE NIGHT (TV Series) (hair stylist - 1 episode)

1990 ANOTHER 48 HRS. (hair stylist)

1989 HARLEM NIGHTS (hair stylist)

1989 LIFE GOES ON (TV Series) (hair department head)

1989 INDIANA JONES AND THE LAST CRUSADE (hair stylist: USA)

1989 POLICE ACADEMY 6: CITY UNDER SIEGE (hair stylist)

1989 WHAT'S ALAN WATCHING? (TV Special) (hair department
      head: second unit)

1988 COMING TO AMERICA (head hair stylist: Los Angeles)

1987 LEONARD PART 6 (hair stylist)

1987 BLACK WIDOW (hair stylist)

1985 THE COLOR PURPLE (supervising hair stylist)

1985 SWEET DREAMS (hair department head)

1985 THE ATLANTA CHILD MURDERS (TV Mini-Series) (hair stylist - 2 episodes)

1984 MURDER, SHE WROTE (TV Series) (hair department head)

1984 HOT PURSUIT (TV Series) (hair department head - 2 episodes)

1984 BOYS IN BLUE (TV Movie) (hair stylist)

1984 THE JESSE OWENS STORY (TV Movie) (hair department head)

1984 CALENDAR GIRL MURDERS (TV Movie) (hair stylist)

1983 WOMEN OF SAN QUENTIN (TV Movie) (hair department head)

1983 FOR LOVE AND HONOR (TV Series) (hair department head)

1983 SUPERMAN III (hair department head - uncredited)

1983 FLASHDANCE (hair stylist)

1982 THE TOY (hair stylist as Bob Stevenson)

1982 FRANCES (hair stylist)

1982 THE POWERS OF MATTHEW STAR (TV Series) (hair department head)

1982 SOME KIND OF HERO (hair department head)

1982 RASCALS AND ROBBERS: TOM SAWYER AND HUCK FINN
(TV Movie) (hair stylist)

1982 TWO TOP BANANAS (TV Short) (hair stylist)

1981 THE ADVENTURES OF HUCKLEBERRY FINN (TV Movie)
(hair department head)

1981 DON'T LOOK BACK: SATCHEL PAIGE (TV Movie) (hair stylist)

1981 SHE'S IN THE ARMY NOW (TV Movie) (hair department head)

1981 STAND BY YOUR MAN (TV Movie) (hair stylist)

1980 HOMEWARD BOUND (TV Movie) (hair stylist)

1980 TENSPEED AND BROWN SHOE (TV Series) (hair department head)

1979 THE FISH THAT SAVED PITTSBURGH (hair department head)

1979 PARIS (TV Series) (hair department head)

1979 THE LAZARUS SYNDROME (TV Series) (hair department head)

1979 SUNNYSIDE (hair stylist)

1978 CORVETTE SUMMER (hairdresser)

1978 BLUE COLLAR (hair stylist)

1978 LOGAN'S RUN (TV Series) (hair stylist - 5 episodes)

1977 WHICH WAY IS UP? (hair stylist)

1977 GREASED LIGHTNING (hair stylist)

1976 CAR WASH (hair stylist)

1976 JUST AN OLD SWEET SONG (TV Movie) (hair stylist)

*1973-75 During this time Robert Stevenson worked uncredited on TV shows and films on the Universal Studios lot. A partial list of the television shows included Adam-12, Alias Smith & Jones, Banacek, Baretta, The Bionic Woman, The Bold Ones, Columbo, Dragnet, Emergency, Ironside, Kojak, Owen Marshall, Marcus Welby-M.D., McCloud, McMillian & Wife, Toma and many others. Film & TV movies included: The Bastards, Evil Roy Slade, The Hounds of Baskerville, Willie Dynamite and others.

*1969-72 Robert Stevenson was an Apprentice in the Makeup Department at Universal Studios.

ACKNOWLEDGMENTS

Almighty God, I thank you for inspiring me to write this book to your glory. I have felt your presence throughout the writing process and along my Hollywood journey.

Robert Louis Stevenson, my husband of forty-plus years, you truly are my God-given treasure. Since you came into my life you have loved me, encouraged me, respected me and inspired me. With God on our side, we have each strived to become the best that we could be. I am so proud of the life we have built together, which has taken us higher than we ever could have imagined. This book is not just my story; it is our story. There is no me without you — the guy from Watts with the girl from Compton, representing South Central Los Angeles!

To my sisters, Carol Tucker and Catherine Bush, and brother, Richard Steverson, the older we get the more grateful I am for our parents and our upbringing. We grew up with two people who always sought to do what was best for our family. Each day we have to strive to inspire our children, grandchildren and family to live by their glorious example.

To my three sons, Jason Woodruff, Damon Woodruff and my baby boy, Teron Stevenson, I am so proud to be your mother. I have been loving each of you from the day you were born. May this book remind you and enlighten you about my struggle for excellence. I trust I have set a good example for becoming all that you can be. As you come to realize that none of us are perfect, you must know that with God is on your side, you will discover His purpose and achieve it.

To Kendra Monet Stevenson Ruffin, my beautiful bonus daughter. You are the boss of this family and no one minds bowing to you. In all that you do, you lift us higher. Thanks for always making every occasion classy, unique and memorable. I am so proud of the woman you have become.

To my grandchildren, Kambria Ruffin, Valentino Martinez, Sage Woodruff, Aman Stevenson, Dayna Woodruff, Delaney Woodruff and great-grandson Nellon Johnson, may my story allow you to recognize that we all make mistakes, and we all get discouraged. However,

ACKNOWLEDGMENTS

no matter what, when you get knocked down, you have to dust yourself off, get back up and keep moving forward. You are each unique
and have special gifts to give to the world. You must stay focused,
encouraged and seek each and every day to be all that God created you
to be. This is my prayer for you.

To my long-time girlfriends, Saundra Lang, Tammi Nash, Gloria
Gibson, Mary McCurry, Tina Ogas, cousins Viola Baecher, Elinor
Reed and Virginia Steverson McKean, thanks for being along for the
ride over many years. I am thankful that we have always offered one
another a listening ear and a shoulder to lean on. Thanks for believing
in me. I hope I have made you proud.

To my goddaughters, Monique Nash, Solombra Ingram, Marissa
Burton, nieces Cynthia Tucker and Brandy Stowers, I hope I have inspired you professionally and personally to shoot for the stars. As you
go forth in your careers, may you pursue even greater opportunities
and achieve the unimaginable. These warm sentiments also go out to
my much appreciated former RSPR staff: the intelligent Ronda Penrice, the bright shining star Sharon Pinnix, God-loving, super special
Steven Williams and my cool-as-a-cucumber my baby boy, Teron Stevenson.

To the entertainment publicists and media of color, please know
that our calling is unique and sorely needed. It is our task to inform
and enlighten everyone about who we are as a people. As the world
struggles to recognize that diversity and inclusion are important, it is
our duty to ring the alarm. Continue to fight the good fight.

Dr. Margena A. Christian, owner and founder of Doc M.A.C. Write
Consulting and Publishing in Chicago, Illinois, I thank you. You are a
wonderful writing consultant, who I have known and respected from
your excellent work as Features Editor with JET magazine back in the
day. I sincerely appreciate you expertly guiding me through all aspects
of the publishing process. Your keen editing, proofreading and writing
services have made me confident of the process and the final outcome.
You are a Godsend. Katara Washington Patton of Chicago, Illinois,
you were an amazing editor, who I can't wait to meet face to face one
day. Raymond A. Thomas, a highly recommended and award-winning
fine artist and former art director for Johnson Publishing Company
Inc., thanks for making me look good.

ACKNOWLEDGMENTS

A very special thank you to Sandra Varner from Oakland, my sister and P.R. specialist/journalist extraordinaire, who was inspired by God to give me the title of this book. In addition, I want to express my gratitude to Stephanie Frederic of FGW Productions for being a cheerleader, who encouraged me to tell my story and share and share my knowledge with others aspiring to seek careers in entertainment.

Finally, 2020 has had a positive impact on me. The pandemic has me sheltering-in-place and, instead of sitting idle, I completed this book. As I wrote, I came to realize how the outrage over social and racial injustice problems we face today are the exact same as we heard in the sixties after the Watts Riot.

When devastating events occur and people peacefully protest, our nation's leaders wake up to take steps to treat our fellow man better. It is because of the job opportunities for minorities that came about after the Watts uprising that my husband Robert and I were able to have meaningful careers in Hollywood. Our successful careers changed the trajectory of our lives and inspired others in our universe to seek the same.

INDEX

CPSIA information can be obtained
at www.ICGtesting.com
Printed in the USA
FSHW021005030421
80066FS